MENTAL FLOSS

THE CURIOUS MOVIE BUFF

MENTAL FLOSS

THE CURIOUS
MOVIE
BUFF

BY **JENNIFER M. WOOD** AND THE TEAM AT
MENTAL FLOSS

A MISCELLANY
OF FANTASTIC
FILMS
FROM THE
PAST 50
YEARS

weldon**owen**

CEO Raoul Goff
VP PUBLISHER Roger Shaw
EDITORIAL DIRECTOR Katie Killebrew
SENIOR EDITOR Karyn Gerhard
VP CREATIVE Chrissy Kwasnik
ART DIRECTOR Allister Fein
VP MANUFACTURING Alix Nicholaeff
PRODUCTION MANAGER Sam Taylor

weldon**owen**

an imprint of Insight Editions
P.O. Box 3088
San Rafael, CA 94912
www.weldonowen.com

ISBN 978-1-681888-84-2

Produced by Indelible Editions

INDELIBLE
EDITIONS

Printed in China
2025 2024 2023 2022 • 10 9 8 7 6 5 4 3 2 1

PICTURE CREDITS

Alamy.com: A7A Collection, 14-15; BFA Collection, 192-193; BFA/Sophie Giraud /New Line Cinema, 118; Collection Christophel, 68, 230, 256; IFA Film, 16, 160; Impress, 198; Keystone Pictures USA, 19; kpa Publicity Stills, 214, 264-265; Lifestyle pictures, 74, 177; M.G.M/PATHE/Album, 268; Moviestore Collection, 76, 190; Neue Constantin Film, 166; Photo 12, 189; Photo12/7e Art/Kintop Pictures, 44; Pictorial Press, 92, 154, 216; PictureLux, 25, 41, 54-55, 88, 152, 162, 234, 247; RGR Collection, 180; Screen Prod, 48-49, 59; TCD/Prod.DB, 39, 51, 66, 73, 123; Warner Brothers/Album, 236; Zoetrope Films, 27; **Bruce Willis/National Museum of American History:** 69; **Free 3D:** Nahdlc, 80; **iStock.com:** nicolamargaret, 120; **Shutterstock.com:** AcantStudio, 23; Airin.dizain, 85; Alberto Zamorano, 77; Alexandru-Radu Borzea, 161; alexblacksea, 163; Alfonso de Tomas, 80; AM-STUDiO, 146; Andrey_Kuzmin, 30; andrey oleynik, 195; Anikei, 226; Anna I Anisimovam, 119; Anton_Ivanov, 137, 150, 240; Anton_Lutsenko, 164, 165; antoniradso, 250-251; Aperture75, 228; ARENA Creative, 98; Artem Samokhvalov, 174; ArtMari, 174; Ashley M Woods, 93; baibaz, 178; Baimieng, 218; Balefire, 139; Barbora Martinakova, 148; BlueMac, 245; BR Photo Addicted, 83; Brian A Jackson, 218; Carl DeAbreu Photography, 237; carrie-nelson, 54; Castleski, 32-33; Cavan-Images, 182; Chase Dekker, 102-103; chasehunterphotos, 162-163; chingyunsong, 210; chippix, 243; Chones, 114-115; Chris Harvey, 132-133; Corrado Pravisano, 201; cvalle, 56, 57; daizuoxin, 139; Daniel Myjones, 175; DarkBird, 263; Denis Makarenko, 103, 155; DenisMArt, 237; dowraik, 142; dubassy, 72; Ecuadorpostales, 173; Eeli Purola, 146; Enrique Ramos, 183; Eric Isselee, 123; Eroshka, 70; eukukulka, 83; Everett Collection, 224; Evgeniy Goncharov photo, 193; EvrenKalinbacak, 262; Excellent backgrounds, 110; eXodusN, 146; Fabio Pagani, 16-17, 18, 104-107, 158-159, 196-197, 247-249, 268-269; Fabricio Dalgo, 23; Fer Gregory, 196; FocusStocker, 45; Fotokkden, 60; Fotystory, 219; Freer, 233; GaViAl, 173; gdvcom, 79; germanjames, 195; gresei, 119; Guzel Studio, 202; Happy monkey, 197; HenriqueWestin, 81; Hitachin33, 84; Hurst Photo, 254; iava777, 111; ilovezion, 165; Image Craft, 90-91; ItzaVU, 254; Ivan Baranov, 96; iYodstocker, 218; Jaguar PS, 179; Jim Vallee, 30; jocic, 60; Jolygon, 220; Kai Beercrafter, 80; Karjalas, 61; Kate.cat, 62; KathySG, 184, 185; koya979, 71; Krakenimages.com, 197; kzww, 257; LEE SNIDER PHOTO IMAGES, 143; Little Adventures, 241; lukeruk, 100; Lunik MX, 110-111; Lutsina Tatiana, 51; Luuk de Kok, 136; Lyudmila Lucienne, 266; M. Unal Ozmen, 263; Madlen, 127; Marcin Roszkowski, 94; MARGRIT HIRSCH, 142; Mark Carrel, 145; Massimo Santi, 238-239; Mega Pixel, 122; MidoSemsem, 60; Militarist, 60, 141; Mirt Alexander, 128; ModernNomad, 46-47; moopsi, 208; MoreVector, 75; mountaintreks, 186; Murilo Mazzo, 194; mypokcik, 203, 204; Nagel Photography, 223; Naypong Studio, 208-209; ND700, 64; NeagoneFo, 252; Nerthuz, 110; netsign33, 246; New Africa, 124, 173, 252; nex999, 34-35; nexus 7, 257; Nina Puankova, 42; Nowik Sylwia, 82; Oksana Kuzmina, 253; onzon, 182; P Maxwell Photography, 24, 85, 179, 242; PainterMaster, 203; Pascal Constantineau, 52; Patricia Chumillas, 92; patti jean guerrero, 141; Petr Smagin, 31; Petr Vaclavek, 50, 51; Philphot, 185; PhotoHouse, 172; Photoprofi30, 129; pics of my life, 262; Pixel-Shot, 259; Piyawat Nandeenopparit, 234-235; Production Perig, 260; Ps.INL, 120, 121; pumbria, 124-127; RAY-BON, 220-222; RetroClipArt, 265; retofuerst, 139; Retouch man, 263; Rob Byron, 36; Robert B. Miller, 188; robypangy, 81; Rodion Kutsaev, 125, 126; Romariolen, 116-117; SAHACHATZ, 130; Sahara Prince, 149-151; Salamahin, 254; SanchaiRat, 211; samui, 25; Sanit Fuangnakhon, 204; Sarunyu L, 46; SayHope, 176; s_bukley, 152; sdecoret, 232-233; sema srinouljan, 52, 53; Separisa, 142; Seregam, 61; Sergey Tinyakov, 134; Sergio33, 197; Sfam Photo, 14-15; SG Arts, 168-169; Shafran, 112-113; SimonWest, 201; Skreidzeleu, 98; solomon7, 237; Soloveva Kristina, 250; somchaij, 140; sore88, 155; sozon, 95; Stefano Buttafoco, 228-229; s-ts, 77; StudioSmart, 127; surawach5, 168; Svetoslav Radkov, 111; sweet marshmallow, 174; Thomas Quack, 141; Triff, 194; tugol, 206-207; Untashable, 216; Valentin Agapov, 212-215; Valentina Proskurina, 203; VanSky, 97; Vecc, 156-157; Vector Factory, 47; VectorPot, 26; Victoria Sergeeva, 153; Virtis, 42; Volodymyr TVERDOKHLIB, 205; Vovantarakan, 86; vvetc1, 63; Willow Hood, 40, 108; xpixel, 124-127; Yellowj, 109; Yeti studio, 192, 193; Yuri Turkov, 232; Zaiachin, 260; Zeeking, 261; Zhukov Oleg, 218; **Wikimedia.org:** Airwolfhound, 28; Alan Light, 67; Alessandro Nassiri, 260; Barbara Krafft, 22; California Historical Society Collection, 58-59; Compass International Pictures, 212; David Martin, 144; Dimension Films, 215; Energy.gov, 243; Filmack Studios/Dave Fleischer, 12; Hal Roach Studios, 37; Heritage Auctions, 104; Lionsgate Home Entertainment, 214; Mark Goff, 107; Mathers, Samuel MacGregor Liddel, 121; The Metropolitan Museum of Art, 143; NASA, 42; New Line Cinema, 213; Paramount Pictures, 213; PHGCOM, 83

CONTENTS

REFRESHMENTS
Candy

DELICIOUS
REFRESHMENTS
Let's all go
to the Lobby
to get Ourselves
a Treat!

INTRODUCTION JENNIFER M. WOOD

When Mental Floss was founded more than twenty years ago, there was generally one way to see a new movie upon its release: go to a theater, purchase a ticket, grab your popcorn, settle into your seat, and spend the next two hours being transported to a land of make-believe. Sure, there were DVDs (Blu-rays were still a few years away), but heading off to the cinema was still a weekly ritual for millions of Americans.

While the way we consume movies has changed a lot over the past two decades—and even more drastically in recent years in response to the COVID-19 pandemic—our appetite for great films has never waned. And with streaming giants like Netflix, Amazon, and Hulu now acquiring and producing their own original movies from top-tier directors such as Martin Scorsese, Spike Lee, and Jane Campion, watching the latest releases from the comfort of your couch is becoming an increasingly common practice. In fact, the evolution of the movie-watching experience has made it so that today's audiences have a literal library of cinema's greatest gems just a couple of clicks away, including century-old filmmaking firsts like Georges Méliès's *A Trip to the Moon* (arguably the first sci-fi film) and Al Jolson's *The Jazz Singer* (cinema's first "talkie").

Naturally, the idea that there are so many movies at your fingertips can be an overwhelming prospect that makes answering the question "What do you want to watch?" impossible at times. (Unless you just answer "*Step Brothers*!" as I often do.) Which is where *The Curious Movie Buff* comes in.

In the pages that follow, you'll find sharp analyses, fascinating facts, moviemaker quotes, and behind-the-scenes tales from the sets of hundreds of the greatest movies going back to 1970, a rich era in which to start any film history lesson. We all know it as the decade that introduced the "blockbuster" to the world with *Jaws* and *Star Wars*, but it's also the era in which maverick directors like Robert Altman, Gordon Parks, and Hal Ashby wrestled the decision-making power away from the major Hollywood studios and started calling the shots, which is how we ended up with movies like *M*A*S*H*, *Shaft*, and *Harold and Maude*.

The Curious Movie Buff contains the kind of in-depth content that readers have come to expect from Mental Floss's team of movie-loving writers and editors. From perennial favorites like *The Godfather* and *Jurassic Park* to more recent classics-in-the-making like *Get Out* and *Parasite*, there are no boundaries to the films we're exploring. And in addition to profiles of particular movies, we've also gathered up lists of movies that share some sort of DNA or element—our favorite heist movies, the best car chases, and the all-time greatest movie endings—to help serve as a guide as to where your movie-watching goes next.

We have loved putting *The Curious Movie Buff* together, and we hope that you walk away from it with dozens of new-to-you films added to your various queues—and hundreds of interesting facts to whip out at your next movie night.

WRITTEN BY: Robert Alan Aurthur and Bob Fosse

DIRECTED BY: Bob Fosse

OTHER MOVIES DIRECTED BY BOB FOSSE:
Sweet Charity (1969); *Cabaret* (1972);
Lenny (1974); *Star 80* (1983)

ALL THAT JAZZ (1979)

While staging Broadway's *Chicago* and editing his 1974 Lenny Bruce biopic *Lenny*, Bob Fosse suffered a heart attack and underwent open-heart surgery. Shortly after, he began work on a new musical dramedy about a director, Joe Gideon, who suffers a heart attack and undergoes open-heart surgery while staging a Broadway musical and editing a biopic about a comedian. The semi-autobiographical overtones didn't stop there: Fosse funneled virtually every facet of his life into *All That Jazz*, from his hacking smoker's cough to his relationship with his nominal wife, Gwen Verdon (the two married in 1960 and separated a decade later, but never divorced and continued their working relationship). He even cast his onetime girlfriend, Ann Reinking, as Gideon's girlfriend.

Such navel-gazing takes a sizable amount of moxie to put on the silver screen at all—and an even more sizable talent to pull off. Fosse, of course, had both, and *All That Jazz* earned a slew of awards. It also became a glittering example of life-imitating-art-imitating-life: Fosse, much like Joe Gideon before him, died after another heart attack in 1987.

RICHARD DREYFUSS WAS ORIGINALLY CAST IN THE STARRING ROLE.

Richard Dreyfuss, winner of the Best Actor Oscar for *The Goodbye Girl* (1977), was originally cast in the role of Joe Gideon, but backed out shortly before filming began because of what were deemed "artistic differences." He said he later regretted the decision.

JOE GIDEON'S MORNING MONTAGE HAS BECOME A POPULAR REFERENCE.

Soundtracked by Antonio Vivaldi's *Concerto alla Rustica*, Gideon begins each day the same way: with eye drops, Alka-Seltzer, a cigarette, shower, Dexedrine, and the phrase "It's showtime, folks," uttered to his mirror in varying degrees of fatigue. Elements of this routine can be seen in a number of other movies and TV shows. In Sofia Coppola's *Marie Antoinette* (2006), the eponymous royal blinks her way through courtly drudgery to the tune of *Concerto alla Rustica*; in *Better Call Saul*'s second episode, "Mijo," Bob Odenkirk's Jimmy gives the mirror his best "It's showtime, folks," before his own Vivaldi-featuring montage starts.

BOB FOSSE WAS IN ROY SCHEIDER'S EAR— LITERALLY—DURING THE OPENING SCENE.

Fosse wanted to create a documentary feel in *All That Jazz*, which is felt at the very beginning of the movie, during an open-call dance audition filmed at Broadway's Palace Theatre. While five cameras roamed the stage, Scheider, who played Joe Gideon, was wearing an earpiece so that Fosse, seated in a booth, could feed him improvised lines and instructions on how to interact with the dancers. Fosse's ostensible reason for using the earpiece was to save time, since the shoot was only scheduled for two days; instead, it lasted a full week.

ERZSÉBET FÖLDI HAD AN UNCONVENTIONAL AUDITION.

In addition to performance skills, the girl cast as Joe Gideon's daughter, Michelle, needed to have trust. So Fosse told hundreds of hopeful youngsters to run across the stage, one by one, and leap into his arms. Twelve-year-old Erzsébet Földi, a student at the School of American Ballet, passed the test and progressed through the rest of the audition process. To help choose between Földi and the other front-runner, Fosse asked them each to light his cigarette. Földi's childlike way of completing the task embodied Michelle's innocence—and earned Földi the role.

THE ACTORS BONDED BEHIND THE SCENES OF "BYE BYE LIFE."

The grand finale, "Bye Bye Life," was shot on location in a black-box theater at SUNY Purchase. While Fosse and the set designers were busy developing the lavish, flashy set, the actors had ample time to kill in their motel rooms. They jokingly nicknamed their group the "Prisoners of the Performing Arts," also known as "POPA," and played charades and other games to entertain themselves. "It was just constant laughter and fun," John Lithgow, who played Gideon's rival Lucas Sergeant, later remembered.

"It's showtime, folks!"

From the politically charged to the positively campy, these movie musicals from the last fifty years are guaranteed to have you singing along from your couch.

MAGNIFICENT MOVIE
MUSICALS

Across the Universe (2007)

Julie Taymor's ambitious ode to the Beatles tracks the band's own evolution from young pop rockers to psychedelic counter-culturalists through a fictional sixties love story between Jude (Jim Sturgess), a working-class Liverpool artist, and Lucy (Evan Rachel Wood), a straitlaced American student-turned-anti-war-activist. In order to distance viewers from the original Beatles tracks, composer Elliot Goldenthal intentionally omitted many memorable guitar riffs, which he called, according to Taymor, "the ghost in the room."

Cabaret (1972)

The ultimate source material for Bob Fosse's gritty yet glittery film adaptation of Joe Masteroff, John Kander, and Fred Ebb's 1966 Broadway musical was Christopher Isherwood's 1939 book *Goodbye to Berlin*—a lightly fictionalized retelling of his experiences of Berlin life during the Weimar Republic. A few of the film's most iconic songs, including "Mein Herr," "Money, Money," and "Maybe This Time," weren't in the original stage production. (Neither was Liza Minnelli, though she did audition for it.)

Chicago (2002)

The stars of Rob Marshall's Oscar-winning movie version of Kander and Ebb's 1975 Broadway musical did their own singing and dancing, though some had little to no previous experience. Richard Gere learned to tap-dance to portray smooth-talking lawyer Billy Flynn and Renée Zellweger, who'd never seen the musical nor heard the songs, trained extensively to play Roxie Hart. Catherine Zeta-Jones, meanwhile, had done musical theater, and John C. Reilly had performed as a tramp clown during his youth.

Dreamgirls (2006)

After several false starts, a movie adaptation of the 1981 Broadway hit *Dreamgirls* finally hit screens in 2006 with an all-star cast featuring Beyoncé, Jamie Foxx, Eddie Murphy, and *American Idol*'s Jennifer Hudson in her film debut. While the original musical tried to distance itself from its inspiration—Motown Records' origin story and the rise of the Supremes—so as not to ruffle feathers, filmmaker Bill Condon made changes to bring it closer to its roots. Key among them was shifting the setting from Chicago to Detroit, Motown's birthplace.

Fame (1980)

Fame, which follows the talented teens at New York City's High School of Performing Arts, is a prequel of sorts to another iconic musical: *A Chorus Line*. In her song "Nothing," the character Diana Morales reminisces about her time at the school. According to director Alan Parker, this inspired *Fame* producer David De Silva to develop an original movie exploring what that would have been like.

Get on Up (2014)

When Chadwick Boseman first got the script for the James Brown biopic *Get on Up*, he'd recently finished filming the Jackie Robinson biopic *42* and flat-out refused to step into another icon's shoes. Director Tate Taylor didn't give up, though, and Boseman eventually accepted the role, delivering a superlative, spirited portrayal of Mr. Dynamite's many sides. Though the bulk of the music comes from Brown's remastered recordings, all the dancing is Boseman.

Grease (1978)

Based on Jim Jacobs and Warren Casey's 1971 musical, this rollicking romp about 1950s high schoolers quickly became a classic and landed several songs on the charts—including Frankie Valli's title track, written by Barry Gibb. *Grease* has also become everyone's favorite example of Hollywood's habit of casting older adults as teenagers. John Travolta (Danny) was twenty-four, Olivia Newton-John (Sandy) was twenty-nine, Stockard Channing (Rizzo) was thirty-three, and Michael Tucci (Sonny) was thirty-one.

Jesus Christ Superstar (1973)

Many religious organizations disapproved of Tim Rice and Andrew Lloyd Webber's hippie-ish rock opera about the days leading up to Jesus Christ's crucifixion. But Pope Paul VI, for one, supposedly enjoyed *Moonstruck* director Norman Jewison's 1973 film version. After a private screening, as Ted Neeley (who played Jesus) remembered it, the pope called it a "beautiful" movie that would help promote Christianity.

La La Land (2016)

Writer and director Damien Chazelle's Oscar-winning flick opens with a flashy musical number in a mundane setting: gridlocked traffic on a Los Angeles freeway ramp. If the scene looked painfully familiar to L.A. commuters, that's because it was filmed on an actual freeway that had to be shut down for a weekend. That balance of Old Hollywood romance with the harsh reality of struggling in one of the least forgiving cities in America is explored throughout the movie's runtime.

Mamma Mia! (2008)

A young woman's lighthearted quest to find out before her wedding which of her mother's three former flames is her father, told through the music of ABBA, was adapted for film by the creators of the original 1999 West End musical—producer Judy Craymer, director Phyllida Lloyd, and writer Catherine Johnson. Two ABBA members make cameos: Benny Andersson is the piano player on the dock during "Dancing Queen," and Björn Ulvaeus plays one of the Greek gods seen during "Waterloo."

Moulin Rouge! (2001)

Baz Luhrmann's over-the-top musical tragicomedy follows the ill-fated romance between "penniless writer" Christian (Ewan McGregor) and glamorous courtesan Satine (Nicole Kidman), all set against the backdrop of Paris's Moulin Rouge circa 1900. Getting the rights to include so many modern pop songs took a good two years, and Luhrmann failed with songs by at least two artists: the Rolling Stones and Yusuf/Cat Stevens.

Purple Rain (1984)

Purple Rain's high-octane performances and chart-topping soundtrack helped make it a blockbuster. But Prince's semi-autobiographical film wasn't originally called *Purple Rain*, nor was it meant to include that song. Its working title was *Dreams*, and of the one hundred songs Prince gave director Albert Magnoli to choose from, "Purple Rain" wasn't among them—it was added after Magnoli saw the singer perform it live.

Saturday Night Fever (1977)

You'll come for the soundtrack, but want to stay for all the dirty, gritty, New York-in-the-1970s realism on display in this disco drama, which helped shoot John Travolta—already famous for the ABC sitcom *Welcome Back, Kotter*—into the stratosphere. With what remains one of the top-selling soundtracks of all time, you might be thinking *Saturday Night Fever* is a fun disco-era romp. But the original release was substantially darker, with an R rating and a contemporary review from the *Washington Post* saying it "assaults you with a flagrantly foul-mouthed script and coarse viewpoint."

A Star Is Born (2018)

Lady Gaga and Bradley Cooper's magnetic chemistry and a slew of evocative songs—many composed with help from Willie Nelson's son, Lukas Nelson—effectively silenced anyone tempted to suggest that the world didn't need yet another iteration of 1937's *A Star Is Born*. Cooper, who also directed and co-wrote the film, cast Lady Gaga after seeing her perform Édith Piaf's "La Vie en Rose" at a cancer benefit. In the movie, Cooper's character Jackson Maine first discovers Gaga's Ally in a drag bar singing that very song.

Tommy (1975)

While the pinball prodigy at the heart of The Who's 1969 rock opera album *Tommy* is born during World War I, Ken Russell's 1975 silver-screen reimagining moves the setting forward by about thirty years. This way, Tommy's (played by The Who front man Roger Daltrey) ascent to fame and enlightenment mostly takes place during the seventies—a better match for the soundtrack, and also a good excuse to feature some of the era's biggest talents, from Tina Turner to Elton John.

West Side Story (2021)

With the help of historical consultants and an almost unimaginably talented cast, director Steven Spielberg and screenwriter Tony Kushner created a less one-dimensional, highly dynamic remake of *West Side Story*. Though Spielberg has said that his team drew inspiration from the 1957 musical rather than the 1961 movie, they did borrow at least one beloved element from the latter: Rita Moreno, who won a Best Supporting Actress Oscar for playing Rita in the original film. In Spielberg's version, she portrays a new character—Valentina, the widow of drugstore owner Doc.

WRITTEN BY: **William Goldman** (based on the book by Carl Bernstein and Bob Woodward)

DIRECTED BY: **Alan J. Pakula**

OTHER MOVIES BY ALAN J. PAKULA: *Klute* (1971); *The Parallax View* (1974); *Sophie's Choice* (1982); *The Devil's Own* (1997)

ALL THE PRESIDENT'S MEN (1976)

The 1970s were a bad time for American politics, but a great time for Hollywood movies about American politics. One of the best was *All the President's Men*, Alan J. Pakula's retelling of how dogged *Washington Post* reporters Bob Woodward (Robert Redford) and Carl Bernstein (Dustin Hoffman) exposed the Watergate cover-up and eventually brought about Richard Nixon's resignation.

ROBERT REDFORD SHAPED THE MOVIE—AND THE BOOK IT WAS BASED ON.

In 1972, when the Watergate story was still unfolding, Redford contacted Woodward and Bernstein to express his interest in their work. He also told them that the most interesting way to tell the story would not be to simply reveal all the information they uncovered, but to lay it out piece by piece, in the order they uncovered it— to make the story a procedural.

While they initially disagreed, not wanting to insert themselves into the news, Woodward and Bernstein soon came to realize Redford was right and took his approach when they wrote the book. "He laid the seed for that in that first phone call," Woodward later said.

REDFORD DIDN'T PLAN TO STAR IN THE MOVIE, BUT THE STUDIO INSISTED.

As producer, Redford's original idea was to make the film in black-and-white, almost documentary style, without any superstar actors. But executives at Warner Bros. knew it was going to be a pricey film and told Redford in no uncertain terms that they needed his name on the marquee to help sell it. Once Redford agreed, it became clear that the other reporter would also have to be played by someone famous, lest viewers perceive a power imbalance between Woodward and Bernstein.

The MPAA initially gave *All the President's Men* an R rating because of its ten or so uses of the word *fuck*. On appeal, the ratings board relented and gave it a PG rating, making it one of the rare PG films to drop the F-bomb at all, let alone ten times.

THE SCREENWRITER WAS HIRED BY ACCIDENT.

Redford was friends with William Goldman, who had won an Oscar for writing *Butch Cassidy and the Sundance Kid*, and invited him to a meeting with Woodward and Bernstein when their book was nearing completion, just to hear the story and give his input. Redford later said, "I didn't mean to involve [Goldman] in the project, and I wasn't commissioning him as the screen-writer." But a few weeks later, a mix-up led to publisher Simon & Schuster sending galley proofs of the book to Goldman's agent, who passed them on to his client, who understood this to mean he was adapting it.

CARL BERNSTEIN AND NORA EPHRON WROTE A DRAFT.

Goldman's first pass at the script yielded something nobody liked—not Redford, not Woodward, and not Bernstein. Unsolicited, Bernstein and his then-girlfriend, writer Nora Ephron wrote their own draft. Goldman was offended by the very idea of two non-screen-writers presuming to revise his work. He was even more furious when Redford weakly suggested that he consider their input. In hindsight, everyone agreed the whole incident was a mistake: "I would say in retrospect that whatever Goldman says about the self-aggrandizing notion of that screenplay, it might well be right," Bernstein said in 2016. "I would not say that our treatment of him was sterling."

THE NEWSROOM SET IS A PRECISE RE-CREATION OF THE REAL THING.

The film was shot on location where possible, but it wasn't feasible to shoot in the *Washington Post*'s newsroom, where they were putting out a paper every day. Instead, a crew took hundreds of photos and measurements of the workspace and built a 33,000-square-foot replica on the Warner Bros. lot in Burbank, California.

A LITTLE BIT OF IT IS PURE FICTION.

Despite the attention to detail and emphasis on accuracy, there's at least one thing in the movie that never happened in real life: Bernstein luring a protective receptionist (Polly Holliday) away from her desk with a fake phone call so he can slip in and see her boss (Ned Beatty). According to Goldman, it's the one element of Bernstein and Ephron's draft that made it into the final picture.

FREEZE-FRAME

To emphasize the mystery and obfuscation of Watergate, cinematographer Gordon Willis shot most indoor scenes with minimal light and a lot of shadows. The one place that's brightly lit, with no shadows? The newsroom, where the truth is revealed for all to see. Symbolism!

POLITICS UNUSUAL:

INTRIGUING POLITICAL MOVIES

They say that politics makes strange bedfellows. They also make for the basis of some great movies.

1 The American President (1995)

Before he was chronicling the triumphs and tragedies of the Bartlet administration for the small screen on *The West Wing*, Aaron Sorkin was following a different fictional commander in chief: Andrew Shepherd (Michael Douglas) and his budding romance with lobbyist Sydney Ellen Wade (Annette Bening). The film doesn't have the same devoted following as *The West Wing*, but it gave birth to many of Sorkin's presidential hallmarks.

2 The Death of Stalin (2017)

The Death of Stalin proved that *Veep* creator Armando Iannucci's penchant for political satire knows no bounds. This wholly irreverent, not wholly accurate dark comedy follows the machinations of Joseph Stalin's top-tier henchmen—including Steve Buscemi as Nikita Khrushchev and Michael Palin as Vyacheslav Molotov—in the wake of their leader's untimely demise. Not everyone appreciated Iannucci's endeavor to find humor in this fraught chapter of Soviet history: Russia banned the movie altogether.

3 Election (1999)

Reese Witherspoon stars as the indomitable Tracy Flick, a type A overachiever dead set on becoming student body president, no matter what it takes. Matthew Broderick—no stranger to teen movies, but a far cry from his Ferris Bueller days here—co-stars as the high school teacher who intends to stop her. Under the steady hand of director Alexander Payne, *Election*— which is based on Tom Perrotta's scathing 1998 novel of the same name—offers up the kind of savage satire that'll make you want to laugh while you squirm. But one thing's for sure: You'll think twice before you run for student office—or tamper with the results.

4 Lincoln (2012)

Daniel Day-Lewis gives a powerful, Oscar-winning performance in *Lincoln*, which recounts the final months of the sixteenth president's life as he fights to end war, mend the wounds of a nation, and ensure the abolition of slavery.

5 The Parallax View (1974)

Warren Beatty is Joe Frady, a newspaper reporter whose ex-girlfriend Lee (Paula Prentiss) comes to him for help after witnessing the assassination of a prominent presidential candidate atop Seattle's Space Needle—having realized that everyone else who was there that day has died under mysterious circumstances. When Lee, too, is found dead, Frady realizes she was on to something. He begins digging for the truth, ultimately discovering that a corporation might be responsible for the number of bodies that keep piling up around him. *The Parallax View* marks the second film in Alan J. Pakula's so-called Paranoia Trilogy, which began with *Klute* (1971) and concluded with *All the President's Men*.

AMADEUS (1984)

WRITTEN BY: Peter Shaffer

DIRECTED BY: Miloš Forman

OTHER MOVIES DIRECTED BY MILOŠ FORMAN:
One Flew Over the Cuckoo's Nest (1975); *Hair* (1979); *Ragtime* (1981); *The People vs. Larry Flynt* (1996); *Man on the Moon* (1999)

Though much has been written about the life of Wolfgang Amadeus Mozart, the most entertaining look at the master composer's life might very well be *Amadeus*, Miloš Forman's film about the artist's life (and rivalries). The Oscar-winning biopic not only brought renewed interest to Mozart's music in the 1980s, but inspired Austrian rocker Falco to write the chart-topping "Rock Me Amadeus." Poor Salieri never stood a chance.

AMADEUS BEGAN LIFE AS A TONY AWARD-WINNING PLAY.

Playwright Peter Shaffer had become intrigued with the legends of Mozart and Salieri's rivalry, which led him to write *Amadeus*. It played in various theaters in London beginning in 1979, then premiered on Broadway in 1980 with Ian McKellen as Antonio Salieri and Tim Curry as Mozart. The production won five Tonys, including Best Play and Best Actor for McKellen, who beat out Curry for the award. Later, when the film arrived, it was Salieri who triumphed: F. Murray Abraham's Salieri beat out Tom Hulce's Mozart for the Best Actor Oscar.

MARK HAMILL WANTED THE LEAD, BUT FORMAN WOULDN'T AUDITION HIM.

Star Wars icon Mark Hamill played Mozart in touring and Broadway productions in 1983, and was interested in reprising the role on the big screen. "Miloš Forman said 'Oh no, you must not be playing the Mozart, because the people not believing the Luke Spacewalker as playing the Mozart,'" Hamill (putting on a Czech accent) said in 1986.

KENNETH BRANAGH THOUGHT HE HAD LANDED THE LEAD ROLE.

In his autobiography, Branagh wrote that he thought he had the part in the bag until he was informed by Forman that they were casting Americans for the leads. Other actors who auditioned for the Mozart role included Curry and Mel Gibson. Though Mozart was a rock star in his day, actual rock star Mick Jagger was also turned down after his audition. Ultimately, Tom Hulce won the lead.

THEY NEARLY BURNED DOWN A PRICELESS LANDMARK.

The movie was filmed at the Tyl Theatre (now known as the Estates Theatre) in Prague, which is the theater where *Don Giovanni* premiered in October 1787. The authenticity of the building was a huge boon for the production, since it had hardly been updated since it was first built in 1783. "We had fire everywhere," choreographer Twyla Tharp recalled in 2015. "We could have burnt down the opera house."

And there nearly was a disaster: While filming in the opera house, an actor wearing a peacock feather on their helmet leaned back—into a lit candelabra. The feather caught fire. They kept filming until a fireman told Forman,

"Please stop the cameras, your actor is on fire."

TOM HULCE PRACTICED PIANO FOR FOUR TO FIVE HOURS A DAY.

In order to look believable on camera, Hulce spent a month with a piano teacher before filming. "I spent four weeks, four to five hours a day learning to play," Hulce told *People* in 1984. And for that scene at the masquerade ball when Mozart plays a tune while lying on his back? That was really Hulce.

HULCE'S LAUGH IS LIKELY FICTITIOUS.

Throughout the movie, Mozart has an infectious cackle. Hulce created the giggle after Forman asked him to come up with "something extreme." But he was only ever able to make the sound while filming. "When we did the looping nine months later, I couldn't find the laugh," Hulce later said. "I had to raid the producer's private bar and have a shot of whiskey to jar myself into it."

As to whether the laugh is historically accurate? Hulce claimed it was, but music professor Robert L. Marshall wrote, "We simply have no contemporary testimony at all as to how Mozart sounded when he laughed."

THE ACTORS FELT INTENSE JEALOUSY, TOO.

Salieri and Mozart were eighteenth-century frenemies: They were contemporaries in a competitive field, and though they needed each other's support, they weren't above petty jealousies and worries about backstabbing. Hulce and Abraham also felt those pressures. "Tom and Meg [Tilly, the actress originally cast as Constanze, but who had to drop out due to a leg injury] were very close," Abraham told the *New York Times* in 1984. "They had these secret jokes and were always laughing together. I was pushed out, and I was resentful. I began to have very nasty feelings that were exactly like Salieri's feelings toward Mozart."

23

HERE'S LOOKING AT YOU:

MEMORABLE BIOPICS

While it might seem fun to be the subject of a feature film, not every person-turned-character has loved seeing their life play out on the big screen. But that doesn't mean we can't enjoy these tiny dives into real life.

1 *12 Years a Slave* (2013)
Steve McQueen had already been considering developing a movie about a free Black man sold into slavery when his wife recommended that he read *12 Years a Slave*, Solomon Northup's 1850s memoir in which that very thing happens. Despite the violent nature of the film—based on McQueen's commitment not to "sugarcoat" the era—Lupita Nyong'o (who won a Best Supporting Actress Oscar for her role as Patsey) described the set as "a very safe and sacred place."

2 *The Aviator* (2004)
Leonardo DiCaprio's pairings with Martin Scorsese have resulted in several critically praised films, including 2002's *Gangs of New York* and 2013's *The Wolf of Wall Street*. Here he portrays pioneering aviator and noted recluse Howard Hughes, a man whose piloting and entrepreneurial prowess were quickly overshadowed by mental illness.

3 *Donnie Brasco* (1997)
To watch Al Pacino as forlorn mafia second-stringer Lefty Ruggiero is to forget about his assured Michael Corleone in *The Godfather*. Paired with Johnny Depp as real-life (though somewhat fictionalized) undercover FBI agent Joe Pistone who infiltrated the Bonanno crime family in the seventies, Pacino is underworld-weary and close to the end of his run. As Depp puts both of them in increasing danger, you get to feeling sorry for the wrong guy. Their performances made *Donnie Brasco* one of the last great mob tales in a pre-*Sopranos* world.

4 *The Elephant Man* (1980)
For all his career weirdness to come, David Lynch played it relatively straight with *The Elephant Man*. That might have been out of respect for Joseph (John) Merrick, the real-life subject of the film who suffered from such severe disfigurement that he was a morbid sideshow attraction in nineteenth-century London. The prosthetics never threaten to overshadow John Hurt, who gives Merrick a humanity not afforded by a cruel society; or Anthony Hopkins, who plays the physician determined to comfort Merrick in what ended up being a short life. Mel Brooks convinced Lynch to make the film but didn't publicize his producing credit: It was feared his name might have people expecting a comedy.

5 *Raging Bull* (1980)
Scorsese kicked off the eighties with what many people consider the best film of his career—a gorgeously shot black-and-white story of volatile boxer Jake LaMotta (Robert De Niro, in an Oscar-winning performance). Though it wasn't a box office success (which caused Scorsese no small amount of anxiety), it was hailed by critics and is now regarded as one of the best boxing movies of all time.

AMERICAN PSYCHO
(2000)

WRITTEN BY: Mary Harron and Guinevere Turner (based on the book by Bret Easton Ellis)

DIRECTED BY: Mary Harron

OTHER MOVIES DIRECTED BY MARY HARRON: *I Shot Andy Warhol* (1996); *The Notorious Bettie Page* (2005); *Charlie Says* (2018)

Before he set the bar for superhero reboots as Christopher Nolan's Caped Crusader, Christian Bale took on the role of yuppie serial killer Patrick Bateman of Bret Easton Ellis's iconic 1991 novel (which was set in 1980s Manhattan). The film wasn't an easy sell—it took nearly a decade to finish—and a range of actors and directors were attached to it over the years. When it finally was released, a misguided marketing campaign—which sold the movie as a straight-up horror film rather than the dark satire and social commentary it was meant to be—left audience members expecting a conventional slasher movie confused and disappointed. Fortunately, *American Psycho* eventually found its audience, which has only grown in the years since.

CHRISTIAN BALE WAS TOLD THAT TAKING THE ROLE WAS CAREER SUICIDE.

"When I offered [Bale] the part, he said he had all these messages on his answering machine telling him this was career suicide. And that just made him more excited," Harron told the *Guardian* in 2000. "That's sort of how I reacted, too." But the studio wanted a bigger name in the role. "They would've taken almost anybody over Christian," Harron said.

AMERICAN PSYCHO BY THE NUMBERS

18 seconds made the difference between an NC-17 or an R rating

While the film's violence might seem to have proposed the biggest obstacle for the MPAA, *American Psycho*'s original NC-17 stemmed largely from an explicit sex scene involving Bateman and a pair of prostitutes. In order to secure an R rating, Harron was forced to cut eighteen seconds out.

LEONARDO DICAPRIO WAS OFFERED THE LEAD—WITHOUT MARY HARRON'S KNOWLEDGE.

At the 1998 Cannes Film Festival, Lionsgate executives announced that Leonardo DiCaprio—fresh off his *Titanic* success—would be playing the lead in *American Psycho*, which was news to both Harron and Bale. So Harron refused to meet with DiCaprio. "Leonardo wasn't remotely right [for the part]," Harron told the *Guardian*. "There's something very boyish about him. He's not credible as one of these tough Wall Street guys. He brought way too much baggage with him; I did not want to deal with someone who had a 13-year-old fan base. They shouldn't see the movie." Ultimately, the studio lined up Oliver Stone to replace Harron.

Legendary feminist Gloria Steinem was a vocal opponent of *American Psycho*—both the book and its proposed movie—for the violence it depicted against women. It was long rumored that she tried to talk DiCaprio out of taking the role. Coincidentally, on September 3, 2000—less than five months after *American Psycho*'s release—Steinem married David Bale, Christian Bale's father.

BALE IGNORED THE FACT THAT HE HAD BEEN RECAST.

Despite DiCaprio and Stone now being attached to the adaptation, Bale proceeded as if nothing had changed about his deal with Harron. "I would call Mary Harron," Bale told the *Wall Street Journal*. "She'd be having a nice dinner with her family—and I'd go, 'So Mary, so when we do this scene . . . ' And she'd go, 'Christian, Oliver Stone is directing, DiCaprio is playing your role.' I said, 'Right, but you said it, *my* role, all right? It is coming back, so let's talk about it, because it's coming back to us.' And she'd go, 'Christian, can you please leave me alone?'" Bale was right to be optimistic; after passing on roles for nine months in the hope that *American Psycho* would come back around, it finally did.

THE FILM MARKED THE FIRST OF BALE'S MANY BODY TRANSFORMATIONS.

In order to achieve Bateman's near-perfect physique, Bale worked out with a trainer for three hours a day, six days per week. *American Psycho* marked the beginning of Bale's numerous body transformations; he lost sixty-three pounds to play an insomniac in 2004's *The Machinist*, then immediately needed to gain the weight back—plus even more muscle—to begin his superhero reign in *Batman Begins*.

APOCALYPSE NOW

(1979)

WRITTEN BY: John Milius and Francis Ford Coppola

DIRECTED BY: Francis Ford Coppola

OTHER MOVIES DIRECTED BY FRANCIS FORD COPPOLA:
The Godfather (1972); *The Conversation* (1974);
The Godfather: Part II (1974); *The Outsiders* (1983)

In the annals of movies whose behind-the-scenes stories were as troubled and disastrous as the stories they depicted, few rank higher than Francis Ford Coppola's *Apocalypse Now*, a loose adaptation of Joseph Conrad's novella *Heart of Darkness*. But the result of more than a year of filming plagued by bad weather, sickness, and Marlon Brando's unpreparedness was a movie that has only risen in people's estimation since then, vividly depicting the insanity of the Vietnam War through the eyes of a rattled U.S. Army captain (Martin Sheen) as he searches for a rogue Army Special Forces officer (Brando).

GEORGE LUCAS WAS SUPPOSED TO DIRECT IT.

The original plan for *Apocalypse Now* was that Coppola would produce with then up-and-comer Lucas directing, shooting it on 16mm black-and-white film in Stockton, California, in a pseudo-documentary style similar to Gillo Pontecorvo's *The Battle of Algiers* (1966). But the project languished for years, and Lucas eventually dropped out to direct a movie he had written—*Star Wars*.

HARVEY KEITEL WAS THE FIRST ACTOR TO PLAY CAPTAIN WILLARD.

Casting Captain Willard proved to be problematic. Coppola first offered the role to Steve McQueen, who turned it down because he didn't want to shoot in the jungle. Al Pacino, James Caan, and Jack Nicholson all said no, too, but Harvey Keitel was game. However, after a few weeks Coppola fired Keitel for reasons that remain a source of disagreement. That's when Martin Sheen stepped in. According to legendary editor Walter Murch, who won an Oscar for his work on the film, there is one shot of Keitel in the movie: Willard walks from the helicopter to the boat, and puts his rifle next to him. It was a wide shot, and the sunset was perfect, so they kept it in.

COPPOLA RISKED EVERY CENT HE HAD.

Coppola invested $30 million of his own money to get the budget he believed he needed. That total included the valuations of his house and his winery, which he signed over as collateral. If the movie tanked, Coppola faced financial ruin, which understandably made the filming process fairly stressful. The director suffered an epileptic seizure while shooting and also had a nervous breakdown.

THE MOVIE WENT FAMOUSLY OVER BUDGET AND WAY OVER SCHEDULE.

Initially, Coppola planned for a fourteen-week shoot in the Philippines in the spring of 1976, but Typhoon Olga ruined nearly all the sets and equipment, forcing the production to shut down for eight weeks. Coppola shot with reckless abandon thereafter, and principal photography didn't conclude until May 1977. Post-production lasted another two years, and the movie was finally released in August 1979. The 1991 documentary *Hearts of Darkness: A Filmmaker's Apocalypse*—directed by Fax Bahr, George Hickenlooper, and Francis's wife Eleanor Coppola—offers a vivid look behind the scenes of the making of the movie, and its many challenges.

COPPOLA HAD TO GET CREATIVE WHILE SHOOTING MARLON BRANDO.

Brando, who previously won an Oscar (which he refused) as Vito Corleone in Coppola's *The Godfather*, showed up in the Philippines weighing more than was expected. This meant that all of his costumes had to be scrapped and the director had to come up with a way to shoot around Brando's weight. Coppola and cinematographer Vittorio Storaro decided that shooting Brando in shadows and silhouettes would solve the problem and make Colonel Kurtz seem more mysterious. (They also utilized six-foot-six Pete Cooper, their on-set Marine coordinator, as a stand-in for Brando in some shots.)

COPPOLA MADE UP THE MOVIE'S ENDING AS HE WENT ALONG.

The original ending in John Milius's script had North Vietnamese forces attacking Kurtz and his followers in a giant climactic battle, but Coppola scrapped that because he felt it didn't fit with the movie he was making. Instead, using the story of the "Fisher King" found in books like *The Golden Bough* and the poetry of T. S. Eliot (a book of which can be seen in Kurtz's possession in the film), Coppola devised a new ending wherein Willard would kill Kurtz and ostensibly become his followers' new king.

'70s

SPECTACULAR SEVENTIES MOVIES

By the end of the 1960s, the battle between "Old Hollywood" (Technicolor musicals, historical epics, and old-fashioned acting) and "New Hollywood" (youth-oriented stories full of sex and violence, political volatility, and realistic performances) was over, and New Hollywood had won. Game-changing films like *Bonnie & Clyde*, *The Graduate*, and *Easy Rider*—all released between 1967 and 1969—had shifted the Hollywood tide while the French New Wave had inspired the kids in film school, and the 1970s proved a remarkably fertile time for the new batch of filmmakers that followed. Miraculously, studios gave these young directors a lot of creative freedom. The result? One of the best decades in all of movie history.

The Godfather (and its sequel), *All the President's Men*, *The French Connection*, *Apocalypse Now*, *Jaws*, *Harold and Maude*, and *Star Wars* are just a handful of the iconic titles that were born in the seventies (and are written about elsewhere in this book). Here are some of the decade's other best works.

Being There (1979)

A TV-obsessed simpleton stumbling his way into the higher echelons of political power sounds totally implausible . . . but that's the premise of this genteel but sharp comedy directed by Hal Ashby, whose other films from this decade—*The Landlord, Harold and Maude, The Last Detail, Shampoo, Bound for Glory,* and *Coming Home*—could all be on this list. Peter Sellers's lead performance, just like the movie, perfectly walks the line between the absurd and the sublime.

Blue Collar (1978)

After making a name for himself as a writer with films like *Taxi Driver,* Paul Schrader chose this story of down-on-their-luck auto workers who plot to rob their union's safe as his directorial debut. It remains, even today, a searing portrait of income inequality, middle-class pain, and the way those with power manipulate the powerless into thinking they might be able to get some of their own. Yaphet Kotto, Harvey Keitel, and Richard Pryor all turn in powerful performances, and the whole film is a master class in how to use the hook of a heist plot to say something bigger.

A Clockwork Orange (1971)

Stanley Kubrick's *A Clockwork Orange,* an adaptation of Anthony Burgess's dystopian novel, still manages to surprise and shock people with its violence, sex, and social commentary. The image of a juvenile delinquent having his eyes propped open to force him to watch films meant to recondition him remains indelible.

Deliverance (1972)

Burt Reynolds began his streak of 1970s movie superstardom with this deeply disturbing tale of thirtysome-things (Reynolds, Jon Voight, Ronny Cox, and Ned Beatty) who decide to go canoeing in Georgia and find themselves in over their heads with the inhospitable locals. The result is a kind of rural horror film that resonates with the perils of paddling outside of your comfort zone.

Enter the Dragon (1973)

Bruce Lee's first major American film is revered as one of the greatest martial arts films ever made. Yet, when it became a hit, distributors began recutting and redubbing all manner of martial arts films for American audiences, creating an influx of cheap Chopsocky and Chopsocky-esque films that often featured Bruce Lee clones with names like "Bruce Li" or "Bruce Le." Sadly, Lee died shortly before the film's U.S. release, so never saw its success.

The Last Picture Show (1971)

It was fitting that as Old Hollywood faded away, an up-and-coming filmmaker like Peter Bogdanovich would make something set in the past, shot in nostalgic black-and-white, that depicted a town where the old ways were dying. Roger Ebert observed that *The Last Picture Show* "is above all an evocation of mood," full of lovely melancholy as its young, restless characters in a moribund Texas town struggle with where to go and what to do next.

Logan's Run (1976)

Ageism is taken to extremes in this standout 1970s sci-fi film about a man (Michael York) who enforces his society's mandate to kill anyone over the age of thirty. When York has a change of heart, he goes on the run himself.

M*A*S*H (1970)

Though it might be better known today simply for the sitcom it inspired, Robert Altman's *M*A*S*H* still stands as a groundbreaking, gleefully irreverent masterpiece in its own right. Anchored by incredible, understated performances from Donald Sutherland and Elliott Gould and driven by the now-famous naturalistic, constantly flowing dialogue, the film remains an intoxicating blend of high- and low-brow comedy, blending the zany with the profound, and the crude with the poignant, to create one of the great anti-war movies.

Network (1976)

Sidney Lumet's *Network* satirized that most American of inventions: the television industry. Nearly every outrageous thing that happens in this depiction of a fictional broadcast network run by ruthless executives has since happened in real life, making the film even more potent now than it was then. Plus, the performances by Faye Dunaway, William Holden, and Peter Finch are terrific fun.

One Flew Over the Cuckoo's Nest (1975)

The 1970s were a fantastic decade for Jack Nicholson, who appeared in fifteen movies including *Five Easy Pieces*, *The Last Detail*, *Chinatown*, and *One Flew Over the Cuckoo's Nest*—and those are just the ones that earned him Oscar nominations. He won for *One Flew Over the Cuckoo's Nest*, in which he plays a sane man in an insane asylum who questions authority and tries to break people out of complacency, themes that still resonate today.

Serpico (1973)

Al Pacino was nominated for an Oscar for his role as Frank Serpico, a real-life New York cop who exposed corruption within the police force. Meanwhile, director Sidney Lumet—who was always interested in social issues, as seen in movies like *12 Angry Men*, *Network*, and *The Verdict*—brought the full force of his righteous indignation to the edge-of-your-seat story.

Sweet Sweetback's Baadasssss Song (1971)

In many ways, *Sweet Sweetback's Baadasssss Song* is a fiery response to the depiction of Black characters in cinema up until that point—characters who often reacted to the prejudices forced upon them. As Sweetback, director, writer, and star Melvin Van Peebles is a proactive force, lashing out against crooked cops trying to frame him for murder with animus of his own. Though he may not be a particularly enviable hero—Sweetback has some sexist blind spots, for one—he was a pivotal adjustment in how the Black experience was communicated on film.

Taxi Driver (1976)

New York City was a violent cesspool in the seventies, and nobody captured it better than Martin Scorsese did in this jarring drama about an unstable cabbie (Robert De Niro) who longs to clean up the sleazy streets. Long before "toxic masculinity" was a common phrase, Travis Bickle was taking women to porno movies and personifying the violent ends to which some men will go to get what they want.

The Texas Chain Saw Massacre (1974)

This low-budget horror flick, basically the godfather of the "teens go somewhere remote and get murdered" genre, isn't nearly as bloody as its reputation suggests. That's partly a testament to director Tobe Hooper's ability to suggest ghastliness without actually showing it, and partly due to the fact that most of the film's many imitators are drenched in gore. Nearly fifty years later, the film's raw, nightmarish final thirty minutes are still horrifically effective.

The Warriors (1979)

Walter Hill's now-legendary action movie about a Coney Island gang trying to get through one hellish night in New York City after being framed for the murder of another gang leader first gained notoriety, ironically enough, for gang violence breaking out at early screenings. While it caused problems early on, *The Warriors* found life beyond that initial theatrical run as a midnight and repertory cinema staple. Looking back on the film in 2014, Hill summed up his own views on why the film endured in an interview with *Esquire*: "It's probably not as apparent now, as half of today's movies are fantastical, but I think the most unusual thing about the film was the fact that it didn't present the gang and gang structure as a social problem. It presented it as simply a fact, the way things are, and not necessarily negative . . . It didn't preach to them about middle-class values. And I think that's what made the movie unique. When you look at the movie, it's more like a musical than some grimly realistic thing."

APOLLO 13
(1995)

WRITTEN BY: William Broyles Jr. and Al Reinert (based on the book by Jim Lovell and Jeffrey Kluger)

DIRECTED BY: Ron Howard

OTHER MOVIES DIRECTED BY RON HOWARD:
Night Shift (1982); *Splash* (1984); *Willow* (1988); *How the Grinch Stole Christmas* (2000); *Frost/Nixon* (2008); *Solo: A Star Wars Story* (2018); *Thirteen Lives* (2022)

In 1970, *Apollo 13* astronauts Jim Lovell, Jack Swigert, and Fred Haise blasted off into space with the goal of becoming the third NASA crew to land on the Moon. But when an explosion cost them fuel cells and oxygen, it created a life-support crisis that kept the world on the edge of its seat. Though the odds of survival were heavily stacked against them, a little ingenuity and a lot of luck went a long way in helping all three men to safely return home.

Ron Howard's dramatization of the 1970 space program crisis was the third highest-grossing film of the year, and remains one of the most faithful depictions of NASA operations ever put on film.

STEVEN SPIELBERG MADE A CRUCIAL SUGGESTION THAT CHANGED *APOLLO 13*.

To simulate weightlessness inside the *Apollo 13* spacecraft, Howard and his crew were contemplating using wires and harnesses, a logistical decision that would have had his cast suspended like marionettes for months of shooting. Instead, Spielberg—a friend of Howard's and frequent collaborator with Hanks—suggested that he look into the KC-135, a NASA-owned airplane that allows people to experience zero gravity by maneuvering forty-five degrees up and then plummeting forty-five degrees down. Howard's test shooting went well—and his producer was persistent enough that NASA granted permission for a crew to film while on board the plane.

THE CAST ENDURED MORE THAN SIX HUNDRED CONTROLLED PLANE DIVES.

Because the KC-135 only achieved weightlessness for its occupants for twenty-five seconds at a time, Howard, Hanks (playing Lovell), and co-stars Kevin Bacon (as Swigert) and Bill Paxton (who portrayed Haise) had to make roughly six hundred dives in order to capture the amount of footage needed. Thirty to forty dives were possible per flight, and the crew took two flights a day. The actors actually got more pre-space experience with a reduced-gravity environment than a lot of real astronauts.

HOWARD REFUSED TO USE ANY STOCK FOOTAGE.

Both NASA and news crews had been meticulous in their coverage of the crew's departure and subsequent reentry, and Howard had investigated the possibility of using it for the film. But when his team began studying the footage, they realized most of it had been seen. Instead, Howard created all shots of the mission, replicating actual scenes and then augmenting them with angles that would have been impossible in real life. It was so convincing that *Apollo 11* astronaut Buzz Aldrin asked where they had found the archived footage.

A PREVIEW AUDIENCE MEMBER HATED *APOLLO 13*'S ENDING.

Test screenings of the film were generally a success, but Howard was fascinated by the opinion of one twenty-three-year-old who seemed to be aggravated at the film's climax, where the astronauts plop into the ocean unharmed. This, he wrote on a comments card, was "Terrible. More Hollywood BS. They would never survive."

"HOUSTON, WE HAVE A PROBLEM" WAS NOT THE EXACT QUOTE.

Lovell's grim announcement of the command module's malfunctions to Mission Control was not quoted word for word in the film. In reality, the ground received the message, "Houston, we've had a problem here." While Hanks's Lovell delivers the line in the movie, in real life, it was Swigert who first said it—though Lovell repeated it immediately as "Houston, we've had a problem."

SWIGERT'S FRIEND WAS UNHAPPY WITH BACON'S PORTRAYAL OF THE ASTRONAUT.

Swigert, who was one of the three astronauts aboard *Apollo 13*, died in 1982. In the film, Bacon embodies Swigert as a roving-eyed bachelor and possibly a carrier of a sexually transmitted disease. (Paxton's Fred Haise comments he might've gotten "the clap.") When the film was released, Barbara Zuanich-Friedman, a friend of Swigert's, penned an op-ed for the *Los Angeles Times* that took producers to task for his portrayal, asserting he was not the playboy Bacon presented. "Hollywood usually stereotypes its bachelors," she wrote, "and Jack, 25 years after the fact, fell prey to that chintzy ploy . . . He would have loved the film. He would have hated his character."

"Failure is not an option."

FAR OUT:

10

OUT-OF-THIS-WORLD SPACE MOVIES

1 Contact **(1997)**
Countless movies have asked whether or not we're alone in the universe, but few have given it more thought than Robert Zemeckis's adaptation of Carl Sagan's bestselling novel. Initially, *Mad Max*'s George Miller was tapped to direct, but he left the production when Warner Bros. decided to take the film in a new direction. "It basically regressed into a much safer, more predictable thing," Miller said in 2015. The filmmaker likened his own interpretation to Christopher Nolan's *Interstellar*.

2 *Gravity* **(2013)**
There are no aliens or intergalactic battleships in *Gravity,* but it ranks among the most thrilling space movies of the 2010s. Sandra Bullock and George Clooney star as a pair of astronauts who find themselves marooned in space when, while working in Earth's orbit, flying debris destroys their shuttle. The straightforward plot left director Alfonso Cuarón plenty of room to showcase the movie's groundbreaking visual effects. To simulate moving in microgravity, the actors were strapped into rigs that lifted and rotated them at different angles. Despite the physically demanding work, Bullock's and Clooney's faces are the only "real" components in many shots; much of the rest is CGI.

3 *Hidden Figures* **(2016)**
Hidden Figures spotlights the long-overlooked contributions Black women made to space exploration. Based on a nonfiction book, it tells the true story of Katherine Johnson (Taraji P. Henson), Dorothy Vaughan (Octavia Spencer), Mary Jackson (Janelle Monáe), and the other Black women who helped launch America's astronauts into space. It covers both the space race and the civil rights movement, as the Black mathematicians became key players in the rush to send an American into orbit and eventually land one on the moon. Though the movie took some creative liberties, Johnson herself approved of it.

4 Independence Day (1996)

Welcome to Earth? More like welcome to a disaster movie resurgence. Disaster movies were a big thing in the 1970s, with box office hits like *Airport* (1970) and *The Towering Inferno* (1974) laying the groundwork for what was to come. But it wasn't until Roland Emmerich's *Independence Day*—with its memorable ensemble cast featuring Will Smith, Jeff Goldblum, and Bill Pullman, along with its groundbreaking special effects—that the genre really found its footing. The film's success inspired a slew of imitators in the latter half of the nineties (see: *Dante's Peak*, *Volcano*, and others). Meanwhile, Emmerich went on to become a titan in the genre with later (albeit lesser) hits like *The Day After Tomorrow* (2004) and *2012* (2009).

5 Interstellar (2014)

Christopher Nolan followed up the final installment of his box office–smashing Batman trilogy with an esoteric space adventure. *Interstellar* tells the story of a group of astronauts from a dystopian future who pass through a wormhole in a quest to find habitable planets for humans to colonize. Though the mix of popcorn sci-fi with philosophical themes was met with mixed reviews, the special effects received universal praise. The VFX team collaborated with theoretical physicist Kip Thorne to create an accurate depiction of a wormhole based on real scientific equations. In addition to its innovative visuals, *Interstellar* also gave us one of Hans Zimmer's most memorable scores and an epic performance in the Matthew McConaughey "McConaissance."

6 The Martian (2015)

Based on Andy Weir's 2011 sci-fi bestseller of the same name, *The Martian* follows Mark Watney (Matt Damon), an astronaut and botanist struggling to survive on Mars after being presumed dead and left behind by his team. While humans are still years away from landing on Mars—let alone living and farming there—there's a reason those notions feel especially convincing in the film. Director Ridley Scott and his team worked with NASA to model their depiction of Mars from real science.

7 Moon (2009)

Sam Rockwell stars as Sam Bell, the lone astronaut on a lunar base harvesting alternative fuel. Unfortunately for the astronaut, whose only companion is a robot named GERTY, things on the base are not quite what they seem. When director Duncan Jones (son of David Bowie) screened the flick for real-life astronauts at NASA, they gave him high marks for nailing "the mundaneness of working in that environment," Jones told *Popular Mechanics*. "You do a lot of really boring stuff again and again and again. There's not a lot to do up there. You've got your job to do and a lot of time to kill."

8 Solaris (1972)

Soviet filmmaker Andrei Tarkovsky's iconic film, which won the Special Grand Prix du Jury at Cannes, follows the travails of a crew on a space station orbiting a fictional planet. It was based on the novel by Stanisław Lem, and though they worked together on adapting it for the screen, Lem was not a fan of Tarkovsky's vision, apparently telling the filmmaker during an argument that "he didn't make *Solaris* at all, he made *Crime and Punishment*."

9 Spaceballs (1987)

Mel Brooks hadn't directed a movie in six years when he released *Spaceballs*, a joke-saturated spoof of *Star Wars* and other popular genre films of the era. Critics speculated he was a little too late (*Return of the Jedi* had been released four years prior), and box office at the time was modest, but *Spaceballs* has since earned its reputation as a cult hit.

10 WALL·E (2008)

On paper, Pixar's *WALL·E* is bleak. It's the twenty-ninth century, the only remaining humans are sedentary blobs aboard starships, and WALL·E (Waste Allocation Load-Lifter: Earth-Class) is the last trash compactor still operating on the landfill wasteland that is Earth. But the wide-eyed, diligent little robot that could is infinitely lovable—and the story of his adventure to one of the starships to save a seedling and a fellow robot is full of hope and humanity. Sound designer Ben Burtt (of *Star Wars* fame) used some 2,400 sounds to bring *WALL·E* to life, from electric toothbrushes and shopping carts to Slinkies—they make a surprisingly good laser-gun sound.

BACK TO THE FUTURE

(1985)

WRITTEN BY: Robert Zemeckis and Bob Gale

DIRECTED BY: Robert Zemeckis

OTHER MOVIES DIRECTED BY ROBERT ZEMECKIS:
Who Framed Roger Rabbit (1988); *Forrest Gump* (1994); *Cast Away* (2000); *Flight* (2012); *Pinocchio* (2022)

On July 3, 1985, Robert Zemeckis unleashed a time travel movie for a whole new generation when he had Marty McFly (Michael J. Fox) hop behind the wheel of a tricked-out DeLorean and zoom back in time—with a little help from Emmett "Doc" Brown (Christopher Lloyd) and some stolen plutonium—to ensure his future existence.

The movie, which was nominated for four Oscars and won one (for Best Sound Effects Editing), became the biggest movie of 1985 and quickly spawned two sequels over the next five years, both of which scored major wins at the box office. Heavy!

THE *BACK TO THE FUTURE* SCRIPT WAS REJECTED MORE THAN FORTY TIMES.

Back to the Future may be considered a classic today, but the initial response to the script hardly predicted how big of a hit it would become. "The script was rejected over forty times by every major studio and by some more than once," screenwriter Bob Gale told CNN in 2010. "It was always one of two things. It was 'Well, this is time travel, and those movies don't make any money' . . . We also got, 'There's a lot of sweetness to this. It's too nice, we want something raunchier like *Porky's*. Why don't you take it to Disney?'"

DISNEY THOUGHT THE MOVIE WAS TOO RAUNCHY.

After hearing "take it to Disney" enough times, Gale and Zemeckis did just that. As Gale told CNN: "We went in to meet with an executive and he says, 'Are you guys nuts? Are you insane? We can't make a movie like this. You've got the kid and the mother in his car! It's incest—this is Disney. It's too dirty for us!'"

MARTY AND DOC'S FRIENDSHIP BEGAN WITH A BREAK-IN.

Have you ever wondered how Marty and Doc became friends? Well, we did—Gale shared the origin of their friendship with Mental Floss: "[He] snuck into Doc's lab, and was fascinated by all the cool stuff that was there. When Doc found him there, he was delighted to find that Marty thought he was cool and accepted him for what he was. Both of them were the black sheep in their respective environments. Doc gave Marty a part-time job to help with experiments, tend to the lab, tend to the dog, etc."

THE TIME MACHINE WAS ORIGINALLY AN OLD REFRIGERATOR.

Well, sort of an old refrigerator. "Way back in that second draft, it was going to be a 'time chamber,' not unlike a refrigerator, and Doc Brown had to carry it on the back of his truck," Gale told CNN.

DOC BROWN ORIGINALLY HAD A PET CHIMPANZEE.

Sid Sheinberg, head of Universal, was anti-chimpanzee: "I looked it up," he told Gale, "no movie with a chimpanzee ever made any money." When Gale and Zemeckis countered that Clint Eastwood's *Every Which Way but Loose* and *Any Which Way You Can* had been popular, Sheinberg replied, "No, that was an orangutan."

RONALD REAGAN QUOTED THE MOVIE IN HIS 1986 STATE OF THE UNION.

It has long been stated that Ronald Reagan was offered the role of Hill Valley's mayor in *Back to the Future Part III*, but turned it down. What is known is that the Reagans were fans of the original *Back to the Future*. So much so that they hosted a screening of it at Camp David, and Reagan even referenced it in his 1986 State of the Union address, stating: "As they said in the film *Back to the Future*, 'Where we're going, we don't need roads.'"

FREEZE-FRAME

In the opening scene, the clocks in Doc Brown's garage are twenty-five minutes behind. One of the clocks features a man hanging from its hands, which is a reference to silent comedy star Harold Lloyd's famous scene from the 1923 film *Safety Last*. It also foreshadows the later scene where Doc hangs from the Hill Valley clock tower in the same way.

TRANSPORTIVE TIME TRAVEL MOVIES

Marty McFly isn't the only hapless protagonist who has run into time travel issues. Here are some other movies that have turned back the clock.

1 **Bill & Ted's Excellent Adventure (1989)**
Party on, dudes! Spaced-out high school pals Bill (Alex Winter) and Ted (Keanu Reeves) head back in time to meet historical figures so they can give a most excellent presentation and graduate. In the original script, the time machine was a 1969 Chevy van; it was changed to a phone booth to avoid comparisons with a certain DeLorean. "Director Stephen Herek had the idea of a phone booth and all of us were so clueless and knew nothing about *Doctor Who*," co-writer Chris Matheson said. "It turned out to be a pretty good idea. It worked."

2 **The Final Countdown (1980)**
Kirk Douglas stars as commanding officer of the USS *Nimitz*, an aircraft carrier that travels back to Pearl Harbor just before the attack of December 7, 1941. Douglas wants to intervene with his modern technology but doesn't know whether his ship will save lives or change history. The U.S. Navy allowed the production to film on the real *Nimitz*.

3 **Frequency (2000)**
John Sullivan (Jim Caviezel) is a homicide detective who misses his late father (Dennis Quaid). When Sullivan discovers he's able to communicate with his dad via a ham radio, it lessens his grief—and helps him solve a murder.

4 **Men in Black 3 (2012)**
This threequel sidelines Tommy Lee Jones's Agent K but has the good sense to cast Josh Brolin as a younger version of the character, whom Will Smith's Agent J encounters when he travels back to 1969 to prevent K's death.

5 **Primer (2004)**
This micro-budget affair—which reportedly cost $7,000 to make—takes a scientific approach to time travel, with engineers Aaron (Shane Carruth) and Abe (David Sullivan) accidentally discovering they can travel a few hours into the past. Despite their academic approach, emotion and greed make a mess of it all.

6 **Somewhere in Time (1980)**
Somewhere in Time puts modern-day playwright Richard Collier (Christopher Reeve) in the arms of early twentieth-century actress Elise McKenna (Jane Seymour) via the power of suggestion. The movie's screenplay was written by sci-fi legend Richard Matheson, whose numerous credits include countless episodes of *The Twilight Zone* as well as the 1954 novel *I Am Legend*, which was adapted into the 2007 movie starring Will Smith.

7 **Time After Time (1979)**
Malcolm McDowell is sci-fi author H. G. Wells, racing forward in time to capture a maniacal Jack the Ripper (David Warner), who used the writer's time machine to travel to 1979 San Francisco. While there, Wells enlists the help of a young bank employee (Mary Steenburgen), and quickly falls in love. McDowell asked the BBC for recordings of Wells but found the writer's South East London accent so unpleasant he refused to try to duplicate it.

8 **Timecop (1994)**
Time Enforcement Commission officer Agent Max Walker (Jean-Claude Van Damme) pursues an evil politician (Ron Silver) into the past to make sure he doesn't realize his ambitions to hold higher office. This spry sci-fi actioner might be the Belgian actor's best film.

9 **Timecrimes (2007)**
This twist-laden Spanish thriller stars Karra Elejalde as a man who stumbles on a time machine and believes he needs to travel back to stop himself from making some fatal errors.

10 **Trancers (1984)**
Jack Deth (Tim Thomerson) is a detective in the twenty-third century who uses the unique time travel method of jumping into an ancestor's body with his consciousness to pursue the villainous Whistler (Michael Stefani)—whose time vessel of a relative happens to be a police officer. Quentin Tarantino has said it's one of the most original time travel films ever made.

WRITTEN BY: Sam Hamm and Warren Skaaren

DIRECTED BY: Tim Burton

OTHER MOVIES DIRECTED BY TIM BURTON:
Pee-wee's Big Adventure (1985); *Beetlejuice* (1988); *Edward Scissorhands* (1990); *Corpse Bride* (2005); *Dumbo* (2019)

BATMAN

(1989)

Superhero movies are bigger than they've ever been before, but one can argue we wouldn't be here at all without 1989's *Batman*. Tim Burton's dark look at the Caped Crusader, which was produced at a time before comic book movies were considered big business, is now a pop culture landmark. Michael Keaton wasn't the first choice for the role of the eponymous superhero, an orphaned billionaire who spends his nights keeping the streets of his beloved Gotham City safe, but he forever changed the genre's landscape.

BATMAN TOOK TEN YEARS TO MAKE.

Executive producers Michael Uslan and Benjamin Melniker lobbied hard for the rights to *Batman*, and finally landed them in 1979, but every studio from Columbia Pictures to United Artists turned it down. In the early eighties, Warner Bros. agreed to back the film, but the script went through several writers and iterations over the next several years. In 1989, *Batman* was finally released; Uslan has been involved in some form in every Batman film since, including as executive producer on Matt Reeves's *The Batman* (2022). Melniker was, too, until his death in 2018 at the age of 104.

AN EARLY SCRIPT FEATURED BOTH THE PENGUIN AND ROBIN.

When Uslan finally got the chance to develop the film, he drafted Tom Mankiewicz, who was a major figure in Richard Donner's *Superman* (1978), to write the script. His script included the Joker, the Penguin, a much greater focus on Bruce Wayne's origin story, and the arrival of Robin late in the film. There would be further rewrites and treatments, but Burton wanted to do his own thing, writing of one treatment he saw that "there was absolutely no exploration or acknowledgement of the character's psychological structure and why he would dress up in a bat suit. In that respect, it was very much like the television series."

TIM BURTON HAD TO FIGHT TO CAST MICHAEL KEATON.

In the 1980s, Michael Keaton was best known for his comedic roles, so the thought of casting him as a vigilante of the night seemed odd; in fact, Uslan thought he was being pranked when Keaton's name popped up. Burton, who had worked with Keaton on *Beetlejuice*, was convinced the actor was right for the role—in part because he felt Keaton was the kind of actor who would need to dress up as a bat in order to scare criminals, while a typical action star would just garner "unintentional laughs" in the suit.

JACK NICHOLSON WAS THE FIRST CHOICE FOR THE JOKER, BUT HE WASN'T THE ONLY CHOICE.

From the beginning, Uslan concluded that Jack Nicholson was the perfect person to play the Joker, and was "walking on air" when the production finally cast him. He wasn't the only actor considered, though: Willem Dafoe, James Woods, Brad Dourif, David Bowie, and Robin Williams were all in contention for the part.

KEATON'S BATMAN MOVEMENTS WERE INSPIRED BY THE COSTUME'S RESTRICTIONS.

Batman fans still love to make jokes about the original costume, and Keaton's inability to turn his head (there's even a dig at that in Christopher Nolan's *The Dark Knight*), but the restrictions of the costume actually inspired how Keaton approached the role. In 2014, Keaton revealed that his performance as Batman was heavily influenced by a moment when, while trying to actually turn his head in the suit, he ended up ripping it. So Keaton suggested to Burton that moving like a statue should be one of Batman's traits.

IT WAS A BOX OFFICE LANDMARK.

Though studio executives resisted the idea of a "dark" Batman movie for years, the film ultimately set a new standard for box office success. It was the first film to ever hit $100 million in ten days, the biggest film in Warner Bros.' history at the time, and the box office's biggest earner of 1989.

BEAUTY AND THE BEAST (1991)

WRITTEN BY: Linda Woolverton

DIRECTED BY: Gary Trousdale and Kirk Wise

OTHER MOVIES DIRECTED BY GARY TROUSDALE AND KIRK WISE: *The Hunchback of Notre Dame* (1996); *Atlantis: The Lost Empire* (2001)

The success of *The Little Mermaid* in 1989 ushered in a new era of cinema for Walt Disney Pictures, one that saw it break records and achieve a number of firsts in animated filmmaking—many of them thanks to *Beauty and the Beast*. The animated love story between an independent-minded village girl named Belle and a prince-turned-Beast who imprisons her until she manages to melt his cold heart was the first animated film to win the Golden Globe for Best Motion Picture—Musical or Comedy, and the first-ever animated film to earn a Best Picture Oscar nomination.

FREEZE-FRAME

Five years after the release of *Beauty and the Beast*, Belle popped up in *The Hunchback of Notre Dame*. (Fittingly, she has her nose in a book.) *Aladdin*'s Magic Carpet and *The Lion King*'s Pumbaa also make cameos in the 1996 animated film. It's hard to spot Pumbaa—and tragic, as he appears to have been slaughtered—but directors Gary Trousdale and Kirk Wise have confirmed all three cameos.

WALT DISNEY HIMSELF CONSIDERED MAKING *BEAUTY AND THE BEAST*.

Walt Disney liked to take his time mulling things over. "When Walt became all wrapped up in the theme parks and live-action films, we tried to get him interested in animation again," Disney animator Frank Thomas recalled. "Walt said, 'If I ever do go back, there are only two subjects I would want to do. One of them is *Beauty and the Beast*.' For the life of me, I can't remember what the other one was."

THREE OF ITS TUNES EARNED BEST ORIGINAL SONG OSCAR NOMINATIONS.

While Alan Menken and Howard Ashman's title tune from *Beauty and the Beast* took home the Best Original Song Oscar in 1992, it was just one of three songs nominated from the movie: "Belle," the opening song, and "Be Our Guest" were also up for Oscars.

THE BEAST IS A MASH-UP OF VARIOUS ANIMALS.

The Beast has the mane of a lion, the beard and head of a buffalo, the brow of a gorilla, the eyes of a human, the tusks of a wild boar, the body of a bear, and the legs and tail of a wolf . . . and a little something extra. Animator Glen Keane claims that "Beast actually has a rainbow bum, but nobody knows that but Belle."

To many movie fans, Disney is synonymous with childhood. The magic may look effortless on screen, but every film in the studio's vault had to go through a complex—and sometimes troubled—production. From their first animated movie to the current CGI era, there's a fascinating story behind your favorite Disney classics.

The Wonderful World of Disney Movies

SNOW WHITE AND THE SEVEN DWARFS RECEIVED A SPECIAL OSCAR.

Snow White was a technological marvel when it premiered in 1937. To celebrate the achievement, the Academy of Motion Picture Arts and Sciences gave Walt Disney an honorary Oscar. They even made a custom award for the movie. That night Walt was presented with one full-size statuette accompanied by seven miniature ones—one for each of the seven dwarfs.

THE DEMO MUSIC WAS A LITTLE TOO ROCK 'N' ROLL FOR ANGELA LANSBURY.

When Angela Lansbury heard the demo of "Beauty and the Beast," it was "kind of a rock song," she told HuffPost. "I told them, 'This is a sweet message, but this really isn't my style. Are you sure you want me to do this?' They told me to sing the song the way I envisioned it, so that's what I did. I created it the way a little English teapot would sing the song."

THE POSTER WAS DESIGNED BY A MASTER OF THE ART.

John Alvin, the artist who created *Beauty and the Beast*'s iconic movie poster, also designed the posters for *E.T. the Extra-Terrestrial*, *Gremlins*, *The Lion King*, *The Color Purple*, and *Blazing Saddles*.

AUDIENCES WERE SUPPOSED TO SEE THE SEQUENCE WHERE THE YOUNG PRINCE IS TURNED INTO THE BEAST.

The original version of the script had the sorceress chasing the prince through the castle hurling magic at him, hitting servants and turning them into objects. Eventually, she hits her target and turns him into an animalistic creature. She leaves, and we see the young Beast looking out from the castle windows, screaming for her to come back and fix him. Wise nixed the sequence. He later said, "The only thing that I could see in my head was this Eddie Munster kid in a Little Lord Fauntleroy outfit."

SPLASH NEARLY KILLED *THE LITTLE MERMAID*.

Disney was producing a sequel to their 1984 live-action mermaid comedy hit *Splash* when writer-director Ron Clements came to the studio with his pitch for *The Little Mermaid*. The idea of releasing two movies featuring mermaids so close together didn't sit well with the studio. Ultimately, it was the draw of returning to the studio's fairy-tale origins that swayed executives Michael Eisner and Jeffrey Katzenberg to push forward with *The Little Mermaid*. Animators did take steps to distance their film from *Splash*, namely by giving Ariel red hair to contrast with Daryl Hannah's blond 'do.

THE GENIE'S TEST ANIMATION FOR *ALADDIN* FEATURED ROBIN WILLIAMS'S STAND-UP.

Robin Williams was Disney's first choice to play the Genie in the 1992 movie, and the filmmakers went to great lengths to convince him to come on board. The animation team's initial test sequence for the character showed him performing snippets from one of Williams's comedy albums. After showing the actor the comedic potential of the medium, Disney was able to convince him to sign on to the project. It was *Aladdin* that really kicked off the whole celebrities-voicing-animated-characters trend.

THE LION KING ALMOST HAD A DIFFERENT OPENING.

The "Circle of Life" sequence is one of the most iconic openings of any Disney movie, but it wasn't always meant to kick off 1994's *The Lion King*. Originally, the filmmakers wanted to open the movie with a dialogue scene introducing the major characters. However, when co-directors Roger Allers and Rob Minkoff heard the final recording of the "Circle of Life," they decided to open with it.

WALT DISNEY ORIGINALLY HAD THE IDEA FOR WHAT WOULD BECOME *FROZEN* IN 1936.

Frozen was seventy years in the making when it finally premiered in 2013. Disney first had the idea to make Hans Christian Andersen's "The Snow Queen" fairy tale into a movie as early as 1936—one year before *Snow White* debuted. He and producer Samuel Goldwyn began development on an adaptation that would have blended animation with live action in a story about Andersen's life, but World War II delayed the project indefinitely. Even after Walt's death in 1966, the studio didn't give up hope of producing the film. After moving through various circles of development for decades, Disney finally green-lit a CGI adaptation of the story in the early 2010s.

BEND IT LIKE BECKHAM (2002)

WRITTEN BY: Gurinder Chadha, Guljit Bindra, and Paul Mayeda Berges

DIRECTED BY: Gurinder Chadha

OTHER MOVIES DIRECTED BY GURINDER CHADHA:
Bride & Prejudice (2004); *It's a Wonderful Afterlife* (2010)

For Jesminder Bhamra (Parminder Nagra), teen life in London is off the beaten path. She's way into football—the European kind—and likes playing pickup games in the park. When her athletic skills get noticed by Jules Paxton (Keira Knightley)—a player for the Hounslow Harriers, a local amateur football squad—Jess ends up landing a spot on the team, and has to battle against both gender and racial discrimination (some of it real, some of it conjured by her overprotective parents). *Bend It Like Beckham* is an atypical sports movie, both because it's about a women's team and because, while full of rousing underdog vibes, it also has something valuable to say about breaking free of societal and familial expectations.

THE STUDIO WASN'T SURE AMERICANS WOULD KNOW WHO DAVID BECKHAM WAS.

Before the movie was released in the U.S., studio brass had to think long and hard about whether American audiences would know who David Beckham was, and whether they'd know what the term "bend" means as it relates to the sport of soccer (aka football). At one point, *Move It Like Mia* was proposed as an alternative title—despite no connection to Mia Hamm. Fortunately, cooler heads prevailed.

GURINDER CHADHA WASN'T A SOCCER FAN.

While *Bend It Like Beckham* is technically a sports movie, it's also much more than that. How else would one explain how and why Chadha—who admittedly knew nothing about soccer—ended up writing and directing it? In 2015, she admitted to the *Telegraph* that when it came to writing anything related to the athletics of the sport, she would just write something like "jargon jargon football jargon" and let her co-writers fill in the blanks.

YES, THOSE ARE THE REAL ACTORS PLAYING THE GAME.

Both Parminder Nagra and Keira Knightley trained hard to make the movie more believable. "I put them into three months [of] solid football training and they had a coach and every day they would [come] in and train," Chadha told blackfilm.com.

BHAMRA AND KNIGHTLEY SUFFERED FOR THE FILM.

If you think that soccer isn't a sometimes brutal sport, think again. According to Chadha, Knightley suffered a few concussions during the course of training and filming. And "Parminder really damaged her toes and was too scared to [kick] the ball in case she broke one," the filmmaker told blackfilm.com. "They really had to go through the pain barrier like other athletes in order to excel. It's only when I said, 'We could always use doubles, don't worry about it,' when the two of them said, 'No way! [We're] definitely going to go for it.' And they did."

IT WAS THE FIRST WESTERN FILM TO BE BROADCAST ON TELEVISION IN NORTH KOREA.

In 2010, *Bend It Like Beckham* became the very first Western-made movie to air on television in North Korea. Though they heavily edited the movie in order to make it work for the broadcasting schedule, it was still a major coup.

"Anyone can cook aloo gobi, but who can bend a ball like Beckham?"

BLACK PANTHER

(2018)

WRITTEN BY: Ryan Coogler and Joe Robert Cole

DIRECTED BY: Ryan Coogler

OTHER MOVIES DIRECTED BY RYAN COOGLER:
Fruitvale Station (2013); *Creed* (2015);
Black Panther: Wakanda Forever (2022)

When Marvel Studios announced a forthcoming slew of new superhero films in 2005, Black Panther was one of the bigger characters on the list. Still, the real promise of a *Black Panther* standalone movie wasn't planted until 2016, when Chadwick Boseman appeared in *Captain America: Civil War* as T'Challa. Finally, in 2018, Wakanda came to life as the centerpiece for a story about its people and its superpowered leader.

The movie's global impact was gargantuan. In addition to earning $1.34 billion worldwide, *Black Panther* also made Academy Awards history: It was the first superhero movie to earn an Academy Award nomination for Best Picture. (Alejandro G. Iñárritu's *Birdman*, which was named Best Picture in 2015, is often deemed—in the words of Slate—an "anti-superhero" movie.)

"You're a good man with a good heart. And it's hard for a good man to be king."

BLACK PANTHER WAS ALMOST MADE IN THE 1990S WITH WESLEY SNIPES.

In the early 1990s, fresh off the success of *Major League* (1989), *New Jack City* (1991), and *White Men Can't Jump* (1992), Wesley Snipes set his eyes on the role of T'Challa. Unfortunately, the right elements never lined up perfectly, so Snipes moved on to make *Blade*—the series that, coincidentally, kept Marvel afloat long enough for them to eventually make *Black Panther* two decades later.

RYAN COOGLER SIGNED ON TO DIRECT THE MOVIE BECAUSE HE COULD BRING HIS OWN CREW.

Under president Kevin Feige, Marvel Studios is known for having a tight grip on its formula, plugging major talent into a system that creates movies that have a dash of originality yet nonetheless feel the same. Ryan Coogler wasn't interested in having his vision diluted, and he only agreed to direct the film because Marvel let him bring his own production team on board: namely, cinematographer Rachel Morrison, production designer Hannah Beachler, and composer Ludwig Göransson, all of whom—except Morrison, who was due to give birth during *Creed*'s production—had worked with Coogler on both the critically lauded *Fruitvale Station* and the *Rocky* spin-off *Creed*.

COOGLER SAW *IRON MAN* ON OPENING DAY WHILE HE WAS IN FILM SCHOOL.

The post-credits sequence in *Black Panther* mirrors *Iron Man*'s press conference ending, with T'Challa addressing the United Nations to announce that Wakanda will share its technology with the world. It was purposeful, both to tie the films together and to nod toward the first Marvel Cinematic Universe (MCU) film, which Coogler saw on opening day when he was still in film school at USC. "What I thought was great about *Iron Man*, which [Marvel does] a great job of in their movies, is that it feels like it's happening in our world even though it's not," the filmmaker told io9. Coogler went from film school to directing a billion-dollar blockbuster in seven years, making him the MCU's youngest director at the time.

DONALD GLOVER WROTE JOKES FOR IT.

In the DVD commentary, Coogler described *Atlanta* creator Donald Glover as "one of the funniest people" he knows and revealed that Glover wrote some gags for the film. The most notable is when the assembled tribes are asked if anyone will challenge T'Challa for the throne, and Shuri (Letitia Wright) raises her hand to complain about everything taking too long.

THE WAKANDA SALUTE EXISTS BECAUSE OF PHARAOHS AND AMERICAN SIGN LANGUAGE.

Crossing arms and saying "Wakanda Forever" has taken on a life of its own beyond *Black Panther*. Coogler explained that the fictional salute was inspired by the way pharaohs are buried and some West African sculptures, with the bonus of meaning "hug" in American Sign Language.

LUPITA NYONG'O PAID FOR SIX HUNDRED CHILDREN IN KENYA TO SEE THE FILM.

The Black Friend author Frederick Joseph launched the *Black Panther* Challenge weeks before the movie hit theaters and raised $50,000 to send kids in Harlem to see it for free. Nyong'o joined in on the kindness, sending six hundred children in Kisumu, Kenya, to see her match wits with Boseman on screen. "I wanted kids from my hometown to see the positive images reflected in the film and superheroes that they can relate to on the big screen," Nyong'o posted to Instagram at the time.

BLADE RUNNER (1982)

WRITTEN BY: Hampton Fancher and
David Webb Peoples

DIRECTED BY: Ridley Scott

OTHER MOVIES DIRECTED BY RIDLEY SCOTT:
Alien (1979); *Thelma & Louise* (1991); *Gladiator*
(2000); *The Last Duel* (2021); *House of Gucci* (2021)

The work of author Philip K. Dick has been like catnip to directors over the years, with Steven Spielberg's *Minority Report*, Paul Verhoeven's *Total Recall*, George Nolfi's *The Adjustment Bureau*, and Richard Linklater's *A Scanner Darkly* among the many celebrated movies that have pulled from his work. The most famous Dick adaptation, however, is Ridley Scott's *Blade Runner*, starring Harrison Ford as Rick Deckard, a Los Angeles cop tasked with hunting down rogue androids, or "replicants." It's a complex plot, and one that the filmmakers quickly learned audiences were having trouble following, so an infamous voice-over was added. Eventually Scott got his way, and the voice-over was chopped from 1992's "Director's Cut" and 2007's "Final Cut" home video releases.

RIDLEY SCOTT DIDN'T READ THE BOOK ON WHICH *BLADE RUNNER* IS BASED.

Blade Runner is (loosely) based on Philip K. Dick's *Do Androids Dream of Electric Sheep?*, which Scott never read. "I actually couldn't get into it," the director admitted. "I met Philip K. Dick later, and he said, 'I understand you couldn't read the book.' And I said, 'You know you're so dense, mate, by page thirty-two, there's about seventeen story lines.'"

PHILIP K. DICK HATED THE SCRIPT (AT FIRST).

Given Scott's feelings toward *Blade Runner*'s source material, it's probably only fair that Dick didn't like the script. The author (who passed away before the film was released) loathed Hampton Fancher's original draft, saying he was "angry and disgusted" at the way it "cleaned my book up of all of the subtleties and of the meaning." Fortunately, he was a fan of David Webb Peoples's rewrite of the screenplay.

FREEZE-FRAME

Another major change between the theatrical and director's cut versions of *Blade Runner* is the ending, which was originally a happy one: Rachael and Deckard drive through the countryside, and we hear in the voice-over that Rachael is a new kind of replicant who can live as long as humans do. For the backdrop of that scene, Scott used outtakes from Stanley Kubrick's *The Shining*.

TEST AUDIENCES HATED THE MOVIE.

After disastrous preview screenings, producers Bud Yorkin and Jerry Perenchio hired a third writer, Roland Kibbee, to write a noirish voice-over for Deckard so that the movie would be easier to follow. Legend has it that Ford intentionally delivered a lackluster performance so that they would ditch the voice-over entirely. Whether or not that's true, Ford was not a fan of the experience, calling it a "fucking nightmare. I thought that the film had worked without the narration. But now I was stuck re-creating that narration. And I was obliged to do the voice-overs for people that did not represent the director's interests."

SCOTT SAYS RICK DECKARD IS DEFINITELY A REPLICANT.

It may be a major point of contention among sci-fi fans, but to director Scott, the answer is clear: Yes, Blade Runner Rick Deckard is a replicant. In the director's cut (not the original theatrical version), there's a short scene where Deckard daydreams about a unicorn; later, near the end of the film, Gaff (Edward James Olmos) leaves an origami unicorn for Deckard to find.

IT MIGHT BE CURSED.

It might not be quite as hard-core-cursed as *Poltergeist* or *The Omen*, but *Blade Runner* has a curse of its own . . . on the businesses whose logos appear in the film. Atari, Pan Am, RCA, Cuisinart, and Bell Phones all suffered severe business problems in the years shortly after the film's release, as did Coca-Cola, whose 1985 "New Coke" experiment was less than successful. Members of the *Blade Runner* production team refer to this as the "product-placement *Blade Runner* curse."

"More human than human' is our motto."

BOYZ N THE HOOD

(1991)

WRITTEN BY: John Singleton

DIRECTED BY: John Singleton

OTHER MOVIES DIRECTED BY JOHN SINGLETON:
Poetic Justice (1993); *Higher Learning* (1995);
Shaft (2000); *2 Fast 2 Furious* (2003);
Four Brothers (2005)

"One out of every twenty-one Black American males will be murdered in their lifetime. Most will die at the hands of another Black male."

That's the statistic that set the tone for audiences as they started watching *Boyz n the Hood*. The film marked the feature directorial debut of John Singleton, who was just twenty-three years old at the time. With its raw story of life in South Central Los Angeles, the film shocked the world with its unrelenting depictions of violence and poverty.

The cast of up-and-comers included several future Oscar winners, including Cuba Gooding Jr. and Regina King, and the film is now considered an undisputed classic that changed how Black stories were told on film.

THE STORY IS LARGELY AUTOBIOGRAPHICAL.
John Singleton pulled from pieces of his own life growing up in Los Angeles when writing the script for *Boyz n the Hood*. He stated in interviews that several elements from his real life made it into the film, from the block where he used to live to the elementary school that he attended, and even a few specific events, including the time his father shot at a fleeing burglar. "It was kind of cathartic," Singleton said. "This movie was my way of kind of getting out of the ghetto as a person."

SINGLETON WAS OFFERED $100,000 TO WALK AWAY.
While pitching the script to different studios, Singleton refused to give out copies unless someone was willing to make a deal where he would get to direct the film, even though he had no prior feature film–directing experience. Columbia Pictures expressed interest in buying the film, and during a meeting Singleton was reportedly offered $100,000 to let a more experienced director take over the project. "I said, 'Well, we'll have to end this meeting right now, because I'm doing this movie. This is the movie I was born to make,'" Singleton recalled in the documentary *Friendly Fire: Making of an Urban Legend*. Columbia's response was to give Singleton the green light and $6 million to make the movie.

IT WAS INFLUENCED BY *STAND BY ME*.

In an interview with Jog Road Productions, producer Steve Nicolaides revealed that Singleton wanted him to produce the film because of his previous work on one of Singleton's favorite films, Rob Reiner's *Stand by Me*. Singleton even added some nods to that film into *Boyz n the Hood*. Reiner himself picked up on one of them—Singleton's choice to mimic a fade-out effect on one of the main characters at the end of the film. "It was an homage," Nicolaides told Reiner during the making of *A Few Good Men*. "I mean, the fat kid wears a striped shirt in it, too."

EVERYONE COULD FEEL THE EMOTION IN THE SCRIPT.

In his commentary, Singleton admitted that he cried while writing Doughboy's monologue for the end of the film, which includes the iconic line "Either they don't know, don't show, or don't care about what's going on in the 'hood." Cube has said that the scenes where he is supposed to cry were the hardest for him because he was used to burying his feelings. Gooding was not as composed: He once punched a hole in a wall during an emotional day.

LIFE IMITATED ART IMITATING LIFE WHEN THE FILM OPENED IN THEATERS.

Boyz n the Hood was met with backlash after some incidents of violence at theaters were reported as being related to the film. In the DVD documentary, Singleton said that he left one showing just before alleged gang violence erupted (he personally witnessed a potential conflict between Crips and Bloods and tried to have security intervene), but he maintained that neither he nor the film were to blame because it was simply a reflection of real life.

According to a *Newsweek* article published that summer, around twenty-one theaters pulled the film after "opening-night violence left two moviegoers dead and more than thirty injured." But Singleton countered, "It wasn't the film. It was the fact that a whole generation [of Black men] doesn't respect themselves, which makes it easier for them to shoot each other. This is a generation of kids who don't have father figures. They're looking for their manhood, and they get a gun. The more of those people that get together, the higher the potential for violence."

CLOSE-UP *Boyz n the Hood* premiered at the 1991 Cannes Film Festival, and the filmmakers worried whether the story would translate culturally (and with subtitles) to French audiences. Any worries were laid to rest when the film was met with a twenty-minute standing ovation.

THE CABIN IN THE WOODS (2012)

WRITTEN BY: Joss Whedon and Drew Goddard

DIRECTED BY: Drew Goddard

OTHER MOVIES DIRECTED BY DREW GODDARD:
Bad Times at the El Royale (2018)

Drew Goddard's meta masterwork is the horror film you can recommend to people who tell you they hate scary movies. As usual, five stereotypical college kids go to a secluded cabin to party but encounter a pain-thirsty Zombie Torture Family. Not as usual, all the action is being orchestrated and monitored from a banal office setting, crafting a clever cover story to explain why the characters can't escape slow-moving zombie killers and other dumb horror movie tropes along the way. Revered by horror lovers and haters alike, Goddard's directorial debut twisted the genre into something new, kicking it in the pants the same way Wes Craven's *Scream* did for slasher films in the 1990s.

THE OPENING SCENE WAS MEANT TO CONFUSE AUDIENCES.

The first scene of the movie features Bradley Whitford and Richard Jenkins chitchatting in a hallway about childproofing cabinets and an office betting pool. While the scene is leading up to something, it was immediately confusing to viewers. The filmmakers admitted that they purposely wanted people to think they'd sat down for the wrong movie (it worked) and had to convince the studio that people wouldn't walk out in order to keep the scene.

IT WAS INSPIRED BY LOS ALAMOS.

Sure, it's a slasher flick, but *The Cabin in the Woods* is really about bored employees ensuring the success of murder machines in the face of the end of the world. It might not be that surprising to learn that Goddard grew up in Los Alamos, New Mexico. "The whole town exists because it's a government lab that designs weapons. And that's the only reason the town exists," Goddard said. "I just keep coming back to where I grew up, watching these decent kind suburban men go to work, every day making these weapons of mass destruction." He and the production used images from Los Alamos in the 1950s to craft the set and even some costumes.

HORROR ICON HEATHER LANGENKAMP DID THE SPECIAL MAKEUP EFFECTS.

Legendary Final Girl Heather Langenkamp is best known for playing Nancy in the *A Nightmare on Elm Street* series, but she and her husband David LeRoy Anderson also do prosthetic makeup, monster costumes, and makeup effects through their company AFX Studio. She's listed in the credits as Heather L. Anderson.

THE FULL LIST OF MONSTERS MIGHT INCLUDE A NOD TO *SIN CITY*.

There are too many baddies mentioned in the film to list here, but among the witches, sexy witches, mermen, and unicorns, there's Kevin. He's a kind-seeming dude who might show you where the movie section is in Best Buy but dismembers people during his time off. It's possible that he's a reference to the relaxed, quietly sadistic slasher played by Elijah Wood in the movie version of *Sin City*.

THE CABIN IN THE WOODS BY THE NUMBERS

The body count is officially around 60, but it's technically much higher.

The next time this question pops up at bar trivia, you'll know that approximately sixty bodies hit the floor during *The Cabin in the Woods*' runtime. But if you want to be annoying about it, the death toll is technically

6,800,000,000

because that was the world population in 2009, when the film was shot, and the story ends with the planet's destruction (which is also why it's weird that people keep asking about a sequel).

CALL ME BY YOUR NAME (2017)

WRITTEN BY: James Ivory (based on the book by André Aciman)

DIRECTED BY: Luca Guadagnino

OTHER MOVIES DIRECTED BY LUCA GUADAGNINO: *I Am Love* (2009); *A Bigger Splash* (2015); *Suspiria* (2018)

I t's not easy to make someone smile through their tears, but that's exactly the way most people responded to *Call Me by Your Name*, the lush tornado of young love set in the Italian countryside. Written by James Ivory and directed by Luca Guadagnino, the movie stars Timothée Chalamet as Elio, an introspective seventeen-year-old, and Armie Hammer as Oliver, the confident graduate student who lives with Elio's family over the summer. Over the course of his stay, their relationship turns seductive and blossoms into a fiercely intense story of first love.

THE ACTORS HAD A MEMORABLE REHEARSAL.
Early in production, Hammer and Chalamet joined Guadagnino in the backyard of the villa where they were filming and the director arbitrarily chose a scene to practice. That scene consisted only of Elio and Oliver rolling in the grass making out, so Hammer and Chalamet got right down to it. Guadagnino stopped them, told them that they needed to feel it, and had the actors try again. After a long kissing session, they looked up to find that the director had already walked off, leaving them alone.

AUTHOR ANDRÉ ACIMAN MAKES A CAMEO IN THE MOVIE.

After other actors weren't available, the production opted to have the book's author, André Aciman, play Mounir, a dinner guest and husband to a character named Isaac, played by producer Peter Spears. "He had been so hands-off with the movie, but we wanted him to be a part of it," Spears told *The Hollywood Reporter*. "He rose to the occasion, and it was pretty great."

THE FILMMAKERS CHANGED THE SETTING FROM 1987 TO 1983.

The novel takes place in 1987, but Guadagnino changed it to 1983 for the film partially because the world was already far deeper into the AIDS crisis by 1987 than by 1983. As Chalamet described it, the time change made it so the film "wasn't as intense and could be a little more utopic." Guadagnino was also twelve in 1983 and wanted to use the music from his childhood.

IT RECEIVED THE LONGEST STANDING OVATION IN NEW YORK FILM FESTIVAL HISTORY.

Before it premiered at Sundance to widespread acclaim, Sony Pictures Classics had already purchased *Call Me by Your Name* for an estimated $6 million. The movie had already made the rounds at several festivals before screening at the New York Film Festival in October 2017, where it garnered ten full minutes of a sustained, standing ovation. At the time, that was more than any other movie in the festival's then-fifty-five-year history.

CALL ME BY YOUR NAME IS DEDICATED TO BILL PAXTON.

The legendary actor, who passed away on February 25, 2017, wasn't involved in producing *Call Me by Your Name* in any way, so the dedication initially seemed puzzling to many. "My husband, Brian Swardstrom, was Bill's best friend and agent for almost his entire career," Spears explained. "Brian is also the agent of Timothée Chalamet (as well as Tilda Swinton, which is how we all met Luca years ago). Brian and Bill came to visit us on the set while we were shooting in Crema, Italy . . . Bill and Luca became friends . . . and Luca chose to honor his memory by dedicating the movie to him."

WRITTEN BY: **Neal Purvis, Robert Wade, and Paul Haggis (based on the book by Ian Fleming)**

DIRECTED BY: **Martin Campbell**

OTHER MOVIES DIRECTED BY MARTIN CAMPBELL: *GoldenEye* (1995); *The Mask of Zorro* (1998); *Green Lantern* (2011); *The Protégé* (2021)

CASINO ROYALE
(2006)

The James Bond franchise was in rough shape by the time 2002's *Die Another Day* landed in theaters. While at the time it was by far the biggest Bond movie (unadjusted for inflation), it was saddled with a bloated plot and plenty of unconvincing CGI—but its biggest sin was that it made 007 (Pierce Brosnan) come off like a decidedly uncool relic of a bygone era. Four years later, the series finally got a much-needed course correction with *Casino Royale*, a reimagining of Bond's early days that placed the character (now played by Daniel Craig) into a more realistic setting and examined just what makes this martini-loving super spy tick.

MORE THAN TWO HUNDRED ACTORS WERE CONSIDERED FOR THE ROLE OF JAMES BOND.

Finding a new James Bond doesn't happen overnight. According to producer Michael G. Wilson, more than two hundred actors were considered over the span of two years before Daniel Craig finally landed the role. Of those hundreds of names, though, Henry Cavill was the only other actor who came close to landing the part, but at just twenty-two years old, he was considered too young. Craig himself nearly turned down the role until he read the script and saw the radical change in direction the movie was going to take.

IT WASN'T THE FIRST (OR THE SECOND) *CASINO ROYALE* ADAPTATION.

Just a year after author Ian Fleming brought 007 into the world with the 1953 novel *Casino Royale*, CBS adapted the book for an episode of the TV series *Climax!*, where Bond was retooled as an American (played by Barry Nelson) and Peter Lorre starred as Le Chiffre. In 1967, the story was adapted again, this time as a big-screen comedy with David Niven in the Bond role and Orson Welles playing Le Chiffre.

QUENTIN TARANTINO WANTED A SHOT AT THE STORY.

Before Craig and director Martin Campbell boarded the project, Quentin Tarantino tried to bring *Casino Royale* to the screen. His idea was to keep Pierce Brosnan in the role—Tarantino revealed to *Empire* that Brosnan was his favorite Bond after Connery—and, according to rumors, have it be set in the fifties or sixties and shot in black-and-white. Uma Thurman was also a possibility to play the doomed love interest Vesper Lynd, a role that eventually went to Eva Green.

CASINO ROYALE TOOK ITS CUES FROM BATMAN.

In 2005, director Christopher Nolan's *Batman Begins* gave audiences a more realistic take on the Dark Knight that was the complete opposite of 1997's campy dud, *Batman & Robin*. The Bond franchise, seeking a similar reinvention, followed suit. "We're trying to do for Bond what *Batman Begins* did for Batman," *Casino Royale* co-writer Paul Haggis said in 2005. Together, the two movies were prime examples of the "gritty reboot" trend that dominated Hollywood through the 2000s.

ONE OF THE MOVIE'S STUNTS SET A GUINNESS WORLD RECORD.

The scene where Bond's Aston Martin crashes and rolls across a darkened road wasn't just great trailer fodder—it was a record-breaking piece of filmmaking. By flipping and rolling seven times at eighty miles per hour, the car broke the record for the most cannon rolls ever (the previous record was six). As the name suggests, a nitrogen cannon was fixed to the car, which caused it to flip when shot.

THERE'S A REAL CONDITION THAT CAUSES PEOPLE TO WEEP BLOOD LIKE LE CHIFFRE.

In the movie, the villain Le Chiffre (Mads Mikkelsen) sports a scar above and below his left eye that causes him to "weep" blood. Though the exact cause is unknown, the blood-soaked tears are based on a real condition known as hemolacria. While it can be caused by an injury, it could also be the product of a tumor, high blood pressure, or a blocked tear duct.

CHINATOWN (1974)

WRITTEN BY: Robert Towne

DIRECTED BY: Roman Polanski

OTHER MOVIES DIRECTED BY ROMAN POLANSKI:
Repulsion (1965); *Rosemary's Baby* (1968);
The Ninth Gate (1999); *The Pianist* (2002);
The Ghost Writer (2010)

Despite the advice given in its closing line of dialogue, the one thing you can't do with *Chinatown* is forget it. Regarded by nearly everyone, from the American Film Institute to IMDb users, as one of the best movies ever made, Roman Polanski's masterpiece is a modern film noir with a labyrinthine plot and deeply sinister undertones. The basics: Los Angeles detective Jake J. J. Gittes (Jack Nicholson) sees a simple investigation into adultery spin out of control into a conspiracy involving the city's water supply. Nicholson delivers a top-of-his-game performance, as do Faye Dunaway, John Huston, and, well, just about everyone in it (including Rance Howard, Ron Howard's dad, as Irate Farmer).

NO SCENES IN THE *CHINATOWN* SCREENPLAY ARE ACTUALLY SET IN CHINATOWN.

Chinatown is a symbol in Towne's screenplay, representing what the writer described as "the futility of good intentions." In his original screenplay, it was just a metaphor, with none of the action taking place there. Polanski suggested it would be more satisfying if the film's climax took us to the very place J. J. Gittes never wanted to return to, literally as well as symbolically.

POLANSKI CONVINCED TOWNE TO CHANGE THE ENDING, TOO.

In the original version, Evelyn Mulwray (Faye Dunaway) fatally shoots her father, but since she refuses to explain her reasons, she's destined for life in prison. "Not a happy ending," Towne said, "but a more complex ending." Polanski wanted to go even darker: Evelyn takes a shot at her dad but only wounds him, while she herself ends up dead, leaving poor Katherine in the hands of the nasty old man. Towne thought that was too melodramatic but ultimately ceded the battle to Polanski. Eventually, Towne acknowledged that Polanski's version was better.

NOAH CROSS REGULARLY MISPRONOUNCING GITTES'S NAME WAS A MISTAKE, NOT A CHOICE.

It certainly suits the character of a rich, evil man not to care whether he gets some dumb detective's name right. But in truth, the reason Cross keeps calling him "Gits" instead of "Git-is" is that the actor, John Huston, couldn't get it right. Polanski had Nicholson add a line trying to correct him, and after that just let it go.

IT WAS INTENDED AS THE FIRST PART IN A TRILOGY—BUT NO, THE ABORTED THIRD PART DID NOT BECOME *WHO FRAMED ROGER RABBIT*.

Part two was *The Two Jakes*, which Towne wrote and Nicholson directed in 1990. Part three, which never did get written, was to have been called *Gittes vs. Gittes* (not *Cloverleaf*, as the legend goes), about the introduction of no-fault divorce in California, possibly with some Howard Hughes intrigue as well. An urban legend has sprung up that this third plot was the basis for *Who Framed Roger Rabbit*, which involves a private detective in 1940s L.A. uncovering a scheme to dismantle public transportation and buy up land for a freeway system. But *Roger Rabbit* came out in 1988, two years before the failure of *The Two Jakes* meant *Gittes vs. Gittes* wasn't going to happen. According to *Roger Rabbit* screenwriter Jeffrey Price, the movie "was helped by the fact that *Chinatown* had come out not too long before that, which was a very big movie. We weren't doing a parody of *Chinatown*, but we benefited from that being the hit it was."

WE DON'T KNOW ANYTHING THAT J. J. GITTES DOESN'T KNOW.

This is the sort of detail that's either "well, duh" obvious or that blows your mind a little when you realize it. The film is entirely from Gittes's point of view: He's in every scene, and there's no information that we learn before he does. When he gets a phone call, we hear the voice but don't see the person at the other end. When he gets knocked unconscious in the orange grove, the movie fades with him, fading back in when he wakes up. To emphasize the point that we're seeing everything from Gittes's perspective, Polanski often put the camera behind Nicholson, so we see his back and shoulders. Watch for it.

TOWNE'S ACCLAIMED SCREENPLAY OWES A LOT TO POLANSKI.

Towne won an Oscar for his screenplay, the only one of eleven nominations that came through for *Chinatown*. (It was the year of *The Godfather: Part II*.) The script is used in screenwriting courses and is often held up as an example of a perfect screenplay. But Towne's first version was 180 pages long (which would have made a three-hour movie), and hopelessly complicated. "It would have been a mess" if they'd filmed that version, Towne later said. It was when Polanski came to L.A. in the spring of 1973 and spent eight weeks painstakingly rewriting the script with Towne that it really came together. They worked on it every day and, by both men's admission, *fought* every day, about everything. Polanski crafted the story structure, and Towne would write the dialogue. Towne's ex-wife (who admittedly had an ax to grind) later told a biographer, "Roman could have easily asked for a [writing] credit on *Chinatown* and he would have gotten it. It wasn't just the ending. Roman simply took it over, structured the whole piece."

CLUE (1985)

WRITTEN BY: John Landis and Jonathan Lynn

DIRECTED BY: Jonathan Lynn

OTHER MOVIES DIRECTED BY JONATHAN LYNN:
My Cousin Vinny (1992); *The Distinguished Gentleman* (1992); *The Whole Nine Yards* (2000); *The Fighting Temptations* (2003)

These days, no one is shocked when Hollywood studios announce they're trying to make a movie based on a toy, let alone a board game. But that wasn't the case in 1985, when *Clue* and its many mysteries hit theaters. The movie follows a group of six supposed strangers who convene at a mysterious house for a dinner party. Mr. Boddy (played by punk legend Lee Ving) dies, and the not-so-strangers try to solve the murder in hilarious ways. Time's been kind to this odd little gem of a movie, thanks to an ever-growing cult following and the ability to watch all three of its alternate endings at once.

JOHN LANDIS WAS THE ORIGINAL DIRECTOR.
John Landis crafted the original premise for *Clue* and initially planned to direct it. After commissioning Jonathan Lynn to write the screenplay, Landis decided to direct *Spies Likes Us* instead, leaving *Clue* without a director. Impressed by Lynn's background in theater, Landis suggested that he direct the film. "He worked so hard and he was passionate about it," Landis said.

CARRIE FISHER WAS THE ORIGINAL MISS SCARLET.
In the film's original cast, its biggest star was Carrie Fisher. Days before she was supposed to show up for rehearsals, though, Fisher entered rehab. While both Lynn and Fisher had hoped she could work out a schedule that would allow her to receive treatment and make the film, *Clue*'s insurers wouldn't allow it, so the role went to Lesley Ann Warren instead.

THE DIALOGUE PACING WAS INSPIRED BY *HIS GIRL FRIDAY*.

Lynn set the film in New England in 1954, deliberately recalling tones of Old Hollywood, and he wanted his cast to keep that in mind. Before they started shooting, Lynn screened the classic 1940 Cary Grant–Rosalind Russell film *His Girl Friday*, a film famous for its rapid-fire dialogue, for his cast. "He wanted us all to have that cadence, that very clipped, quick delivery on our lines," Warren recalled.

COLLEEN CAMP HAD TO FIGHT HARD FOR THE ROLE OF YVETTE.

According to Colleen Camp, the role of Yvette the maid was a coveted one in Hollywood, and everyone from Jennifer Jason Leigh to Madonna was interested in the part. Determined to win it for herself, Camp showed up to her audition in a rented maid's outfit and won the role.

MRS. WHITE'S ROLE GOT LARGER WHEN MADELINE KAHN CAME ABOARD.

According to Lynn, the role of Mrs. White was "underwritten" in the first draft of the script. When comedy legend Madeline Kahn became interested in the part, Lynn went back and expanded the role.

THE FILM'S MOST FAMOUS SPEECH WAS IMPROVISED.

Lynn was not a fan of improvisation, but Kahn was. So when Mrs. White is supposed to talk about how much she hated Yvette, Kahn lets loose a riff involving "flames" on the side of her face, and it was so good it just had to stay in the movie.

THERE WAS ORIGINALLY A FOURTH ALTERNATE ENDING.

Clue famously features three different solutions to the mystery, and they originally played in different theaters across the country (which is part of the reason the film was a box office flop; no one knew which version to see). In the planning stages of the film, though, Landis wanted *four* endings, one of which was eventually scripted and later scrapped by Lynn because it just wasn't working. So what was it? Well, Lynn claims he doesn't remember, but the original movie storybook says it involved a scheme by Wadsworth to poison everyone.

FREEZE-FRAME

The Singing Telegram Girl, who only has a few seconds of (living) screen time in the film, was played by the Go-Go's rhythm guitarist Jane Wiedlin.

WRITTEN BY: Amy Heckerling

DIRECTED BY: Amy Heckerling

OTHER MOVIES DIRECTED BY AMY HECKERLING:

Fast Times at Ridgemont High (1982);
National Lampoon's European Vacation (1985);
Vamps (2012)

CLUELESS (1995)

More than a dozen years after connecting to eighties teens with *Fast Times at Ridgemont High*, writer-director Amy Heckerling went back to high school with *Clueless*. With loads of sass and style, the movie spoke to a whole new generation of teens, and even gave them some seriously quotable new phrases to do it with ("As if!"). The film made a household name of Alicia Silverstone, who stars as Cher Horowitz, a spoiled but well-meaning high schooler who is desperate to help the people around her become their best selves. In the process, she often forgets to think about herself and overlooks the love that's been sitting right under her nose. *Clueless* won the hearts of a generation and became one of the most beloved coming-of-age comedies of all time.

CLUELESS IS MODERN-DAY JANE AUSTEN.

Heckerling found her inspiration for Cher's bumbling journey of love from Jane Austen's classic novel *Emma*. "I remembered reading *Emma* in college and being struck at how much it reminded me of old TV shows like *Gidget*," Heckerling recounted to *Entertainment Weekly*. "There's something so basic about it."

THE "HAITIANS" MISPRONUNCIATION WAS ALL ALICIA SILVERSTONE.

You know how Cher rallies for America opening its borders to the Haiti-ans? The script read "Haitians" and Silverstone made an honest mistake. But before producers could rush in and correct her, Heckerling demanded they let her go. "I had to stop them," she said. "It was much funnier the way she said it. That was Cher."

REESE WITHERSPOON COULD HAVE PLAYED CHER.

Witherspoon already had a few film roles to her credit, while Silverstone only had the Lolita-like horror movie *The Crush* on her feature filmography. But with no pressure from the studio to cast stars, Heckerling had the freedom to pick the ingénue whom she felt captured "a vague notion in my head of Cher as a pretty, sweet blonde, who, in spite of being the American ideal, people still really like."

SILVERSTONE HAS AEROSMITH TO THANK FOR THE ROLE OF CHER.

Heckerling's casting director first pitched Silverstone for Cher based on her performance in *The Crush*, but Heckerling wanted that fascinating blonde girl from the music video for Aerosmith's "Cryin'." Lucky for Silverstone, she was one and the same.

PAUL RUDD WANTED TO PLAY CHRISTIAN . . . OR MURRAY.

Though he was ultimately cast to play Cher's brainy stepbrother Josh, Paul Rudd had initially wanted to portray Christian. He was intrigued by a Hollywood script having a "cool gay kid" character. When that didn't pan out, he asked to audition for Murray, a role that ultimately went to Donald Faison. Rudd told *Entertainment Weekly*, "I thought he was kind of a funny hip-hop wannabe. I didn't realize that the character was African American."

THE SUCK AND BLOW SCENE REQUIRED SOME MOVIE MAGIC.

While "Suck and Blow" might have seemed like a fun and sexy party game, it was in fact a pain to shoot. Turns out the cast wasn't up to sucking or blowing well enough to make the game work with an actual credit card. So a prop card made of cardboard was brought in.

CLUELESS IS PART OF AN UNOFFICIAL TRILOGY.

Heckerling is well known for her forays into coming-of-age stories: The first was her directorial debut, the beloved 1982 comedy *Fast Times at Ridgemont High*. *Clueless* came in 1995 and was followed up with the Jason Biggs–fronted *Loser* in 2000. Each comedy not only centered on teens but also aimed to capture the adolescent zeitgeist of their eras in a way that made them accessible and cool to all ages.

"He does dress better than I do. What would I bring to the relationship?"

HIGH SCHOOL 101: TOTALLY RELATABLE TEEN MOVIES

Better Luck Tomorrow (2003)

Justin Lin (who would later become known for his work in the *Fast and Furious* franchise) made a splash in Hollywood with his breakthrough film *Better Luck Tomorrow*. The movie follows a group of Asian American high school students who go from overachievers to clandestine criminals. It was produced on a shoestring budget of $250,000—$10,000 of which was provided by MC Hammer. The rapper had so much faith in Lin that he immediately agreed to sign on as producer when the filmmaker called him asking for cash.

Booksmart (2019)

Booksmart forgoes any typical high school antagonist—mean girl, boy, parent, teacher, etc.—to focus on the central besties: Molly (Beanie Feldstein) and Amy (Kaitlyn Dever), two high-achieving seniors determined to make up for four years of too-responsible behavior with one wild night. The film marked Olivia Wilde's directorial debut; and though she didn't write the script, the idea for the bad drug trip where the girls turn into Barbie dolls was all hers.

The Breakfast Club (1985)

Watching this John Hughes film—in which an athlete (Emilio Estevez), a brain (Anthony Michael Hall), a basket case (Ally Sheedy), a criminal (Judd Nelson), and a princess (Molly Ringwald) are stuck in weekend detention together and find that they have plenty in common despite their differences—is basically a rite of passage for any teenager. It's difficult to imagine any of the actors in any other roles, but Hughes initially wanted Ringwald to play loner Allison. Ringwald, however, wanted to play popular girl Claire, and Hughes let her have it, casting Sheedy as Allison instead. As for why the movie is called *The Breakfast Club*? Hughes got the name from a friend's son; it was what he called his school's morning detention. (Previously, he had been calling the movie the much less memorable *Detention*.)

Bring It On (2000)

Jessica Bendinger originally planned to make a documentary about the national cheerleading scene. But after that idea failed to garner any interest, she pivoted to writing the film that became *Bring It On*. Kirsten Dunst (who initially turned down the role) stars as cheer captain Torrance Shipman, opposite Gabrielle Union as Isis, the leader of a rival team. The Toros and Clovers battle to take the top spot at Nationals, but are hampered by plagiarized routines and plenty of squad drama. It's a good thing Bendinger's original documentary plans didn't pan out—that version of the story wouldn't have featured any of *Bring It On*'s signature spirit fingers, as that isn't a real cheerleading move.

Cooley High (1975)

Unlike the blaxploitation films of its era, *Cooley High* spotlights the relatable hijinks and struggles of Black teenagers living in the 1960s. It follows two best friends (played by Glynn Turman and Lawrence Hilton-Jacobs) from Chicago's Near North Side in their final weeks of high school. Screenwriter Eric Monte went on to work for such popular sitcoms as *Good Times* (which he co-created). His late-seventies show *What's Happening!!* was loosely based on *Cooley High*.

The Edge of Seventeen (2016)

Nadine (Hailee Steinfeld) is dealing with a lot: the grief of her dad's death, strained relationships with her mother and very popular brother (whom her best friend has a crush on), and her own self-loathing. Writer-director Kelly Fremon Craig so accurately captured the timeless tragicomedy of being a teenager in part because, on the recommendation of producer James L. Brooks, she spent six months interviewing actual high schoolers.

Eighth Grade (2018)

Writer-director Bo Burnham channeled his experience with anxiety onstage into his debut feature about the horrors of being a thirteen-year-old girl. Though it's filled with funny moments, *Eighth Grade* was a surprisingly serious turn from a comedian who got his start making irreverent jokes on You-Tube. It deals with themes like mental health and growing up on the internet—topics that Burnham revisited in his comedy special *Inside* three years later. Elsie Fisher received accolades for her performance as Kayla, but the gig didn't necessarily make navigating her own adolescence easier. When she returned to school after wrapping up filming for *Eighth Grade*, she didn't get a part in her high school play.

Fast Times at Ridgemont High (1982)

In 1979, *Rolling Stone* reporter Cameron Crowe went undercover at a California high school and his experiences formed the basis of the 1981 book, *Fast Times at Ridgemont High: A True Story* (which is now out of print). One year later, Amy Heckerling directed the big-screen adaptation of his work, pulling Crowe aboard as screenwriter; together, they created one of the most enduring teen comedies of the 1980s. The cast is packed with pre–Brat Pack up-and-comers, including Sean Penn (as lovable stoner Jeff Spicoli), Judge Reinhold, Phoebe Cates, and Cates's famous red bathing suit. But really, it's Jennifer Jason Leigh's poignant portrayal of hopelessly naïve teen Stacy Hamilton that gives this lewd, crude, often hilarious coming-of-age tale its heart and soul.

House Party (1990)

House Party started as a student film for writer-director Reginald Hudlin, but morphed into something greater. Hudlin, a fan of John Hughes, wanted to capture the teen experience with this tale of a high schooler named Kid (Christopher "Kid" Reid) trying to make his way to a killer party being hosted by his BFF, Play (Christopher "Play" Martin). Although DJ Jazzy Jeff and the Fresh Prince (aka Will Smith) were the hip-hop duo Hudlin originally had in mind for the lead roles, it's hard to imagine another pair crushing the film's iconic dance-off better than New York City's own Kid 'n Play. The film spawned four sequels, and is being rebooted for a new generation of youngsters by LeBron James.

Love & Basketball (2000)

Romance and love of the game collide in this coming-of-age drama about childhood pals Monica (Sanaa Lathan) and Quincy (Omar Epps) who share passion on and off the court, but struggle to keep it going as their individual career ambitions pull them in opposite directions. In making the film—which was semi-autobiographical and produced by Spike Lee—writer-director Gina Prince-Bythewood aimed to create a "Black *When Harry Met Sally . . .*," but also wanted to tell a story wherein a woman could have it all: a great love, an incredible career, and, most importantly, to not have to choose one over the other.

Mean Girls (2004)

In *Mean Girls*—which Tina Fey wrote after reading Rosalind Wiseman's *Queen Bees & Wannabes: Helping Your Daughter Survive Cliques, Gossip, Boyfriends & Other Realities of Adolescence*—Cady Heron (Lindsay Lohan) is the new kid at a suburban Illinois high school after a childhood spent in Africa. The story of her assimilation into (and then sabotage of) the cutthroat popular clique known as "the Plastics" is so quotable that it's practically its own language: "She doesn't even go here," "You go, Glen Coco," "Get in loser, we're going shopping." The list is endless.

"Get in loser, we're going shopping."

COMING TO AMERICA

(1988)

WRITTEN BY: Eddie Murphy, David Sheffield, and Barry W. Blaustein

DIRECTED BY: John Landis

OTHER MOVIES DIRECTED BY JOHN LANDIS: *National Lampoon's Animal House* (1978); *The Blues Brothers* (1980); *An American Werewolf in London* (1981); *Trading Places* (1983)

Is there an Eddie Murphy role that isn't memorable? Even *Norbit* was nominated for an Oscar. From Buckwheat on *Saturday Night Live* to Dr. Dolittle, the veteran comedian has embodied some of the most beloved characters ever to hit the screen. *Beverly Hills Cop* might have been the film that proved Murphy could be a solo movie star, but looking back on his launchpad period in the 1980s, *Coming to America* stands out as the best of this comedic juggernaut's efforts. As an African prince who relocates to Queens, New York, to find the perfect wife, Murphy's hilarious performance(s) turned a silly little film into a certified comedy classic. Supporting turns from Arsenio Hall (also in multiple roles), James Earl Jones, and John Amos only add to the powerhouse aura of the film.

FREEZE-FRAME

Only true horror fans might have spotted this: Tobe Hooper, the late horror director behind *The Texas Chain Saw Massacre*—and a dear friend of Landis's—appeared in the McDowell's party scene.

PAULA ABDUL CHOREOGRAPHED THE OPENING DANCE SCENE AT THE PALACE IN ZAMUNDA.

In an interview with *Rolling Stone*, the choreographer-turned-pop-star listed her *Coming to America* scene as one of the top moments of her choreography career. "This was one of my moments of having to really prove myself, because I was still pretty new in my career as a choreographer," Abdul said. She told how Landis wanted to hire Janet Jackson's choreographer for the gig (which she was), but seemed surprised when they met. "He looked at me and said, 'What are you, a teenager?' And I said, 'Yes, I am!'"

LANDIS AND MURPHY CLASHED ON SET.

Despite working together previously on 1983's *Trading Places*, Landis and Murphy had a less-than-amiable professional relationship. "We had a good working relationship, but our personal relationship changed because he just felt that he was a superstar and that everyone had to kiss his ass," Landis told Collider. "He was a jerk. But great [in the film]—in fact, one of the greatest performances he's ever given."

"Zamunda" is an altered version of a famous writer's name.

As noted in the DVD commentary of the film, screenwriters Barry Blaustein and David Sheffield named the kingdom of "Zamunda" after Bob Zmuda, Andy Kaufman's writing partner and close friend.

MCDOWELL'S WAS ACTUALLY A WENDY'S IN QUEENS.

The real-life location of the McDowell's is along Queens Boulevard, where a Wendy's used to be located (it has since been demolished). While it may be fictional, McDowell's has its own Yelp page; one reviewer noted how Akeem, Murphy's character, "used a handle of his mop in some martial art sequence I've never seen before. Totally stunned (and saved) everyone."

COMING TO AMERICA MARKED CUBA GOODING JR.'S FEATURE DEBUT.

According to IMDb, his character is known as "Boy Getting Haircut" in the famous barbershop scene.

JAMES EARL JONES AND MADGE SINCLAIR, THE KING AND QUEEN OF ZAMUNDA, WERE ALSO THE KING AND QUEEN IN THE LION KING.

The duo must have truly impressed Disney, because the on-screen couple landed the coveted gig of voicing Mufasa and Sarabi, respectively, in the 1994 animated masterpiece.

IT PAYS TRIBUTE TO ROOTS.

In the barbershop scene, the Jewish man calls Akeem "Kunta Kinte," a reference to *Roots*. In fact, John Amos—who starred in *Coming to America* as Lisa's father Cleo—played the adult version of Kunta Kinte in the groundbreaking 1977 miniseries.

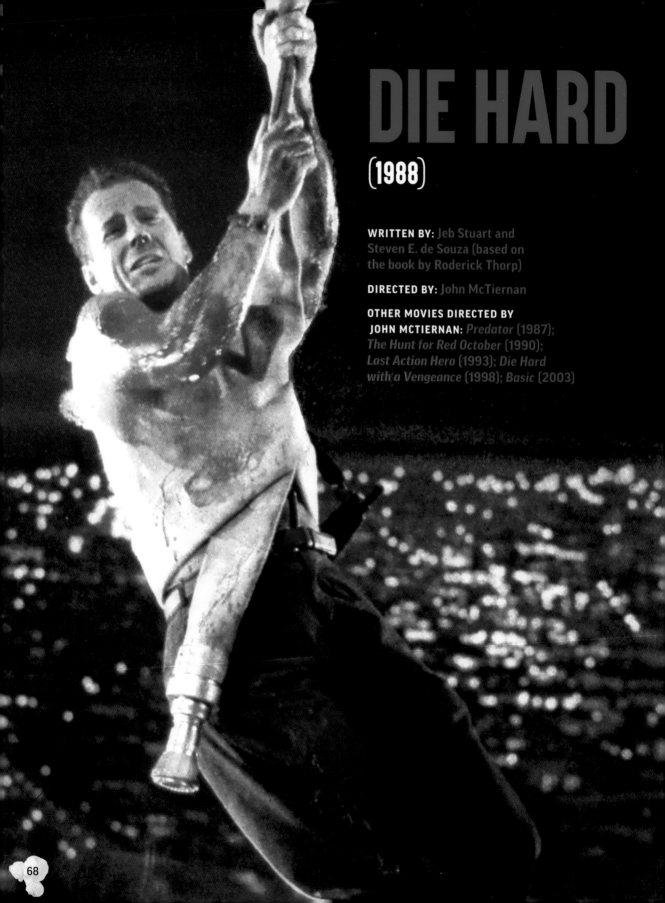

DIE HARD

(1988)

WRITTEN BY: Jeb Stuart and Steven E. de Souza (based on the book by Roderick Thorp)

DIRECTED BY: John McTiernan

OTHER MOVIES DIRECTED BY JOHN MCTIERNAN: *Predator* (1987); *The Hunt for Red October* (1990); *Last Action Hero* (1993); *Die Hard with a Vengeance* (1998); *Basic* (2003)

A renegade cop, a team of terrorists with a secret motive, a Christmas party gone awry, a skyscraper loaded with explosives, and Reginald VelJohnson—*Die Hard* really *does* have everything. Director John McTiernan made sure that all those elements came together for a film that still works like a Swiss watch, perfectly timed without a millimeter of space wasted. From its instantly quotable screenplay to Alan Rickman's unforgettable performance, it's easy to see why the movie became one of the most influential entries in the history of the action genre. For proof, just look at the endless list of action films that can be described as "*Die Hard* on a [insert random location here]."

BRUCE WILLIS WAS FAR FROM THE STUDIO'S FIRST CHOICE FOR THE LEAD.

If *Die Hard* was to be a success, the studio knew they needed a bona fide action star in the part, so they set about offering it to a seemingly never-ending list of A-listers of the time. Rumor has it that Sylvester Stallone, Harrison Ford, Robert De Niro, Charles Bronson, Nick Nolte, Mel Gibson, Richard Gere, Don Johnson, Burt Reynolds, and Richard Dean Anderson (yes, MacGyver!) were all considered for the role of John McClane. And all declined it.

WILLIS WAS CONSIDERED A COMEDIC ACTOR AT THE TIME.

Die Hard's producers had nothing against Bruce Willis, of course. He just wasn't an immediate choice for the role because, up until that point, he was known solely as a comedic actor, not an action star. Ultimately, it was Willis's believability as an "Everyman" that landed him the role. Following the success of the film, the action genre really became Willis's bread and butter.

WILLIS WAS BARELY VISIBLE ON THE MOVIE'S INITIAL POSTER.

Because the studio's marketing gurus were unconvinced that audiences would pay to see an action movie starring the funny guy from *Moonlighting*, the original batch of posters for the film centered on Nakatomi Plaza instead of Willis's mug.

WILLIS WAS PAID $5 MILLION, WHICH WAS A MAJOR PAYDAY.

Even with all the uncertainty surrounding whether he could pull the film off, Willis was paid $5 million to make *Die Hard*, which was considered a rather hefty sum at the time—a figure reserved for only

the top tier of Hollywood talents. So how did that happen? In Brian Abrams's *Die Hard: An Oral History*, Arnold Rifkin—Willis's agent—explained, "I needed a number that would make him the highest paid actor for a minute in time. That would be the justification if it didn't work. If it worked, the rest was irrelevant."

YOU CAN SEE (BUT CANNOT TOUCH) MCCLANE'S SWEATY TANK TOP.

In 2007, Willis donated McClane's blood-soaked tank top to the National Museum of American History at the Smithsonian.

McCLANE HAS FOUR FEET.

As Willis spends much of the movie in his bare feet running through broken glass, he was given a pair of rubber feet to wear as a safety precaution. Which is understandable, but if you look closely in certain scenes, you can see the fake appendages.

DIE HARD WAS ALAN RICKMAN'S FEATURE FILM DEBUT.

In 1987, the casting director saw Alan Rickman playing the dastardly Valmont in a stage production of *Les Liaisons Dangereuses* and knew they had found their Hans. Although Rickman had been acting since the 1970s, he came to Hollywood late; he was forty-two years old when *Die Hard*, his first movie, premiered.

RICKMAN'S DEATH SCENE WAS KIND OF TERRIFYING.

At least it was for Rickman. In order to make it look as if he was falling off a building, Rickman was supposed to drop twenty feet onto an airbag while holding onto a stuntman. But in order to get a genuinely terrified reaction out of him, they dropped him on the count of two (some say one)—not three, as was planned.

ONE LINE STOLE THE MOVIE.

It was a simple line—"Yippee-ki-yay, motherfucker!"—but it became the film's defining moment and the unofficial catchphrase that has been used in all its sequels.

THE CREDIT FOR "YIPPEE-KI-YAY" BELONGS TO WILLIS . . . MAYBE.

In a 2013 interview, Willis explained that the movie's most famous line came from him. "I was just trying to crack up the crew and I never thought it was going to be allowed to stay in the film," Willis said. However, de Souza also claimed credit, saying in 2015, "Bruce and I grew up watching the same TV shows. Roy Rogers used to say 'Yippee ki yah, kids.' So it had to become 'Yippee ki yah, motherfucker' in the movie. That line was from me."

"Yippee-ki-yay, motherfucker!"

HERO WORSHIP: WHY IS THE WORLD SO OBSESSED WITH *DIE HARD*?

Few films in the history of cinema are as endlessly rewatchable as *Die Hard*. But why do we find so much comfort in a 1988 action flick?

In Brian Abrams's *Die Hard: An Oral History*, screenwriter Steven E. de Souza shared his thoughts on what makes McClane so compelling: "He was an underdog. That's why the movie worked," de Souza said. "It's hard to feel sorry for Stallone or Schwarzenegger, which is why they have to work so hard to have ninety-five guys attack them at once . . . *Die Hard* really captured the possibility that you could win but die."

"Wish fulfillment" is a phrase sometimes used in the context of action heroes, but John McClane is not someone we'd necessarily want to trade places with. "Most of us are never going to hold a gun to somebody's head," clinical psychologist Dr. Abigael San told Mental Floss in 2020. "But we might have been in situations of conflict and being pulled in different directions, where we had maybe overplayed the power of something, and there might be a kind of resonance and reflection in what we see on screen."

MOVIES THAT WERE SUPPOSED TO BE SEQUELS TO OTHER MOVIES

Die Hard is based on Roderick Thorp's 1979 novel, which was a sequel to his 1966 novel *The Detective*, which was adapted into a film starring Frank Sinatra in 1968. As such, 20th Century Fox was contractually obligated to offer the role of John McClane in *Die Hard* to Sinatra first. According to de Souza, Sinatra said "I'm too old and too rich to act any more," which was fortunate for Willis.

But why let a good screenplay go to waste? Sometimes planned sequels get repurposed and recycled into something completely new.

Colombiana (2011)

With the success of *Léon: The Professional* (1994), director Luc Besson and his protégé Olivier Megaton tried to make a sequel called *Mathilda*. After years of running into roadblocks—including Natalie Portman's rise to stardom—Besson and Megaton reworked their script for *Mathilda* into *Colombiana*, starring Zoe Saldana instead.

The Hateful Eight (2015)

Quentin Tarantino originally conceived of *The Hateful Eight* as a sequel to *Django Unchained* (2012). But as he began writing, the filmmaker realized that something didn't feel right about having Django in the middle of the new story. "I thought it should be a room of bad guys, and you can't trust a word anybody says," Tarantino said during a Q&A at the Alamo Drafthouse Cinema in Austin, Texas, in 2015.

Minority Report (2002)

After *Total Recall* became a box office hit in 1990, writer Gary Goldman optioned the rights to the Philip K. Dick story "The Minority Report," which director Paul Verhoeven felt could be turned into a *Total Recall* sequel. However, Carolco Pictures, which owned the rights to both *Total Recall* and *Minority Report*, went out of business, so the sequel project ended up with Steven Spielberg and Tom Cruise, who ran with the *Minority Report* half.

DO THE RIGHT THING

(1989)

WRITTEN BY: Spike Lee

DIRECTED BY: Spike Lee

OTHER MOVIES DIRECTED BY SPIKE LEE:
She's Gotta Have It (1986); *Mo' Better Blues* (1990); *Malcolm X* (1992); *25th Hour* (2002); *Da 5 Bloods* (2020)

*D*o the Right Thing—Spike Lee's incendiary profile of racial tension and police overreaction—arrived like a shot in the arm of the American consciousness when it landed in theaters in the summer of 1989. The movie rumbled with youthful energy, dry comic wit, boombox-blasted politics, and an operatic magic unique to New York City.

It's a fierce polemic. It's a snapshot of stereotyping. It's a chill hangout movie. It was also a showcase of Lee's directorial know-how, just when experience was shaping his raw creative talent.

LEE SWITCHED STUDIOS TO AVOID A SAPPY ENDING.

Paramount executives dropped a bomb on Lee close to the end of preproduction, demanding an unrealistically uplifting ending. "They wanted Mookie and Sal to hug and be friends and sing 'We Are the World,'" Lee told *New York* magazine. "They told me this on a Friday; Monday morning we were at Universal." Obviously, he did the right thing.

LEE HIRED THE NATION OF ISLAM'S PARAMILITARY AS SET SECURITY.

The production descended on a street in Brooklyn's Bedford-Stuyvesant neighborhood in late summer 1988, building Sal's Famous Pizzeria and painting murals, but largely leaving the neighborhood in its natural state for the shoot. To ensure safety, they hired members of Fruit of Islam, then run by Louis Farrakhan, to act as on-set security. One of their first jobs was boarding up known crack houses and guarding them to deter drug abusers from returning.

BARACK AND MICHELLE OBAMA SAW *DO THE RIGHT THING* ON THEIR FIRST DATE.

"He was trying to show me his sophisticated side by selecting an independent filmmaker," Michelle Obama said, reflecting on her first date with her future husband—and the future president. On the twenty-fifth anniversary of Lee's film, Barack recorded a video message thanking Lee for helping him impress Michelle.

***DO THE RIGHT THING* WAS INSPIRED BY A REAL-LIFE INCIDENT.**

On December 19, 1986, four Black men—Michael Griffith, Timothy Grimes, Curtis Sylvester, and Cedric Sandiford—were traveling when their car broke down. Sylvester stayed with the car while the other three walked three miles to the predominantly Italian American Howard Beach neighborhood of Queens, New York, where they got into an argument with some white teenagers before heading to New Park Pizzeria for a meal and a telephone. When they left the eatery, they were accosted by a larger group of white men, including the ones they'd encountered earlier. Sandiford and Griffith were beaten; Griffith tried to run but was chased onto the Belt Parkway, where he was hit by a car and killed. The incident was such a part of *Do the Right Thing*'s DNA that Lee wanted to have his character, Mookie, shouting "Howard Beach!" while defacing Sal's Famous Pizzeria.

IT CONTAINS NODS TO A FEW CLASSIC FILMS.

Lee, an avid cinephile and a student of film history, is such a massive fan of Charles Laughton's *The Night of the Hunter* (1955) that he dropped part of it into the middle of *Do the Right Thing*. Radio Raheem (Bill Nunn) carries the knuckle ring version of Robert Mitchum's *The Night of the Hunter* character's "Love" and "Hate" tattoos, and he explains their existence using almost the exact same monologue.

FREEZE-FRAME

Even the opening credits of *Do the Right Thing* are iconic. Rosie Perez's frenetic, emotional dance to the bowel-shaking bass boom of Public Enemy's "Fight the Power" sets the stage as well as any of Shakespeare's prologues. "Spike didn't tell me he needed anger and angst and exhaustion," Perez explained. "Instead, he just said, 'I need you to *kill* it.' I thought, OK. I thought I killed it in the first hour. Freakin' eight hours later, this freakin' man had me still dancing."

DRIVE (2011)

WRITTEN BY: Hossein Amini
(based on the book by James Sallis)

DIRECTED BY: Nicolas Winding Refn

**OTHER MOVIES DIRECTED BY
NICOLAS WINDING REFN:** *Bronson* (2008);
Valhalla Rising (2009); *Only God Forgives*
(2013); *The Neon Demon* (2016)

Boasting an old-fashioned movie star performance from Ryan Gosling as a taciturn, toothpick-chewing Hollywood stunt driver with a sideline in heist getaways, *Drive* is both an art-house movie and an action movie, a hyper-stylized, ultraviolent, tragically romantic neo-noir. It also features one of the greatest jackets ever filmed. Directed by Nicolas Winding Refn and featuring Carey Mulligan, Bryan Cranston, Albert Brooks, and Oscar Isaac, it topped endless critics' year-end lists, and sold a lot of toothpicks.

WE HAVE REO SPEEDWAGON TO THANK FOR *DRIVE*.

If one particular playlist had been a smidge different in 2009 or so, *Drive* might never have happened. Ryan Gosling was brought onto the project by producer Marc Platt and told he could pick his own director; Gosling wanted Refn, who had directed Tom Hardy in the 2008 powerhouse prison drama *Bronson*. Refn was interested, as a tarot card reader in Paris had told him he would have a good experience in Hollywood. So they went out for dinner and, by all accounts, had a terrible time.

As Gosling drove Refn home, he put the radio on to fill the awkward silence. The REO Speedwagon song "Can't Fight This Feeling" came on the radio, and they both joined in with it. "I started singing along and all that isolation and loneliness was overcome," Refn told the *Guardian*. "We understood each other. The film is that scene, really."

REFN AND GOSLING HAD VERY DIFFERENT VIEWS OF THE MOVIE.

While Gosling has described *Drive* as "a violent John Hughes movie," suggesting that "if *Sixteen Candles* had a head-smashing, it would be a masterpiece." Refn saw it as more of a fairy tale. "I read Grimm fairy tales to my daughter a few years ago, and the idea with *Drive* was similar," he told the *Guardian*. "You have the driver who's like a knight, the innocent maiden [Carey Mulligan], the evil king [Albert Brooks], and the dragon [Ron Perlman]. They're all archetypes." Of Gosling's nameless knight, the Driver, he says, "He's the man we all aspire to be . . . but he wasn't meant to live in the real world. He's too noble, too innocent."

THIRTEEN (AUTHENTIC VERSIONS) OF GOSLING'S ICONIC SATIN JACKET EXIST.

The Driver's satin jacket, embroidered with a large scorpion, is a nod to the fable, told in the movie, of the scorpion and the frog—the scorpion dooming both the frog and itself due to its inescapably violent nature (well, it probably is; the jacket's designer, Erin Benach, refuses to say whether the jacket or the fable's inclusion in the movie came first, and it's nowhere to be found in the original screenplay). The jacket was also inspired by KISS and the 1963 movie *Scorpio Rising*. Gosling originally wanted a look along the lines of 1950s Korean souvenir jackets, but Benach thought they were too billowy. Thirteen identical jackets were used in filming, with thousands of knockoffs available online shortly after the film's release.

GOSLING BARELY SPEAKS DURING THE MOVIE.

The Driver's other two trademarks came about during production. His near-silence—he speaks just 116 lines in the whole film—was a reaction to Gosling having just made and promoted the dialogue-heavy *Blue Valentine* and being "tired of talking."

ALBERT BROOKS SHAVED HIS EYEBROWS OFF FOR THE ROLE.

Cast against type, Albert Brooks (who Gosling says "was confused as to why we would want him for that part") shaved his eyebrows off to make himself look less expressive as the ruthless mobster Bernie Rose. Despite all the critical acclaim, *Drive* ended up with only one Oscar nomination. Brooks, who many had felt was in line for a Best Supporting Actor nod, took to Twitter after the nominations were released, announcing, "I got ROBBED," before clarifying, "I don't mean the Oscars, I mean literally. My pants and shoes have been stolen."

ONE DISPLEASED AUDIENCE MEMBER TOOK DRASTIC ACTION AGAINST THE STUDIO AND THE MOVIE THEATER SHE VISITED.

One viewer expecting a very different film attempted to sue both the distributor FilmDistrict and the cinema she visited (the Emagine in Novi, Michigan), claiming that the trailer presented something much more akin to a *Fast & Furious*–type experience. She also claimed the film was anti-Semitic, later attempting to get a judge who tried to dismiss the case removed from it on the grounds that he must also be anti-Semitic. A continuation of the case was active until 2018, but seems to have exhausted appeal options.

EVIL DEAD II

(1987)

WRITTEN BY: Sam Raimi and Scott Spiegel

DIRECTED BY: Sam Raimi

OTHER MOVIES DIRECTED BY SAM RAIMI: *Darkman* (1990); *The Quick and the Dead* (1995); *A Simple Plan* (1998); *Spider-Man* (2002); *Drag Me to Hell* (2009); *Doctor Strange in the Multiverse of Madness* (2022)

Before director Sam Raimi found big box office success with the original *Spider-Man* trilogy, he was best known as the cult filmmaker behind *The Evil Dead* series. With 1981's *The Evil Dead*, Raimi and star Bruce Campbell offered their irreverent take on a hapless dope named Ash terrorized by ghouls in a wood-enshrouded cabin. The success of that film led to *Evil Dead II: Dead by Dawn*, a pseudo sequel-slash-remake that married the first film's grotesque aesthetic with a slapstick bent reminiscent of Raimi's beloved *The Three Stooges*. While Ash would live on in 1993's *Army of Darkness* and the 2015–2018 Starz series *Ash vs. Evil Dead*, it's this first sequel that typically stands as the character's big moment.

STEPHEN KING MADE IT POSSIBLE FOR *EVIL DEAD II* TO BE MADE.

King loved the first *Evil Dead* movie so much that he provided a blurb that was used in its marketing—but that wasn't the horror icon's only contribution to the franchise. When Campbell, Raimi, and producer Rob Tapert decided to pursue a sequel following a disastrous reaction to their 1985 film *Crimewave*, which was co-written by the Coen brothers, it was King who went to bat on their behalf with producer Dino De Laurentiis, with whom he had a deal to make adaptations of his work.

EVIL DEAD II IS A "REQUEL."

The film starts off with Ash and his girlfriend encountering demonic forces in a secluded cabin, a similar—though not identical—story to the first film. This could lead some viewers to infer it's a remake, since Ash would have to be colossally stupid to go back there. Campbell said they didn't have the rights to their first film, so for the recap they needed new footage. This means *Evil Dead II*, according to Campbell, could be called a "requel."

BRUCE CAMPBELL HAD TO DEAL WITH A "BLOOD FLOOD."

In one memorable scene, Ash is tormented by his own severed hand and subsequently endures a tsunami of blood being sprayed directly in his face as something akin to waterboarding. While lying flat on his back, a fifty-five-gallon drum of stage blood was positioned directly over Campbell's face. "They're gonna pull the plug and gravity is going to do the work," Campbell told *Entertainment Weekly*. "In the movie, you see it come rocketing out and just hit me square in the face. It was a bull's-eye." Campbell said he blew "red snot" out of his nose for a week.

IT WAS NEARLY RATED X.

The geysers of blood and gore that permeate almost every frame of *Evil Dead II* are so exaggerated that many viewers find it absurdist and amusing—but not the Motion Picture Association of America (MPAA). Producers were dreading that the ratings board would slap the movie with an X. To avoid that fate, the De Laurentiis Entertainment Group (DEG) had to get creative. They "sold" the rights to a DEG employee, who was the president of Rosebud Releasing Corporation. Rosebud was able to release the film without a rating, which DEG—as an MPAA signatory member—would not have been allowed to do. Why not cut some of the gore to get an R? DEG executive Lawrence Gleason told the *Los Angeles Times* that they could have forced Raimi to edit the film down. "But with an R rating, it would have been about 62 minutes long," Gleason said.

FREEZE-FRAME

When Ash storms the nearby work shed to arm himself for a showdown with the Deadites, keen-eyed horror fans can spot Freddy Krueger's razor glove hanging on the wall. Its appearance was part of a long-standing tradition between Raimi and *A Nightmare on Elm Street* director Wes Craven, with the two regularly referencing the other's work in shots.

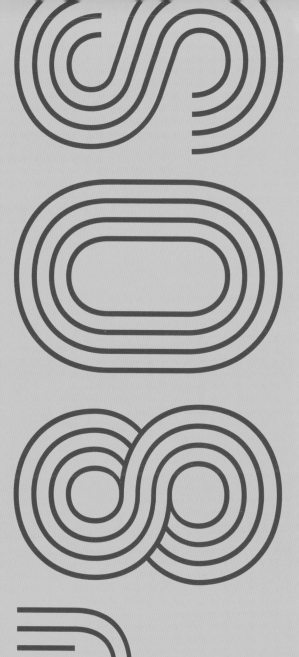

IRRESISTIBLE EIGHTIES MOVIES

In the 1970s, Hollywood studios gave bold young directors free rein, resulting in a new golden age of movies (and a lot of sleepless nights for studio execs). In the 1980s, burned by the excesses and high-profile disasters of the previous decade, the studios took charge again and started churning out safe, reliable, assembly-line product. But you can't keep creative minds down. Despite the limitations and studio-mandated box office expectations, a number of excellent movies managed to get made, including some that achieved greatness by reinventing old genres and tropes.

Blue Velvet (1986)

This glimmering nightmare about the seedy underbelly of suburbia is director David Lynch at his David Lynch–iest. *Blue Velvet* is a mesmerizing horror-noir about a naïve young man (Kyle MacLachlan) who gets involved with a nightclub singer (Isabella Rossellini) being tormented by a maniacal drug dealer (Dennis Hopper). Hopper's performance makes for one of the most terrifying villains (non-supernatural division) in all of film.

E. T. the Extra-Terrestrial (1982)

The 1980s were a pretty great decade for Steven Spielberg, who followed up *Raiders of the Lost Ark* with this instant sentimental classic about a boy and his alien friend. Spielberg's sappiness would get the better of him in duds like *Always*, but here he found the right blend of emotion and nostalgia by giving it a bitter undercurrent to remind us that even the sweetest memories often have tinges of sorrow.

The Goonies (1985)

In an era where favorite movies were rented, rewound, and watched countless times, *The Goonies* stands as one of the most worn-out VHS tapes of the eighties. Director Richard Donner and writer Chris Columbus assembled a troupe of kid actors (Sean Astin, Corey Feldman, Jeff Cohen, Ke Huy Quan, and Josh Brolin) to see them off on an adventure to retrieve a lost treasure that once belonged to pirate One-Eyed Willy. Today, *The Goonies* is not only a classic but a reminder of when kids' movies could still charm adults.

Gremlins (1984)

Practical puppets steal the show in this story of a young adult (Zach Galligan) who befriends a Mogwai named Gizmo. The fluffy creature is cute, but breaking the rules of his breed—getting him wet and feeding him after midnight are prohibited—leads to an outbreak of ferocious relatives in this black comedy about the perils of non-native species.

Heathers (1989)

High school rom-coms don't get much darker than this cult hit, which sees a mysterious new student (Christian Slater) seduce one of the school's most popular girls (Winona Ryder), then lure her into a murder spree. Croquet, scrunchies, corn nuts, and some truly memorable one-liners abound.

The Last Emperor (1987)

Italian master Bernardo Bertolucci (*Last Tango in Paris*) earned a Best Director Oscar for this sumptuous biography of China's last emperor, much of it shot on location in Beijing's awe-inspiring Forbidden City. That fact alone is impressive, as are the nineteen thousand extras used over the course of the movie. But more important is Bertolucci's marvelous ability to help us understand an entire nation of people through the eyes of one venerated figure.

Ordinary People (1980)

Robert Redford's directorial debut, a searing story about a family in crisis after the death of a son/brother, earned him the only competitive Oscar of his career (so far) and established him as the latest well-liked actor who was perhaps even better behind the camera. Sitcom stars Mary Tyler Moore and Judd Hirsch also proved their mettle as serious actors, making *Ordinary People* a surprise on several counts.

Poltergeist (1982)

Steven Spielberg produced—and, according to Hollywood lore, may have helped direct—this Tobe Hooper film about a suburban family under siege by a paranormal spirit intent on disrupting their lives. Spielberg's humor and heart is present, but so are some genuinely unsettling scares. Turns out there's good reason to fear clowns and trees.

Ran (1985)

Legendary director Akira Kurosawa (*Seven Samurai, Rashomon*) spins *King Lear* by having a patriarch in feudal Japan try to put away the bloodshed of his past by handing the keys to his kingdom over to his three sons. But their youth knows no wisdom, and wars are the result. *Ran* juggles its themes masterfully, taking its musings on fathers and sons and blending them with the regrets of old age and the thrill of wartime spectacle. For Kurosawa, who tried for years to get the project made, *Ran* is the rarest of films: It's the culmination of an artist having mastered their genre.

Scarface (1983)

Scarface's place in movie history was cemented by Al Pacino's manic and downright frightening performance as gangster Tony Montana. But beneath that, there's a sprawling, ultraviolent crime drama that is a must-see for any fan of the genre.

The Shining (1980)

Stephen King famously didn't like Stanley Kubrick's adaptation of his horror novel, but cinephiles—especially devotees of Kubrick—found much to love in the ominous, idiosyncratic, ultimately terrifying story of a man going stir-crazy at an isolated hotel. The methods to Kubrick's madness are a story in themselves (see the fun documentary *Room 237*), and *The Shining* remains one of the more unnerving studies of a damaged mind.

Some Kind of Wonderful (1987)

One of John Hughes's final teen movie efforts might just be his most sophisticated. It reads in some ways like a retake on the class-divide dynamics of *Pretty in Pink*, but with some notable upgrades. It's deeper than Hughes's previous teen romantic comedy takes, in that it's less like a fairy tale and more like a real high school romance. The trio of Eric Stoltz, Lea Thompson, and Mary Stuart Masterson is still one of cinema's great unsung love triangles.

The Untouchables (1987)

To tell the explosive story of Eliot Ness pursuing gangster Al Capone, you need a director as brash as Brian De Palma and a screenwriter as percussive as David Mamet. Like Scorsese, De Palma brought his facility with balletic violence with him from the seventies, in the service of a story that affords Kevin Costner, Robert De Niro, and Sean Connery the opportunity to do stellar, testosterone-fueled work.

Who Framed Roger Rabbit (1988)

Robert Zemeckis, ever interested in the pursuit of new technology, pulled off several miracles with this detective noir story that has invited comparisons to *Chinatown*. The interaction between live-action humans and animated characters was groundbreaking, and in many ways is still unsurpassed. Getting cooperation from the many competing rights-holders to include characters such as Bugs Bunny and Mickey Mouse was a feat in and of itself. It's also a deliriously loony comedy teeming with meta-references and in-jokes, plus a fantastic performance by the stellar Bob Hoskins.

Wings of Desire (1987)

Wim Wenders's romantic fantasy about angels and mortals falling in love features Peter Falk as a former angel who got bored with immortality and became human. This rich, enchanting masterpiece was remade in 1998 as *City of Angels*, but the original stands as a lovely, imaginative, and affectionate look at humanity, with an air of bittersweetness to the black-and-white way angels see the world.

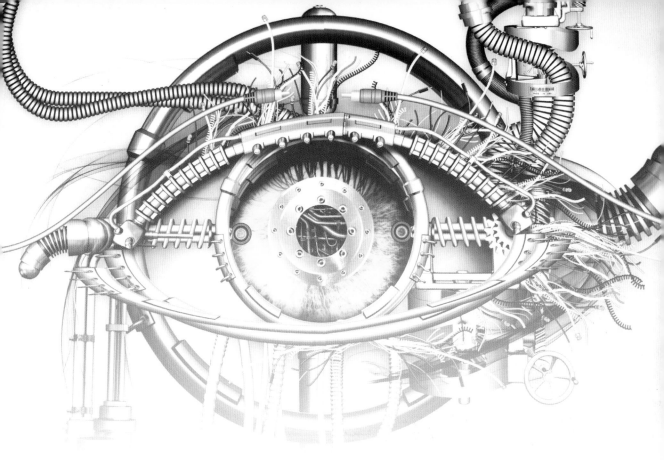

EX MACHINA (2015)

WRITTEN BY: Alex Garland

DIRECTED BY: Alex Garland

OTHER MOVIES DIRECTED BY ALEX GARLAND:
Annihilation (2018)

Alex Garland spent over a decade working as a screenwriter before making his directorial debut with *Ex Machina*, a cerebral sci-fi look at what it is—or isn't—to be human. It follows Caleb (Domhnall Gleeson), who is recruited by reclusive tech billionaire Nathan (Oscar Isaac) to perform a Turing test on his creation Ava (Alicia Vikander), a strikingly humanlike robot. This leads to questions of empathy, ethics, and the nature of existence, all shrouded in mystery, alcohol, and the occasional touch of disco dancing.

THE HOUSE FEATURED IN THE FILM IS A HOTEL IN NORWAY.

The Juvet Landscape Hotel in Norway was used for many shots of Nathan's home. The hotel prides itself on being "in the middle of nowhere" and is situated "in a remote part of a remote village in a remote region." The nearest airport is Ålesund, about sixty miles away.

THE THOUGHT EXPERIMENTS ARE REAL.

They come from the world of philosophy. The "Mary in the black-and-white room" scenario—which was designed to highlight the difference between knowledge and actual sensory, subjective experiences, or qualia— was coined by Frank Jackson in 1982 and was expanded into several books.

THE MOVIE WASN'T AS FUTURISTIC AS GARLAND INTENDED.

Garland has described the technology of the film as being "ten minutes in the future," while also lamenting that some of it was less futuristic than he thought, saying "some of it's by design, and some of it's by stupidity or ignorance."

"It was so outdated," Garland told Consequence about Nathan's high-tech house. "Some of the tech stuff, I didn't realize until later, was just me being down at the discos, sort of hopelessly out of touch . . . I read, I don't know, twenty years ago, that Bill Gates has this house with key cards that lets you into different areas, and I thought, that's very futuristic. Twenty years later I'm writing the screenplay, and I sort of put the future into it, which is actually from twenty years in the past."

THE DANCE SCENE IS A "DISCO NON SEQUITUR."

The dance sequence, in which Nathan and Kyoko (Sonoya Mizuno) perform a routine together, has been termed a "disco non sequitur" by Isaac, a demonstration of just how much time Nathan has spent with his robots, programming and practicing an elaborately choreographed routine for nothing but his own amusement. Garland specifically cut the dance in a manner he deemed "aggressive," deliberately ending it just as the audience starts to have fun.

A LOT OF TIME AND WORK WENT INTO THE VISUAL EFFECTS.

The Oscar-winning visual effects got more of a show-case than in a lot of effects-heavy movies. According to visual effects supervisor Andrew Whitehurst, a typical VFX shot in an action film is less than one second long, while it was closer eight seconds in *Ex Machina*. The filmmakers were keen to avoid having Ava look like Vikander was merely wearing a costume, which is where her transparent mesh skin came from—a technically complex but incredibly effective choice. The type of camera used (a Sony F65 with an anamorphic lens) meant Ava was slightly distorted when out of focus, a new and ridiculously difficult problem for the VFX technicians to deal with.

DON'T HOLD YOUR BREATH WAITING FOR A SEQUEL.

Despite the ending potentially setting up future stories, Garland is adamant that he won't be returning to the world of *Ex Machina* for any kind of sequel. "I imagined it as a completely self-contained story and I still feel that way about it," he told Deadline in 2015.

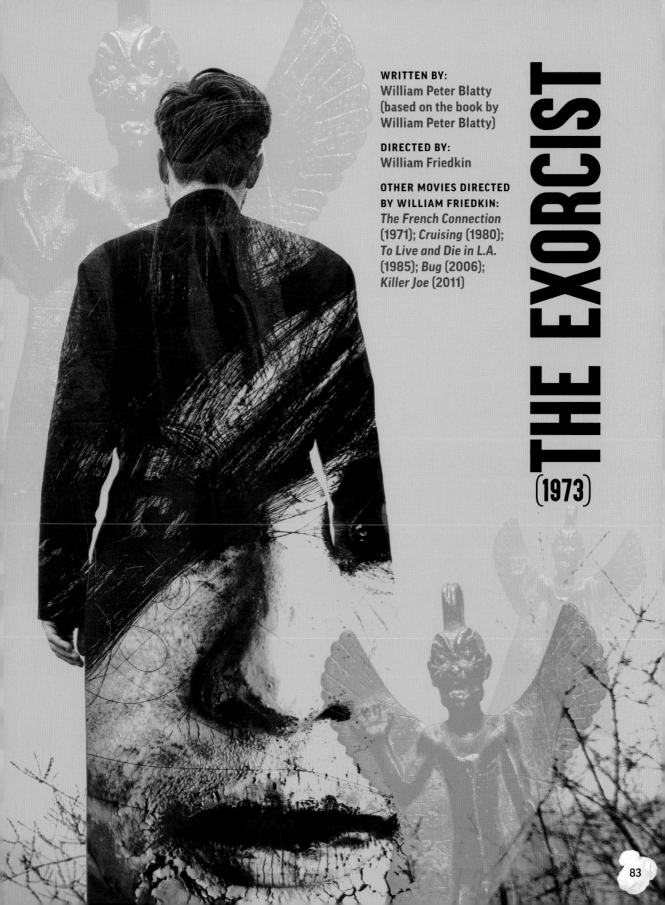

WRITTEN BY:
William Peter Blatty
(based on the book by
William Peter Blatty)

DIRECTED BY:
William Friedkin

**OTHER MOVIES DIRECTED
BY WILLIAM FRIEDKIN:**
The French Connection
(1971); *Cruising* (1980);
To Live and Die in L.A.
(1985); *Bug* (2006);
Killer Joe (2011)

THE EXORCIST

(1973)

When director William Friedkin's *The Exorcist* opened, it quickly became one of the most critically acclaimed and financially successful horror films of all time. Even today, the supernatural thriller—in which Regan MacNeil (Linda Blair), the twelve-year-old daughter of a successful actress (Ellen Burstyn), becomes possessed by an evil demon—still has the ability to shock audiences. Unlike the slasher movie antagonists of the 1980s, Friedkin's adaptation of William Peter Blatty's novel was uninterested in winking at the audience. He was interested only in terrifying them, which he did to unprecedented effect.

Local newscasts reported viewers fainting, vomiting, and fleeing the theater. The movie provoked such extreme responses in viewers seeing it for the first time decades ago that some theaters even had ambulances parked outside ready to attend to overstimulated guests.

THE EXORCIST IS BASED ON A TRUE STORY.
William Peter Blatty's novel is based on the real-life 1949 exorcism of a young boy, known by the pseudonym Roland Doe. The story became national news and caught the interest of Blatty, who was a student at Georgetown University at the time.

THE VHS WAS BANNED IN THE U.K. FOR MORE THAN A DECADE.
While *The Exorcist* was a box office hit when it was released in the U.K. in 1974, a handful of local religious groups protested the film and ended up getting it banned in certain areas. But it faced an even bigger challenge several years after arriving on VHS. When the movie was originally released in 1981, British law didn't require that a movie have a certificate of video release from the British Board of Film Classification (BBFC). That rule changed with the 1984 Video Recordings Act, which led to the movie being pulled from shelves in 1988; in 1999, it finally returned to home video, as the BBFC determined that while it was still a powerful film, it was not as objectionable as when it had originally debuted.

CHAIN-SMOKING AND WHISKEY HELPED ACHIEVE PAZUZU THE DEMON'S RASPINESS.
Mercedes McCambridge, whom Orson Welles once dubbed "the world's greatest living radio actress," provided the voice for Pazuzu, the demon that inhabits Regan. In order to achieve the perfect level of raspiness, McCambridge relied on a diet of raw eggs and whiskey and did a lot of chain-smoking.

MARLON BRANDO WAS REPORTEDLY THE STUDIO'S FIRST CHOICE FOR FATHER MERRIN.
Friedkin vetoed this decision, believing that any movie starring Marlon Brando would immediately become a "Brando movie," which would detract from the story at hand. The role eventually went to Max von Sydow (who was forty-four years old at the time, so he spent three hours in the makeup chair each day to be aged the required thirty or so years).

JASON MILLER WAS ADDED TO THE CAST AT THE LAST MINUTE.
Stacy Keach was originally cast in the role of Father Karras, but then Friedkin saw a performance of *That Championship Season*, the Pulitzer Prize–winning play written by Jason Miller. Friedkin knew that Miller would be perfect in the role of Karras, so they bought Keach out and brought in Miller.

MANY PEOPLE BELIEVED THE SET WAS CURSED.
Filming took place in both New York City and Washington, D.C. After a number of eerie incidents on the New York set, including a studio fire that required rebuilding the sets of the house, Blatty and Friedkin regularly brought in a priest, Father King, to bless the cast, crew, and set when production moved to D.C. According to legend, by the end of the film's production, nine people associated with its making had died.

HORROR MOVIES INSPIRED BY REAL-LIFE EVENTS

While most horror movies are complete works of fiction, the genre occasionally offers up stories that are based on terrifying and jaw-dropping real-life events.

The Amityville Horror (1979)

PREMISE: A young family moves into a house where a murder was committed and experiences strange and terrifying occurrences.

REAL-LIFE INSPIRATION: Based on the book of the same name, *The Amityville Horror* follows the paranormal events that terrorized the Lutzes. In 1975, they moved into 112 Ocean Avenue, where Ronald DeFeo Jr. had brutally murdered his family thirteen months before they arrived. While in their new home, the Lutzes claimed they saw green slime on the walls and red-eyed pigs staring into their kitchen and living room, though there are many people who are skeptical of their claims. After less than a month, the Lutzes moved out of their home in Amityville, New York.

The Conjuring (2013)

PREMISE: Two paranormal investigators help a family who move into a secluded home plagued by weird events.

REAL-LIFE INSPIRATION: *The Conjuring* is based on real-life paranormal investigators Ed and Lorraine Warren and their experience with the Perrons, a family who moved into a Rhode Island farmhouse and claimed to have experienced ghostly and terrifying occurrences in 1971.

"When [my previous movie] *Insidious* came out and was successful the story about the Warrens came to me and I was like, 'Oh, my gosh, this is really cool,'" director James Wan told *Entertainment Weekly* in 2013. "But I didn't just want to make another ghost story or another supernatural film. One thing I had never explored was the chance to tell a story that's based on real-life characters, real-life people. So those were the things that led me to *The Conjuring*." The Warrens also had a possessed Raggedy Ann doll that was the inspiration for the spin-off film *Annabelle*.

A Nightmare on Elm Street (1984)

PREMISE: A supernatural killer stalks his prey while they dream during deep sleep.

REAL-LIFE INSPIRATION: Wes Craven based *A Nightmare on Elm Street* on a series of newspaper articles from the *Los Angeles Times* about a strange phenomenon where young Asian refugees mysteriously died in their sleep. It was reported that many refused to sleep, citing terrifying nightmares that they feared would lead to death.

Open Water (2003)

PREMISE: Two scuba divers become stranded in shark-infested waters after their tour group accidentally leaves them behind.

REAL-LIFE INSPIRATION: *Open Water* is based on American tourists Tom and Eileen Lonergan, a couple who were lost at sea when their tour group left them behind while scuba diving near the Great Barrier Reef in Australia in 1998. When the diving company realized the mistake two days later, they organized a search party, but the Lonergans were never found. Months later, fishermen found a diver's slate (an underwater communication device) with an S.O.S. message on it that read, "[Mo]nday Jan 26; 1998 08am. To anyone [who] can help us: We have been abandoned on A[gin]court Reef by MV Outer Edge 25 Jan 98 3pm. Please help us [come] to rescue us before we die. Help!!!"

THE FLY

(1986)

WRITTEN BY: Charles Edward Pogue and David Cronenberg

DIRECTED BY: David Cronenberg

OTHER MOVIES DIRECTED BY DAVID CRONENBERG: *The Brood* (1979); *Scanners* (1981); *The Dead Zone* (1983); *Naked Lunch* (1991); *A History of Violence* (2005); *Eastern Promises* (2007); *Cosmopolis* (2012)

In 1958, audiences sat down to watch a film about a scientist whose DNA is fused with a fly's during a teleportation experiment gone awry. Nearly thirty years later, in 1986, audiences went to see a David Cronenberg film with the same basic premise, but got something entirely different from the original—and some literally left the theater sick from seeing it.

Creature effects artists Chris Walas and Stephan Dupuis set a brand-new standard for gore with their work on *The Fly* and were handed a Best Makeup Oscar in 1987 for their efforts. Meanwhile, Jeff Goldblum and Geena Davis's undeniable chemistry—the couple was married from 1987 to 1991—provided the movie with enough heart and charm to balance out the more nausea-inducing moments.

"Be afraid, be very afraid."

IT WAS PRODUCED BY MEL BROOKS.

Mel Brooks is a master of comedy, but a fan of the horror genre. When producer Stuart Cornfeld began looking for money to make *The Fly*, Brooks was the first person he went to (the pair had previously collaborated on David Lynch's *The Elephant Man*). It was Brooks who encouraged Cronenberg to take the movie as far as he wanted. "There were no restraints," Cronenberg recalled. "They were willing to lose that percentage of the audience that would have liked the love-interest stuff, but couldn't take the horror."

THE CREATURE EFFECTS TEAM HAD A SPECIFIC TYPE OF ACTOR IN MIND FOR THE LEAD, AND JEFF GOLDBLUM WASN'T IT.

As makeup would be an essential part of making *The Fly* work, creature effects artist Chris Walas asked Cronenberg to "Get somebody with no ears and no bridge of the nose, so that way we have a lot more control with the makeup." When Goldblum was mentioned as a top choice for the lead, Walas and his team agreed that, physically, he was not what they wanted. But as fans of the actor, they wanted to make it work.

THE STUDIO THOUGHT CASTING GOLDBLUM WAS A TERRIBLE IDEA.

When Cornfeld told the studio they wanted Goldblum to play the lead Seth Brundle, former 20th Century Fox president Larry Gordon reportedly called it an "absolutely horrible mistake," but green-lit the decision because he felt it was the filmmakers' mistake to make.

CLOSE-UP

"Be afraid, be very afraid" is a quote that many people have heard, but not everyone knows it comes from *The Fly*. Cronenberg revealed in a commentary track that the iconic line originated with producer Mel Brooks while discussing how characters should react to the early stages of Seth Brundle's transformation. The quote became one of the film's taglines.

TYPHOON THE BABOON WAS A CHALLENGING CO-STAR.

Those involved with the making of the film, including Cronenberg, remember that the baboon (whose name was Typhoon) was very much a wild animal, and not an actor. Visual effects supervisor Hoyt Yeatman said that Typhoon was once startled by the flashing lights in the telepod and broke the door off to get out. The wrangler and Jeff Goldblum (who is six foot four) were the ones who had to keep the primate in check.

SOME PARTICULARLY GRAPHIC SCENES WERE CUT.

After screening the film for audiences, Cornfeld and his team decided that some scenes just did not work and cut them from the film. After Brundle—in an advanced stage of fly-dom that viewers know as "Brundlefly"—dissolves a leg with his own vomit, a scene was shot that involved close-ups of him consuming the severed foot (which actor John Getz kept in his refrigerator after filming). Another scene in the lab involved an experiment by Brundlefly that resulted in a crazed half-baboon, half-cat hybrid, which Seth ended up killing with a lead pipe. Ultimately, the scenes were cut from the final print.

"When we screened it, besides being a little too intense, one woman had thrown up," Cornfeld said. "It taught us a very valuable lesson . . . If you beat an animal, even a cat-monkey, to death with a lead pipe, your audience is no longer interested in your problems."

WRITTEN BY: Ernest Tidyman
(based on the book by Robin Moore)

DIRECTED BY: William Friedkin

OTHER MOVIES DIRECTED BY WILLIAM FRIEDKIN:
The Exorcist (1973); *Cruising* (1980); *To Live and Die in L.A.* (1985); *Bug* (2006); *Killer Joe* (2011)

THE FRENCH CONNECTION (1971)

In 1970, producer Philip D'Antoni and director William Friedkin set out to make a film based on the true story of one of the biggest drug busts in American history. They battled through studio rejection, casting drama, and a book that Friedkin couldn't even get through to produce what became one of the most iconic crime thrillers of all time. *The French Connection* won five Academy Awards, including Best Picture, after its 1971 release, and still stands as one of the greatest films of the 1970s because of its gritty visual style, powerhouse performances, and one of the greatest car chase sequences ever put on film.

IT WAS TURNED DOWN BY ALMOST EVERY STUDIO.

In early 1969, D'Antoni managed to set up *The French Connection* at National General Pictures, seemingly cementing backing for the film. Within a few months, though, things fell apart, leaving D'Antoni and eventually Friedkin on the hunt for another studio. It wasn't easy. "This film was turned down twice by literally every studio in town," Friedkin recalled. "Then Dick Zanuck, who was running 20th Century Fox, said to me, 'Look, I've got a million and a half bucks tucked away in a drawer here. If you can do this picture for that, go ahead. I don't really know what the hell it is, but I have a hunch it's something.'"

GENE HACKMAN WAS NOT THE FIRST CHOICE FOR POPEYE DOYLE.

When it came time to cast the brash detective Popeye Doyle, D'Antoni was gravitating toward Gene Hackman. Zanuck was interested, but Friedkin was not. The director wanted Jackie Gleason and also considered columnist Jimmy Breslin. Eventually, with no convincing backup actor "in the bullpen," D'Antoni issued an ultimatum to Friedkin: Cast Hackman or risk losing the production window on *The French Connection.*

"I said 'Phil, you wanna do this with Hackman, I don't believe in it, but I'll do it with you,'" Friedkin recalled. "'We'll give it our best shot.'" Hackman won the 1972 Academy Award for Best Actor for his performance as Popeye Doyle.

THE FAMOUS CAR CHASE WAS SHOT WITHOUT PERMITS.

The French Connection is perhaps best remembered today for its iconic chase sequence, in which Popeye Doyle commandeers a car to pursue Nicoli, Charnier's chief enforcer, who is in control of an elevated train overhead.

To get permission to use the correct train for the sequence, Friedkin recalled giving a New York transit official "$40,000 and a one-way ticket to Jamaica," because the official was certain he'd be fired for allowing them to shoot the sequence. The rest of the chase, including all the dynamic work with the car under the train tracks, was shot without permits. Friedkin used assistant directors, with the help of off-duty police officers, to clear out traffic on the blocks ahead of the shoot, but they weren't always entirely successful. At least one of the crashes in the finished film was a real accident.

FRIEDKIN DOESN'T KNOW WHAT THE ENDING MEANS.

The French Connection's ending is almost as famous as its chase scene. The cops manage to capture many of the people behind the heroin shipment, but Doyle isn't satisfied with that. He pursues Charnier into the bowels of an abandoned building, determined to catch him. Upon seeing a shadowy figure in the distance, Popeye fires several times, only to discover the man was not Charnier but one of the two federal agents helping them with the case.

Unfazed and still determined, Popeye heads off into the darkness, and we hear a single gunshot ring out. The title cards tell us that Popeye didn't catch Charnier, so who was he shooting at? "People have asked me through the years what [that gunshot] meant," Friedkin said. "It doesn't mean anything—although it might . . . It might mean that this guy is so over the top at that point that he's shooting at shadows."

"Anybody want a milkshake?"

UP TO SPEED:

THRILLING MOVIE CAR CHASES

For many moviegoers, there's nothing more thrilling than watching two or more cars pushed to their absolute limit, whether on the open road or while weaving through crowded city streets. Many movies try to get it right, and lots do, but there are a select few who nail it on a masterpiece level.

1 *Baby Driver* (2017)

Many, many films incorporate pop music needle drops into their biggest action sequences, but few have ever done it quite as intricately as *Baby Driver*. Edgar Wright's action film about a tinnitus-afflicted getaway driver who does his best work when his music is blasting combines the speed and thrills of classic car chases with the cinematic language of the movie musical to create something magical. There are several wonderful chase sequences in *Baby Driver*, but arguably it never gets better than the film's instantly magnetic opening sequence, set to "Bellbottoms" by the Jon Spencer Blues Explosion.

2 *The Blues Brothers* (1980)

This John Belushi and Dan Aykroyd vehicle, which remains one of the most successful *Saturday Night Live* sketch adaptations of all time, leans heavily on a sense of outsize action that runs throughout the film. The story is ostensibly about a pair of well-meaning guys who just want to earn some extra money to save the orphanage they grew up in, but along the way they run into explosions and car chases that they must calmly steer through on their way to fulfill a relatively simple "mission from God." The film has not one, but two great chases that lean into the lunacy of this, and while the early chase through the mall is a masterpiece, the sheer cartoonish absurdity of the final pursuit through the streets of Chicago is the one most people remember.

3 *The Bourne Supremacy* (2004)

When you think "spy movie," you tend to think of the slickest-possible presentation and the coolest-looking car. It's playing against those sorts of conventions that makes the Moscow chase sequence in *The Bourne Supremacy* so effective. Anchored by the intensity of Matt Damon's performance and Paul Greengrass's handheld camera style, the chase plays like a montage of desperation as Bourne flees his pursuers in a beat-up taxicab while nursing a shoulder wound. We know Jason Bourne's not going to die, but watching this chase you're still not sure which will give out first: Bourne's body or the taxi.

4 *Death Proof* (2007)

Quentin Tarantino has been remixing classic genre tropes and moments from his vast knowledge of cinema throughout his entire career, so he was bound to get around to doing a car chase eventually. That definitive moment finally arrived in *Death Proof*, and it's perhaps most notable not because of Tarantino's ability to play with genre conventions, but his ability to adhere to them. It plays in many ways like a classic car chase straight out of the 1970s, and it works as a moment of pure adrenaline because Tarantino shoots it like one. His unflinching camera simply refuses to give the scene a break, repeatedly reminding us that what we're watching is as real, and as exciting, as it gets.

5 Fast Five (2011)

The *Fast & Furious* franchise is renowned for its ability to up the ante with new car stunts in every single installment, to the point that the central ensemble was literally chasing a submarine across the ice in one film. Even as the set pieces have gotten bigger, though, the climactic vault heist from *Fast Five* remains a high-water mark for many fans. The setup is fairly simple: Brian (Paul Walker) and Dom (Vin Diesel) yank a massive vault out of its housing, then drive it through the streets of Rio in matching Dodge Chargers. What makes it truly special are the many ways in which the sequence evolves through little details, from the vault tearing through a line of posts as soon as it hits the streets to Brian backing his car into the vault to drive backward for a while. It's a gem in a series full of gems.

6 Ronin (1998)

The best car chases don't always feature cool cars and even cooler characters, as John Frankenheimer's *Ronin* proves with its masterful centerpiece chase. The two cars involved are relatively unremarkable, but Frankenheimer dials up the intensity through everything from the use of tunnels and bridges to little details like hubcaps spinning off in the middle of turns. Even more remarkable than the chase itself, though, is the way the sequence works as a character piece to really emphasize the danger. No one in either car seems like they're having a good time, and Robert De Niro looks practically freaked out in a lot of the shots. It all adds to the sensation that everything could go horribly wrong at any moment, which only makes it more thrilling.

7 Smokey and the Bandit (1977)

No discussion of great movie car chases is complete without *Smokey and the Bandit*, the film that made the Pontiac Trans Am an essential part of American pop culture. Hal Needham's classic road movie is packed with wonderful car moments and great stunts, so much so that it's difficult to pin down just one as the best part of the film. The task is made more difficult by the sheer amount of swagger that exists between Burt Reynolds's performance and Needham's direction. Even when the danger is dialed up to eleven, the film is so breezy and light that you almost forgot someone could die doing this kind of driving. The jump across Mulberry Bridge feels like a perfect encapsulation of these seemingly opposing ideas, as Bandit quips, "That's not good" upon seeing the roadblock and then "That's worse" upon seeing troopers speeding up from the other direction. It's a brilliant blend of comedy and great stunt work.

8 To Live and Die in L.A. (1985)

William Friedkin, who masterminded the car chase in *The French Connection*, somehow produced another all-timer more than a decade later. *To Live and Die in L.A.* is not a masterpiece in the same way that *The French Connection* is, but its centerpiece chase scene—in which a pair of Secret Service agents flee two gunmen after an operation gone wrong—is a masterpiece for the 1980s in the same way the train versus car chase was for the 1970s. What begins with weaving through trucks in an industrial area soon explodes out onto L.A.'s freeways, and culminates in some of the most daring driving ever captured on film.

GET OUT
(2017)

WRITTEN BY: Jordan Peele

DIRECTED BY: Jordan Peele

OTHER MOVIES DIRECTED BY JORDAN PEELE:
Us (2017); *Nope* (2022)

SPOILERS! Jordan Peele surprised a lot of people when he went beyond his *Key & Peele* sketch comedy roots and made his debut feature a horror film. While there are a few uncomfortable laughs to be found in *Get Out*, the bulk of the movie is a descent into madness. The film follows Chris (Daniel Kaluuya) as he visits his girlfriend Rose's (Allison Williams) wealthy white parents at their home, where Chris begins to suspect that something's not right. He's right, because the Armitage family is trying to sell his body to the highest bidder.

GET OUT WAS INSPIRED BY AN EDDIE MURPHY ROUTINE.

As one origin point for the film, Jordan Peele points to the classic bit in *Eddie Murphy: Delirious* where Murphy asks why white people don't just leave a house when a ghost shows up. "In *The Amityville Horror* the ghost told them to get out of the house," Murphy riffs. "Now that's a hint and a half for you ass. If a ghost said, 'Get the fuck out,' I would just tip the fuck out the door."

"THE SUNKEN PLACE" REPRESENTS THE MARGINALIZATION OF BLACK AMERICANS.

The metaphor is multilayered, but the main theme of the film's horror is the real-world concept of a system silencing you no matter how loudly you shout. On the Blu-ray, Peele also explicitly stated that the Sunken Place is "a metaphor for the marginalization of the Black horror movie audience. We are a loyal horror movie fan base, and we're relegated to the theater, not on the screen."

PEELE HAS VOICE CAMEOS AS A DEER AND IN A COMMERCIAL IN THE MOVIE.

Peele provided the moan of the dying deer at the beginning of the film, as well as the voice of the narrator for the United Negro College Fund PSA, who keeps insisting that

"a mind is a terrible thing to waste."

SPOILERS! THE ORIGINAL ENDING WAS MUCH DARKER.

The ending we all feared was initially the one Peele wanted for the film. He planned on having the police show up to arrest Chris for the carnage at the Armitage house, with Rod (Lil Rel Howery) visiting Chris in jail and hinting that he'd get life in prison with the system stacked against him. Ultimately, test audiences were rooting for Chris and wanted to see him triumph, so Peele opted to oblige them.

GET OUT HAS BEEN TAUGHT IN UNIVERSITIES.

In the fall of 2017, author Tananarive Due taught "Sunken Place: Racism, Survival, and Black Horror Aesthetic" at UCLA. Peele even dropped by the class to expand on, among other things, the film's metaphorical connection to the modern prison industrial complex.

PEELE MADE OSCAR HISTORY.

In 2018, Jordan Peele won the Oscar for Best Original Screenplay for *Get Out*—making him the first Black filmmaker to receive the honor.

WRITTEN BY: Mario Puzo and Francis Ford Coppola

DIRECTED BY: Francis Ford Coppola

OTHER MOVIES DIRECTED BY FRANCIS FORD COPPOLA:
The Conversation (1974); *Apocalypse Now* (1979);
The Outsiders (1983); *Bram Stoker's Dracula* (1992);
Tetro (2009)

THE GODFATHER TRILOGY
(1972-1990)

The original *The Godfather* (1972) and its 1974 sequel, *The Godfather: Part II*, exist on the same "unassailable" level of cinema history that's typically reserved for only a handful of other films, including *Citizen Kane*. An operatic look into the machinations of the Corleone crime family, including patriarch Vito (Marlon Brando/Robert De Niro) and conflicted son Michael (Al Pacino), these are the rare movies that carry the kind of reputation that few people would ever dare challenge. Perhaps that's why a lot of people, especially the ones loudly declaring *The Godfather*'s greatness, seem to ignore the very existence of *The Godfather: Part III*, an underwhelming epilogue to the saga.

Regardless of your feelings about the final film in *The Godfather* trilogy, there's no denying that it might just be cinema's most enduring tribute to family loyalty and the American Dream.

FRANCIS FORD COPPOLA WAS OFTEN ON THE VERGE OF BEING FIRED.

Coppola wasn't the first director Paramount had in mind for *The Godfather*. Elia Kazan, Arthur Penn, Richard Brooks, and Costa-Gavras all turned the job down. After filming began, executives didn't like the brooding, talky drama that Coppola was shooting, and were constantly threatening to fire him (even going so far as to have stand-in directors waiting on set). One version of the story goes that it wasn't until after he shot the scene where Michael kills Sollozzo and McCluskey that the studio was sold on Coppola's vision. The other version says Coppola fired the underlings plotting against him.

PARAMOUNT DIDN'T WANT MARLON BRANDO FOR THE ROLE.

When Coppola initially mentioned Brando as a possibility for Vito Corleone, studio executives were completely against the idea based on prior dealings with the notoriously eccentric actor. They pushed Coppola to cast Laurence Olivier as Vito, before eventually agreeing to pursue Brando under three stringent conditions: (1) He would have to do a screen test (which was practically unheard of for an actor of his caliber); (2) if cast, he would have to forgo his usual movie star salary; and (3) he would have to personally put up a bond to make up for any potential losses caused by his notoriously bad on-set behavior.

Coppola surreptitiously lured the famously cagey Brando into what he called a "makeup test," which in reality was the screen test, the studio demanded. When Coppola showed the studio the test, they liked it so much they dropped the second and third stipulations.

AL PACINO WASN'T THE FIRST CHOICE TO PLAY MICHAEL.

The studio wanted Robert Redford or Ryan O'Neal to play Michael Corleone, but Coppola always wanted Pacino. Other actors, including Martin Sheen and James Caan (who would go on to play Sonny), screen-tested for the part.

ROBERT DE NIRO AUDITIONED FOR SONNY.

Coppola thought his personality was too violent for the role. De Niro would later appear as the young Vito Corleone in *The Godfather: Part II*, and won a Best Supporting Actor Oscar for his work.

COPPOLA TOOK ADVANTAGE OF MISTAKES.

Lenny Montana, who played Luca Brasi, was a professional wrestler before becoming an actor. He was so nervous delivering his lines to a legend like Brando during the scene in the Godfather's study that he didn't give one good take during an entire day's shoot. Because he didn't have time to reshoot the scene, Coppola added a new scene of Brasi rehearsing his lines before seeing the Godfather to make Montana's bad takes seem like he was simply nervous to talk to the Godfather.

THE GODFATHER'S CAT WAS A STRAY.

During his daily walks to the set, Coppola would often see a stray cat, and on the day of shooting the scenes in Vito's study, Coppola took the cat and told Brando to improvise with it. The cat loved Brando so much that it sat in his lap during takes for the whole day.

PACINO WAS THE ARCHETYPAL METHOD ACTOR.
He reportedly really had his jaw wired shut for the first part of the shoot after his character was punched in the face.

THE INFAMOUS HORSE'S HEAD WAS REAL.
The horse head in the movie producer's bed wasn't a prop. The production got a real horse's head from a local dog food company.

THE "TAKE THE CANNOLI" LINE WAS IMPROVISED.
The line in the script only had actor Richard Castellano as Clemenza say, "Leave the gun" after the hit on the mobster who ratted on the Corleones. He was inspired to make the addition after Coppola inserted a line in which the character's wife asks him to buy cannoli for dessert.

very generous award. And the reasons for this being are the treatment of American Indians today by the film industry."

In 1975, De Niro won his first Oscar, for Best Supporting Actor, for playing the younger version of Don Corleone in *The Godfather: Part II*. De Niro was also a no-show to the ceremony—he was busy filming Bernardo Bertolucci's *1900* and admitted that he didn't expect to win. Coppola accepted the statuette on De Niro's behalf, calling it a "richly deserved award," without recognizing publicly that history had just been made. It's a distinction that remained unchallenged until 2020, when Joaquin Phoenix picked up an Oscar for playing the Joker, following Heath Ledger's Joker win a little over a decade earlier. But those were very different characters with the same name; Brando and De Niro played the same character, just at different times.

"Leave the gun,

COPPOLA SUGGESTED THAT MARTIN SCORSESE DIRECT *THE GODFATHER: PART II*.
After *The Godfather*'s tumultuous production, Coppola wasn't interested in diving back into the world of the Corleone family, but the studio wanted a sequel. So Coppola suggested they hire Scorsese, who was fresh off *Mean Streets*, to direct. Paramount disagreed, and eventually got Coppola to helm the sequel by letting him tell parallel stories that featured flashbacks into Vito Corleone's early life—and by agreeing to pay the director the (then) outrageous sum of $1 million, which Coppola had asked for as a bluff.

MARLON BRANDO AND ROBERT DE NIRO WERE THE FIRST ACTORS TO WIN OSCARS FOR PLAYING THE SAME CHARACTER.
In 1973, Brando won the Oscar for Best Actor for his role as Don Corleone in the original *The Godfather*. He famously asked Native American actress Sacheen Littlefeather to attend the ceremony on his behalf; she declared that Brando "very regretfully cannot accept this

DE NIRO ONLY SPEAKS EIGHT WORDS OF ENGLISH IN *THE GODFATHER: PART II*.
De Niro spent months studying Sicilian in order to play the role of Vito, since the character speaks almost exclusively in it. He also visited Sicily for research, saying, "Sicilians have a way of watching without watching; they'll scrutinize you thoroughly and you won't even know it."

THE GODFATHER: PART II WAS ONE OF THE LAST MAJOR TECHNICOLOR FILMS.
Technicolor started releasing films using its dye-transfer process during the Golden Age of Cinema. *The Godfather: Part II* is the last major release to use the process, though it would continue in China until the early '90s. Later that decade, Technicolor announced an "enhanced dye-transfer" process that was used on films like *Batman and Robin* and *Toy Story 2*. But just a few years after its introduction, that was also abandoned.

COPPOLA HAD NO PLANS TO MAKE A THIRD *GODFATHER* FILM.

After *The Godfather* and *The Godfather: Part II*, Coppola thought that the saga of the Corleone family was complete and had no intention of making *Part III*. But after the making of *One from the Heart* in 1982, Coppola found himself in such a dire financial situation that he agreed to Paramount's request for another sequel.

ROBERT DUVALL WAS WRITTEN OUT OF *THE GODFATHER: PART III* DUE TO A SALARY DISPUTE.

Despite Coppola's intentions to reassemble as many members of the original *The Godfather* cast as possible, Robert Duvall balked after learning that Pacino was being paid "three or four times" what he had been offered. When they couldn't reach an accord, Coppola wrote Duvall's character Tom Hagen out of the script and created a new family attorney character played by George Hamilton.

WINONA RYDER WAS ORIGINALLY CAST IN THE ROLE OF MARY.

A who's who of up-and-coming Hollywood actresses were attached or considered for the role of Michael's daughter, Mary Corleone, including Julia Roberts and Winona Ryder, who initially accepted the part before dropping out due to "nervous exhaustion."

SOFIA COPPOLA REPLACED RYDER AT THE LAST MINUTE.

At the eleventh hour, Francis chose his daughter Sofia to step into the role of Mary, a choice that invited complaints of nepotism. When those complaints were made public via media outlets at the start of production, they affected Sofia's confidence and dogged the film as a whole—and still do to this day. In the commentary track for the original cut, Coppola observed the parallels between the story of the movie and its making, saying, "There is no worse way to pay for your sins than for your children to be included in your punishment."

take the cannoli."

GOODFELLAS

(1990)

WRITTEN BY: Nicholas Pileggi and Martin Scorsese

DIRECTED BY: Martin Scorsese

OTHER MOVIES DIRECTED BY MARTIN SCORSESE:
Mean Streets (1973); *Taxi Driver* (1976); *Raging Bull* (1980); *Casino* (1995); *Gangs of New York* (2002); *The Aviator* (2004); *The Departed* (2006); *The Wolf of Wall Street* (2013); *The Irishman* (2019); *Killers of the Flower Moon* (2022)

Whereas Francis Ford Coppola's *Godfather* films tried to examine the criminality of the Corleone family from a historical and socioeconomic perspective interlaced with the origins of America itself, Martin Scorsese took a different tack. *Goodfellas*—Scorsese's mob masterpiece—trekked through the invigorating minutiae of a young lieutenant and his hard-stolen success in a world that didn't recognize his brand of overachieving, which is also why it couldn't stop him sooner.

Ray Liotta's portrayal of mobster-turned-informant Henry Hill jolts through the details of his life of crime, from the wild affluence to the peaks and valleys of living outside the law, while Scorsese's propulsive direction draws a powerful question mark about whether it's worse to be a criminal or just to get caught—and what each viewer's answer says about them.

THE FIRST SCENE FILMED WASN'T DIRECTED BY MARTIN SCORSESE.

For *Goodfellas*, the first scene that was shot was the Morrie's Wigs commercial. To get the feel just right, Scorsese contacted Stephen R. Pacca, who had created his own low-budget ads for his replacement window company, to write and direct the ad.

FRANK VINCENT AND JOE PESCI GO BACK A LONG WAY.

Before whacking Frank Vincent as Billy Batts during the most disappointing "welcome home" party in human history, Pesci gave Vincent a proper beatdown in *Raging Bull*. Vincent would eventually have his revenge, brutally whacking Pesci's character in *Casino*. But Pesci and Vincent go way back off-screen as well, having started their entertainment careers as bandmates and partners in a comedy duo in the late 1960s.

THE COPACABANA TRACKING SHOT IS MEANT TO SEDUCE EVERYONE.

The Copacabana tracking shot, one of the most famous shots in cinema history, shows Henry and Karen (Lorraine Bracco) walking from their car on the street, through a kitchen, and into the famous New York City nightclub. According to Scorsese, it "had to be done in one sweeping shot, because it's his seduction of her, and it's also the lifestyle seducing him."

PAUL SORVINO HAD TROUBLE CONNECTING TO HIS CHARACTER'S CRUELTY.

Sorvino came very close to quitting the project because he didn't think he could pull it off. "What I wasn't sure I would find was that kernel of coldness and absolute hardness that is antithetical to my nature except when my family is threatened," Sorvino told the *New York Times*.

THE MOVIE'S BODY COUNT IS SURPRISINGLY SMALL.

Despite its reputation as a violent movie, the number of on-screen deaths seen in *Goodfellas* is a surprisingly tame five (Spider, Billy Batts, Stacks Edwards, Morrie, and Tommy)—or ten if you include the results of Jimmy Conway's handiwork following the Lufthansa heist.

THE "FUNNY HOW?" SCENE WASN'T IN THE SCRIPT.

The most famous (and most quoted) scene comes at the beginning, when Pesci's Tommy DeVito jokingly—yet uncomfortably—accosts Henry for calling him "funny." In addition to being the driving force behind the scene on-screen, Pesci is also responsible for coming up with the premise. While working in a restaurant, a young Pesci apparently told a mobster that he was funny—a compliment that was met with a less-than-enthusiastic response. Pesci relayed the anecdote to Scorsese, who added it in.

CLOSE-UP

Tommy's mother's painting of two dogs sitting in front of an old man ("One's going east, and the other one is going west. So what?") was actually painted by co-writer Pileggi's mother.

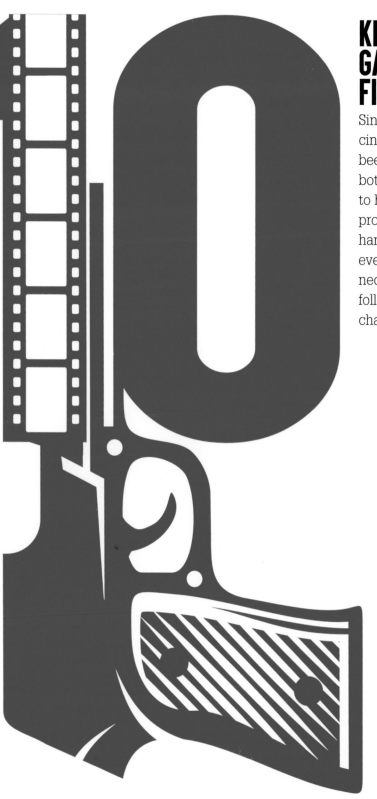

KILLER GANGSTER FILMS

Since the earliest days of cinema, gangsters have been the characters we've both loved and loved to hate. These films are proof that crime pays off handsomely on-screen— even if we wouldn't necessarily want to follow in the criminal characters' footsteps.

1 Battles Without Honor and Humanity (1973)

Kinji Fukasaku's *Battles Without Honor and Humanity* examines the evolution of warrior codes—from sword fights to gunfights—in post–World War II Japan. Fukasaku aims not only for an artful interpretation of real events but utilizes narration, newsreel data, and other techniques to give his storytelling a vivid sense of authenticity.

2 Carlito's Way (1993)

While *Scarface* might be showier, this 1993 effort—which reunited director Brian De Palma with Al Pacino—is the superior film, in that it keeps Pacino on a tighter leash playing gangster cues in a more minor, albeit more deeply felt, key. But as Carlito's increasingly corrupt attorney Dave Kleinfeld, it's Sean Penn who enjoys the film's biggest opportunity to chew scenery.

3 Eastern Promises (2007)

David Cronenberg directed this full-throated story of a Russian mob enforcer (Viggo Mortensen) trying to juggle his responsibilities babysitting his best friend/boss's petulant son (Vincent Cassel) while also dealing with the death of a young sex worker whose child leads back to a ring of kidnappings by the mafia. Mortensen's buck-naked knife fight in a bathhouse is certainly the film's showstopper, but the script—written by *Peaky Blinders* creator Steven Knight—also explores the ties that bind and some that shackle.

4 Get Carter (1971)

British crime films exploded in popularity in the late sixties and seventies, and Michael Caine was often the face of its jazziest, most violent expressions. Here, Caine plays Jack Carter, a London gangster who travels home to discover that his brother was murdered—and decides to take revenge.

5 Infernal Affairs (2002)

Andrew Lau and Alan Mak directed this film that became the inspiration for Martin Scorsese's *The Departed*. The notion of cops and crooks being opposite sides of the same coin is an idea that has long been explored in cinema, but *Infernal Affairs* gives the contrast explicit dimensions when a cop is sent to infiltrate a Triad criminal organization at the same time a low-level Triad member is instructed to become a mole in the police force.

6 The Long Good Friday (1980)

The idea of "going legit" is one that is regularly explored in gangster movies, but few do it more effectively than director John Mackenzie's film about Harold Shand (an electrifying Bob Hoskins) and his imploded aspirations to become a businessman.

7 Miller's Crossing (1990)

Joel and Ethan Coen created this featherweight noir about a gangster's right-hand man (Gabriel Byrne) and the trouble in which he finds himself after his boss (Albert Finney) and another rival (Jon Polito) go to war over the ne'er-do-well brother (John Turturro) of his sometime lady friend (Marcia Gay Harden).

8 Once Upon a Time in America (1984)

Sergio Leone turned down the chance to direct *The Godfather* to focus on his own crime saga, which he delivered twelve years later. Several different versions of the film, of varying lengths, were released over the years in different countries, which forced *Once Upon a Time in America* to have to wait to find its audience. The four-hour-long "Extended Director's Cut" was released in the U.S. in 2014 and brought its transcendent virtues vividly into focus.

9 A Prophet (2009)

Jacques Audiard's Oscar-nominated film follows a naïve young convict named Malik (Tahar Rahim) as he becomes part of a crime organization while behind bars. Slowly watching as he ascends the ranks beneath his brutal Corsican mob boss, Malik becomes a proxy for the failed, forgotten, and seemingly weak who decide to make something of themselves out of sheer determination and will.

10 Sexy Beast (2000)

Jonathan Glazer is the creative force behind this hypnotic story of a retired gangster (Ray Winstone) enlisted by an insistent former colleague (Ben Kingsley) to stage a robbery at the behest of crime boss Teddy Bass (Ian McShane). Winstone's understated role as the reluctant bag man opposite Kingsley gives his co-star ample time to destroy the scenery and anything else in his way, but it's McShane in the Big Bad role who steals the show.

GRIZZLY MAN (2005)

DIRECTED BY: Werner Herzog

OTHER MOVIES BY WERNER HERZOG:
Nosferatu the Vampyre (1979); *Fitzcarraldo* (1982); *Rescue Dawn* (2006); *Into the Abyss* (2011)

Throughout his sixty-year career, Werner Herzog has seamlessly transitioned between narrative and nonfiction features, with a string of documentaries that have focused on everything from Tibetan Buddhism to some of the oldest art known to man. *Grizzly Man*, about the life (and brutal death) of amateur naturalist Timothy Treadwell, is among the best-known of Herzog's real-life stories.

Treadwell spent thirteen summers living among the bears in Alaska's Katmai National Park, filming footage and styling himself as a rogue protector who could get close enough to the grizzlies to pet them. In 2003, he and girlfriend, Amie Huguenard, stayed in the park later than usual, into the pre-hibernation season. Ultimately, a bear mauled them both to death; Treadwell left behind his footage and many questions, which Herzog mined for his film.

WERNER HERZOG'S INVOLVEMENT BEGAN WITH A LOST PAIR OF READING GLASSES.

Herzog was hunting through his pockets and a bunch of papers on the desk of producer Erik Nelson looking for his reading glasses when an article about Timothy Treadwell caught his eye. Nelson encouraged him to read it because they were going to make a movie about it.

"I read it and immediately hurried back to his office, and I asked, 'Who is directing it?,'" Herzog told NPR. "He said, 'I'm kind of directing it.' And there was some sort of hesitation, and with my thick German accent I said, 'No, I will direct this movie.' And that was it. We shook hands and I made it."

TREADWELL WAS HOPING TO TURN HIS FOOTAGE INTO HIS OWN MOVIE.

Treadwell spent thirty-five thousand hours living among the bears. Herzog started with a hundred-plus hours of footage Treadwell shot of his time in the park. Though there was an enormous amount of material, it was all meticulously curated by Treadwell. As *Grizzly Man* points out, Treadwell captured his encounters with the bears as if he were hosting a nature documentary. He released an hour-long edit of footage that Herzog saw during production but did not share it outside a very close circle of collaborators.

HERZOG WAS SURPRISED BY THE INTENSITY OF TREADWELL'S FOOTAGE.

The director and his team were tasked with transforming more than a hundred hours of footage into a 104-minute documentary, which also had to include their own footage and narration. Herzog found the intensity of Treadwell's footage "unexpected."

"It was always clear to me that it wouldn't be a film on wild nature, that it would be much more a film on our nature," Herzog told CHUD.com.

HERZOG NEVER PLANNED TO USE THE AUDIO OF TIMOTHY'S AND AMIE'S DEATH.

When Treadwell and Huguenard realized a bear was encroaching on their tent, one of them must have hit record on the camera—which then captured audio of their deaths. Herzog filmed himself listening to it for the first time, and it's clear that what he's listening to is horrifying. He quickly promised not to use any of these recordings in the film, both out of respect for the dead and to avoid making what he called "a snuff film."

THE MOVIE ISN'T ABOUT BEARS BEING DANGEROUS.

The message of the movie is easy to miss because Treadwell's death looms so large, but Herzog's intention was never to suggest that Treadwell was wrong about bears being safe. "Grizzly bears normally do not kill and attack human beings," the director said. The point Herzog wanted to make was that Treadwell wrongly believed that nature could be tamed.

FREEZE-FRAME

After listening to the audio of Treadwell and Huguenard's deaths, which Herzog called "the most terrifying thing I've ever heard in my life," he told their friend Jewel Palovak to get rid of the tapes. "But that was stupid," he later told *Paste*. "Silly advice born out of the immediate shock of hearing." Palovak placed the tapes in a bank vault instead.

LIFE LESSONS: RIVETING DOCUMENTARIES

The late, great documentarian Albert Maysles once explained the power of nonfiction moviemaking by saying, "When you see somebody on the screen in a documentary, you're really engaged with a person going through real life experiences, so for that period of time, as you watch the film, you are, in effect, in the shoes of another individual. What a privilege to have that experience."

Indeed it is—at least if the filmmakers behind the project are doing it right and finding some small way to extend our personal knowledge of the human experience. And maybe even teach us something at the same time.

13TH (2016)

Following the breakout prestige of *Selma*, Ava DuVernay constructed an exploration of the criminalization of Black individuals in the United States, crafting a throughline from slavery to the modern private prison boom. Eschewing an overdramatized style, DuVernay calmly, patiently lays out facts and figures that will make your jaw drop.

Awesome; I F**kin' Shot That! (2006)

A year before YouTube launched, the Beastie Boys gave fifty fans in their Madison Square Garden audience camcorders to capture the concert. The result is a genuine, fans'-eye view of the experience, and a chaotic mash-up of perspectives.

Blackfish (2013)

Gabriela Cowperthwaite's 2013 documentary about captive orcas quickly proved to be bad business for SeaWorld. Attendance and revenue dropped, and the House

of Representatives got involved. Finally, SeaWorld announced the park would end its orca breeding program and modify all orca performances so the animals would no longer be forced to vamp for audiences.

Bowling for Columbine (2002)

Michael Moore became a new kind of folk hero when he confronted Kmart executives over their sale of firearms and ammunition, and the company later announced it would stop selling ammunition in all of its stores. The chain of events unfolds in Moore's Oscar-winning documentary, which explores the causes of mass shootings and America's broader relationship with guns.

The Central Park Five (2012)

The so-called Central Park jogger case electrified New York City in 1989. After Trisha Meili was raped and beaten in the middle of her nighttime run in the park, the NYPD moved quickly to put the

perpetrator behind bars. Too quickly, it turns out. Five juveniles were charged on faulty evidence and sentenced to prison. They remained trapped behind bars until 2002, when the real culprit confessed and cleared the boys (by then men) with his DNA match.

Crip Camp: A Disability Revolution (2020)

Barack and Michelle Obama executive-produced this insightful and moving portrait of Camp Jened, a summer camp in New York that welcomed kids with disabilities and helped forge a movement in the 1970s to achieve equal rights for those with physical challenges.

Crumb (1995)

With his salacious eye for voluptuous doodles, cartoonist Robert Crumb became notorious in the 1970s. Like most nonconformists, he has a story to tell, one director Terry Zwigoff illustrates to great effect in *Crumb*. The middle of three brothers, Crumb presents as a cynic, collector (of records), and cultural curiosity, with his artwork drawing scorn for their sexual charge and use of racist stereotypes. Crumb the person is not easily understood— and perhaps shouldn't be—but *Crumb* the movie invites a curiosity over what makes this man tick.

Gimme Shelter (1970)

This profound doc captured the Rolling Stones touring at a time when they were one of the biggest bands in the world and only getting bigger. The music is powerful and immediate, and the film closes with their appearance at the Altamont Free Concert, which turned deadly. After a day of skirmishes between concertgoers and the Hells Angels, who were acting as security for the show, a fan with a gun was stabbed to death.

Grey Gardens (1975)

Five years after *Gimme Shelter*, documentarian brothers Albert and David Maysles trained their camera on a much more personal story: Edith Ewing Bouvier Beale, aka "Big Edie," and her daughter Edith Bouvier Beale, called "Little Edie," the aunt and first cousin, respectively, of former First Lady Jacqueline Kennedy Onassis. Though they grew up in a world of privilege, a bitter divorce and financial hardship left the two women with little more than the twenty-eight-room East Hampton mansion known as Grey Gardens. The Maysles treat their subjects with the utmost respect, allowing them to tell their story directly to the camera.

Harlan County, USA (1976)

For eighteen months, filmmaker Barbara Kopple lived in the dark. She shadowed the coal miners at the heart of *Harlan County, USA*, a searing indictment of exploitative labor practices. Risking their lives and often sacrificing their long-term health, the Kentucky miners go on strike, and Kopple documents the violent struggle with the mining company that follows. Decades later, the sight of a workforce crying for fair treatment is as prescient as ever.

The Invisible War (2012)

Kirby Dick's *The Invisible War* offers a harrowing look at the way rape cases in the U.S. military are mishandled. Mere days after watching it, Secretary of Defense Leon Panetta announced a policy change in the way these crimes are investigated. This was before the documentary opened. After its debut, one of the generals featured in the film was replaced, politicians including Senator Kirsten Gillibrand proposed even more radical policy changes, and the Pentagon introduced two new programs to "change the culture" surrounding rape allegations.

Jesus Camp (2006)

Jesus Camp follows children attending a Christian summer camp in Devils Lake, North Dakota—only the young campers at Kids on Fire don't make friendship bracelets or tell ghost stories around the campfire. Instead, they fill their days with sermons preaching Islamophobia, homophobia, and a militant call to action against anyone opposing Christian beliefs. Kids on Fire received so many outraged calls and emails after this movie was released that camp director Becky Fischer

had to shut it down. She didn't quit, though; she just rebranded.

Metallica: Some Kind of Monster (2004)

Metallica was at the top of a very high mountain in 2000, having sustained and grown their popularity through the 1990s into the rarified mainstream air of Grammy Awards and blockbuster movie soundtracks. Then the mountain crumbled beneath them, and they attempt a last-ditch effort to stay together (after bassist Jason Newsted's exit) by spending time exploring their emotions and group dynamic with a performance enhancement coach.

Paradise Lost Trilogy (1996–2011)

The *Paradise Lost* trilogy didn't just bring widespread attention to the West Memphis Three murder case, it also earned the defendants crucial celebrity support. Johnny Depp, Peter Jackson, and Eddie Vedder personally donated millions of dollars to help Damien Echols, Jason Baldwin, and Jessie Misskelley Jr. appeal their conviction. And it worked. The three men were released in 2011, after serving more than eighteen years in prison.

RBG (2018)

Throughout her life and long career, late Supreme Court justice Ruth Bader Ginsburg became involved in seminal decisions on everything from abortion to equal rights. This doc, released two years before her death, details her journey from law school to setting precedent on some of the nation's most pressing issues—and becoming a role model in the process.

Stop Making Sense (1984)

There's little left to say about the concert film perfection of Jonathan Demme capturing the Talking Heads over four nights at the Pantages Theater in Hollywood. It's a glorious exploration of the band's strange and deeply human stage show that flowed through their funky series of great songs while lead singer David Byrne rocked his iconic oversized suit. It's a master class in theatricality and a booster shot of joy. Get the VHS or LaserDisc if you can because there's even more music to love on them.

Summer of Soul (2021)

Questlove directed this look back at the 1969 Harlem Cultural Festival, which was hailed as one of the greatest music concerts of all time but never received the attention of Woodstock or other gatherings of the time.

Super Size Me (2004)

Less than two months after Morgan Spurlock's *Super Size Me* premiered at the Sundance Film Festival, McDonald's announced the end of "super-sizing." The fast-food corporation claimed the decision had nothing to do with Spurlock's grotesque Big Mac binging, but considering the rapid timeline, no one really believed Mickey D's.

The Thin Blue Line (1988)

Errol Morris tore into the evidence and testimony against Randall Dale Adams, a former death row inmate accused of murdering a police officer, in this 1988 true-crime documentary. His counterargument was so convincing that it helped overturn Adams's conviction.

Waiting for Superman (2010)

The plight of the American educational system is put to task in this landmark film from director Dave Guggenheim, who focuses on the trials and tribulations of five young students navigating the problematic public school landscape.

Wattstax (1972)

Dubbed "Black Woodstock" by some cultural critics, the benefit concert marking the seventh anniversary of the 1965 Watts riots featured a vivid tapestry of gospel, funk, and R & B artists interwoven with speeches from Jesse Jackson, Fred Williams, and Melvin Van Peebles. It's an amazing slice of history, made even more impressive by the gargantuan effort that made it possible: The concert itself only had one night to set up and one night to tear down so as not to jar the NFL schedule at the Los Angeles Coliseum, and the audience couldn't be seated near the stage for fear that it might mar the field (they stormed it anyway to do the Funky Chicken).

Woodstock (1970)

If rock 'n' roll emerged from unruly teenage years into conflicted young adulthood in the 1960s, nothing stamped that image in henna ink better than Woodstock and the documentary that accompanied it. The bands that appear are legendary: The Who, Joe Cocker singing The Beatles, Janis Joplin, Jimi Hendrix, and many more. It's a flyby of the three days of peace, love, and music that you could play on repeat with summery ease.

WRITTEN BY: John Carpenter and Debra Hill

DIRECTED BY: John Carpenter

OTHER MOVIES DIRECTED BY JOHN CARPENTER: *Assault on Precinct 13* (1976); *The Fog* (1980); *Escape from New York* (1981); *Christine* (1983); *They Live* (1988); *Ghosts of Mars* (2001)

HALLOWEEN

Virtually every slasher film out there owes a bloody debt to *Halloween*, John Carpenter's minimalist horror classic. Released in 1978, the film set the template for a masked and silent killer stalking beautiful people—in this case, Jamie Lee Curtis as high schooler Laurie Strode. Generations of filmmakers (and many, many *Halloween* sequels) later, few have come close to equaling the dread and tension brought by Michael Myers, aka the Shape, stalking his first All Hallows' Eve.

IT TOOK LESS THAN TWO WEEKS TO WRITE THE SCRIPT.

The movie was originally going to be called *The Babysitter Murders*, but producer Irwin Yablans suggested that the story may be more significant if it were based around a specific holiday, so the title was changed to *Halloween*. Carpenter and co-screenwriter Debra Hill wrote the original script in just ten days.

THE MOVIE MARKED JAMIE LEE CURTIS'S FEATURE DEBUT.

Curtis had never made a feature film before, but was called back to audition for the part of Laurie Strode three separate times. Carpenter initially wanted actress Anne Lockhart for the role, but cast Curtis after her final audition, where she nailed the scene of Laurie looking out her window to see Michael Myers in her backyard.

THE PRODUCTION PROCESS WAS INCREDIBLY SHORT.

The twenty-day shoot commenced in the spring of 1978, and the film was released in October of the same year. The seasonal restrictions created some interesting hurdles for the production, including a lack of fall scenery. Dozens of bags of fake leaves painted by production designer Tommy Lee Wallace were reused for various scenes.

THE SCRIPT DIDN'T CALL FOR A SPECIFIC KIND OF MASK.

The mask for Michael Myers was only described as having "the pale, neutral features of a man," and for the movie the design was boiled down to two options: Both were cheap latex masks that Wallace bought at local toy stores for under two dollars apiece and painted white. One was a replica mask of a clown character called "Weary Willie" popularized by actor Emmett Kelly, and the other was a stretched-out Captain Kirk mask from *Star Trek*. Carpenter chose the whitewashed Kirk mask because of its eerily blank stare that fit perfectly with the Myers character.

ONE *HALLOWEEN* CHARACTER WAS NAMED AFTER ANOTHER FAMOUS HORROR MOVIE CHARACTER.

Donald Pleasence's character, Dr. Sam Loomis, was named after the character of the same name (minus the "Doctor") from Alfred Hitchcock's *Psycho*. Curtis's mother, Janet Leigh, appeared in *Psycho* as Loomis's girlfriend Marion and was killed in the film's famous

shower scene. For the Loomis character in *Halloween*, Carpenter originally wanted either Peter Cushing or Christopher Lee, but both passed on the film because the pay was too low.

MOST OF *HALLOWEEN*'S MAIN CAST PROVIDED THEIR OWN WARDROBES.

Curtis bought her costumes at JC Penney, all for under one hundred dollars.

THE ADULT VERSION OF MICHAEL MYERS IS PLAYED BY THREE DIFFERENT PEOPLE.

Michael Myers was primarily played by actor Nick Castle, Carpenter's friend from USC film school who would go on to co-write the 1981 film *Escape from New York* with the director. The Shape was also played by production designer Tommy Lee Wallace whenever needed, and when Myers is unmasked at the end of the film, he is played by actor Tony Moran, who would go on to appear in guest spots on TV shows like *The Waltons* and *CHiPS*. Moran was paid $250 for a day's work and a single shot in *Halloween*.

CARPENTER COMPLETED THE ENTIRE SCORE FOR *HALLOWEEN* IN JUST THREE DAYS.

The director usually does all the music for his own films, and his theme for the movie came from something he learned for the bongos that his father, who just so happened to be a music professor and composer, had taught him when he was a child.

WRITTEN BY: Colin Higgins

DIRECTED BY: Hal Ashby

OTHER MOVIES DIRECTED BY HAL ASHBY:
The Landlord (1970); *The Last Detail* (1973);
Shampoo (1975); *Coming Home* (1978);
Being There (1979); *The Slugger's Wife* (1985)

HAROLD AND MAUDE (1971)

You'd be hard-pressed to find a true cinephile who doesn't own a copy of *Harold and Maude*. The 1971 box office failure, directed by Hal Ashby and written by Colin Higgins, may have had a rocky debut, but it has since become a New Hollywood classic. The brutally dark rom-com tells the story of a death-obsessed young boy (Bud Cort) who falls for a free-spirited seventy-nine-year-old woman (Ruth Gordon), much to the chagrin of his oblivious, blue-blooded mother (Vivian Pickles). Not only has the film found a second life at film festivals, outdoor park screenings, art-house cinemas, and on home video, but it's also become a must-see movie for anyone serious about filmmaking.

HARRISON FORD WORKED FOR SCREENWRITER COLIN HIGGINS—AS A CARPENTER.

According to the Criterion Collection cut, Higgins employed Harrison Ford, then working as a carpenter, to build a hot tub and deck for his backyard while the movie was in production.

CORT AND GORDON'S REAL-LIFE RELATIONSHIP ALMOST MIRRORED THAT OF THEIR CHARACTERS.

In the April 2001 issue of *Vanity Fair*, Cort revisited the cult classic and reminisced on his chemistry with his co-star. "During the making of the film, [Ruth] was very standoffish. Then, the day my father died, the first call I got was from Ruth, saying 'Let me tell you about the day my father died,'" he told the magazine. "And suddenly we became the characters pretty much that we were in the film."

ELTON JOHN PASSED ON DOING THE SOUNDTRACK.

According to the Criterion Collection version of the film, producer Charles Mulvehill initially approached Elton John to write the music for the movie, as Ashby was a fan of the pop star. John passed—but not before suggesting his friend Cat Stevens for the job. Stevens said yes, and his music has become inextricably linked to the movie.

ALI MACGRAW, ROBERT EVANS'S THEN-WIFE, WANTED THE LOVE SCENE BETWEEN HAROLD AND MAUDE TO BE CUT.

Of course, her Paramount boss husband tried to oblige. Ashby furiously objected, saying, "That's sort of what the whole movie is about, a boy falling in love with an old woman; the sexual aspect doesn't have to be distasteful." About the less-than-explicit scene, *Being Hal Ashby* author Nick Dawson wrote, "Ashby wanted to show the beauty of young and old flesh together, some-thing that he knew the younger generation, the hippies, the heads, the open-minded masses, would dig, but Evans said it would repulse most audiences, so it had to go." In the end, Ashby won by sneaking the footage into the film's trailer.

CORT REFUSED TO DO ANY PR FOR THE FILM IF THE STUDIO DIDN'T GIVE ASHBY CREATIVE CONTROL OVER THE EDIT.

During postproduction, Paramount Pictures stripped Ashby of his power to edit his own movie. So, in solidarity with his director, Cort told the film's PR team that he wouldn't do any publicity for the film unless Ashby got his movie back. According to the *Guardian*, control over the footage was handed back to Ashby— save for a kissing scene between *Harold and Maude* that Paramount head honcho Robert Evans despised.

"It's best not to be too moral. You cheat yourself out of too much life."

OFFBEAT ROMANTIC COMEDIES

While many romantic comedies end with that most Hollywood "Happily Ever After," even those people who don't traditionally consider themselves "a rom-com fan" can usually find a movie resonates with them, as rom-coms represent a wide range of films, from the biting to the effervescent.

1 *The Big Sick* **(2017)**
Based on the real-life love story of husband-and-wife writers Kumail Nanjiani (who also stars) and Emily V. Gordon, *The Big Sick* is a romantic comedy about what happens when life, and the looming possibility of death, get in the way to such an extent that your love story is sometimes more about holding on than it is about holding each other. Director Michael Showalter's absurdist tendencies are softened a bit by the heart of the film, but they're still just present enough to play up how strange this journey is for the people at the core of it, and that makes the emotional payoff all the more intense.

2 *Boomerang* **(1992)**
This Reginald Hudlin flick packs a cast of all-stars—including Eddie Murphy, Halle Berry, and a scene-stealing Grace Jones—and a script full of memorable lines into this story of a man who's thrown for a loop when he finds a woman (Robin Givens) who's actually better at playing his own suave one-night stand game than he is. *Boomerang* is an ahead-of-its-time classic.

3 *But I'm a Cheerleader* **(1999)**
In Jamie Babbit's cult classic ode to living your truth and finding love on your own terms, Natasha Lyonne and Clea DuVall shine as two young women who fall for each other while they're supposed to be getting "cured" at a gay conversion therapy camp. *But I'm a Cheerleader* takes place in a space where every color is bright and everything is coordinated, suggesting a world of absolutes that the characters must navigate in order to discover that who they really are is not so easily defined.

4 *Defending Your Life* **(1991)**
Leave it to Albert Brooks to craft the perfect encapsulation of love overcoming fear via an extended fantasy saga about the bureaucracy of the afterlife. Brooks's comedies are so often focused on skewering the hyper-commercial, status-obsessed culture in which they were made, and that's still present here. But what holds up best about *Defending Your Life* is just how well it works as a sheer expression of the transformative power of love. By the end, all traces of cynicism and fear have faded, and in their place is an honest expression of joy. Brooks's casting of Meryl Streep as his love interest didn't hurt, either.

5 The Incredible Jessica James (2017)

There's nothing like this odyssey through dating life in the App Era. Former *Daily Show* correspondent Jessica Williams owns the hyper-confident, profoundly magnetic main role as a woman with ambitions in every corner of her life. Her unlikely romance with divorcé Boone (Chris O'Dowd) is predicated on refusing to obsess over their exes' social media accounts anymore, but it blossoms into exactly the best kind of supportive, frantic affair that the genre promises.

6 Moonstruck (1987)

Moonstruck is a film so embedded in pop culture that it's delivered not one but two moments iconic even to viewers who've never actually seen the film. More than three decades after its release, "Snap out of it!" remains one of the most memorable romantic comedy lines ever, and Cher's dazzling display of morning-after bliss as she kicks a can through the streets of New York City remains an indelible symbol of what it's like to fall for someone completely.

7 Palm Springs (2020)

Andy Samberg and Cristin Milioti are a perfect rom-com pair, playing to each other's strengths in a way that makes it feel like they've been at it for years. And the time-loop concept at the core of the story works wonderfully as both a metaphor for navigating long-term relationships and a clever premise to show what happens when you care enough to break through to the next stage of the commitment.

8 She's Gotta Have It (1986)

Spike Lee's feature directorial debut also sees him playing one of three men under the thumb of Nola Darling (Tracy Camilla Johns). None of them can stand Nola's gender-reversing approach to casual relationships, and the three hope to goad her into living a monogamous life. Nola, however, wants to pursue happiness on her own terms, not society's. Lee's love letter to Brooklyn is still a standout in his filmography, which quickly grew to include 1989's *Do the Right Thing* and 1992's *Malcolm X.*

9 To All the Boys I've Loved Before (2018)

Based on Jenny Han's wildly popular novel, this thoroughly modern rom-com with nods to eighties classics serves as a powerful reminder that, if you're going to write love letters to all your crushes, make sure your precocious little sister doesn't mail them. That's exactly what happens to Lara Jean Covey (Lana Condor), a shy teen trying to keep her head down while harboring strong feelings for her lifelong friend Josh (Israel Broussard), who's off-limits because he dated Lara Jean's sister. It's a tangled web worthy of Shakespeare that's funny and sweet.

10 When Harry Met Sally . . . (1989)

Before Nora Ephron wrote and directed *Sleepless in Seattle* (1993) and *You've Got Mail* (1998), she penned the screenplay for *When Harry Met Sally . . .* The witty dialogue and heartfelt themes that would become emblematic of her style are baked into this classic romantic comedy. The story follows Sally (Meg Ryan) and Harry (Billy Crystal) as they go from bickering acquaintances to best friends to reluctant lovers over the span of twelve years. The movie is regarded by many rom-com fans as the platonic ideal of the genre. It's also the first thing many people think of when they visit Katz's Deli in New York.

11 While You Were Sleeping (1995)

Due to a comedy of errors, Chicago Transit Authority worker Lucy (Sandra Bullock) ends up spending the holidays with the family of Peter (Peter Gallagher), a handsome commuter she fantasizes about who is now in a coma, and whose family believes her to be his fiancée. But she ends up falling for his brother (Bill Pullman).

> **"When you realize you want to spend the rest of your life with somebody, you want the rest of your life to start as soon as possible."**
>
> — *When Harry Met Sally . . .*

HEAT (1995)

WRITTEN BY: Michael Mann

DIRECTED BY: Michael Mann

OTHER MOVIES DIRECTED BY MICHAEL MANN:
Manhunter (1986); *The Last of the Mohicans* (1992); *The Insider* (1999); *Collateral* (2004)

On December 15, 1995, *Heat*—an almost three-hour-long epic heist film—was released in theaters. Written and directed by Michael Mann, it featured no special effects, was filmed in sixty-five real locations around L.A. (no soundstages), and approached its material with a kind of realism rarely seen in films before or since, which is one reason why many critics and fans consider it to be one of the greatest crime dramas of all time.

It also didn't hurt that the movie starred Robert De Niro as criminal mastermind Neil McCauley and Al Pacino as Vincent Hanna, the LAPD lieutenant hot on the tail of McCauley and his crew as they attempt to pull off one huge score.

IT'S BASED ON A MEETING BETWEEN A REAL-LIFE DETECTIVE AND A BANK ROBBER.

In 1963, a Chicago detective named Chuck Adamson dined in a local coffee shop with convicted bank robber Neil McCauley. A year after the fated meeting, Adamson tracked McCauley and his crew to an in-progress supermarket heist. A chase ensued, and McCauley was shot. Adamson befriended Michael Mann when they worked together on *Thief* and *Crime Story*, but the genesis for *Heat* came from the idea of two men on opposing sides of the law coming together and understanding each other. De Niro's character in *Heat* is named for McCauley.

THE IDEA TO PAIR DE NIRO AND PACINO CAME DURING A BREAKFAST MEETING.

Mann and producer Art Linson had breakfast at the now-closed Broadway Deli in Santa Monica, where McCauley and Eady (Amy Brenneman) meet in the film. Mann asked Linson if he wanted to co-produce the film with him. "And he said, 'You're out of your mind. You've got to direct it.' Then we came up with the idea of Bob and Al."

VAL KILMER'S GUN-HANDLING SKILLS WERE IMPRESSIVE.

One of *Heat*'s most iconic moments is the climactic ten-minute shoot-out scene, which was filmed every Saturday and Sunday in downtown L.A. for six weeks. The actors trained with men from the British Special Air Service (SAS) and at the L.A. County Sheriff's combat shooting ranges. "[The actors] got so good that the footage of Val Kilmer, firing in two directions and doing a reload without a cut, [was] used at Fort Bragg for Special Forces training," Mann told Deadline.

MANN SHOT THE FILM'S CLIMAX AT THE AIRPORT BECAUSE IT LOOKED "SURREAL."

The ending takes place in an abandoned field near an airport, outside of the city. "I wanted to find a landscape that was so transient that it started to achieve a surreal effect on you but still maintained the gritty reality of the movie," Mann told Deadline.

AFTER *HEAT* CAME OUT, COPYCAT CRIMES OCCURRED ALL OVER THE WORLD.

In Cali, Colombia, in 2003, eighteen masked robbers drove a bus into an armored van and stole $350,000 in cash, which mirrors a scene in *Heat*. In 1997, a forty-four-minute shoot-out occurred in North Hollywood in which the gunmen robbed a Bank of America wearing heavy body armor and carrying assault rifles. It was later revealed that the gunmen, who were both killed, had cited *Heat* as an influence for the robbery.

115

10

ARRESTING HEIST MOVIES

In the history of cinema, there have been hundreds of heist films ranging in size from small jobs to massive capers. But only a select few stand out as the perfect combination of planning and execution, of character chemistry and filmmaking intricacy. Here are ten of them.

1 *Bottle Rocket* **(1996)**
Wes Anderson's debut feature is his take on "what if a group of total idiots tried to pull a heist," with everything the Wes Anderson style implies about that. The practice heist, in which the main characters (played by Owen and Luke Wilson) steal from a predetermined list of items within one of their family homes, remains a classic Anderson moment.

2 *Dog Day Afternoon* **(1975)**
Some heist films spend most of their time setting up the caper, while others leap right into it. No matter where they start, there's usually a clear indication there was a plan. Sidney Lumet's white-hot bank robbery picture starring Al Pacino and John Cazale makes it clear that the crooks at the center *did* have a plan. It was just a plan with a lot of flaws, and the very human response to how those flaws reveal themselves throughout the film makes for one of the most raw displays of empathy in crime cinema history.

3 *Hell or High Water* **(2016)**
Chris Pine and Ben Foster shine as two brothers who have planned a high-stakes series of bank robberies, complete with a money-laundering scheme, to save their family's land. The plan is elegant in its simplicity, but grows increasingly complicated as a wise Texas Ranger (Jeff Bridges) closes in.

4 Inside Man (2006)

The plan for the perfect robbery is revealed to the audience at the same speed as it's revealed to the NYPD detective (Denzel Washington) and the secretive fixer (Jodie Foster) who are watching it unfold from the outside as the robbery's mastermind (Clive Owen) moves forward with an agenda we can't see coming. Spike Lee pushes the film at a breathless pace, delivering twist after twist with the grace of a master, until we finally see the whole game board.

5 Ocean's Eleven (2001)

Steven Soderbergh's impossibly star-packed heist movie, which is a remake of Lewis Milestone's 1960 equally star-packed heist movie (that original featured the Rat Pack), is an endlessly entertaining, utterly stylish, and effortlessly witty take on the subgenre that has just about everything you could ever want in a heist film.

6 Out of Sight (1998)

Before he made the *Ocean's* trilogy, Soderbergh turned his eye for genre cinema to this adaptation of Elmore Leonard's novel of the same name, about a U.S. marshal's budding romance with a bank robber she just happens to meet as he's escaping prison. George Clooney and Jennifer Lopez bring the sex appeal, Don Cheadle and Steve Zahn bring the comedy, and Soderbergh brings his eye for setups and payoffs to one of the best crime films of the 1990s.

7 Thief (1981)

Michael Mann remains one of crime cinema's greatest living practitioners, and he came out of the gate swinging with his directorial debut. *Thief* is the story of a safecracker (James Caan) who longs for a fulfilling life beyond criminal pursuits after he gets out of prison. Of course, in classic crime cinema fashion, he finds that having it all isn't as within reach as he'd like. *Thief* features some of the best scenes of fiery, authentic safe-cracking in cinema, and remains one of the highlights of both Mann's and Caan's stellar careers.

8 The Thomas Crown Affair (1968)

If you wanted to make a cool movie in the 1960s, casting Steve McQueen got you halfway to where you wanted to be. *The Thomas Crown Affair* stars McQueen as a bored millionaire who can basically do whatever he wants with his time, and what he wants is to stage extremely intricate robberies just to see if he can. Then along comes Faye Dunaway, and Crown's plans get just a little more complicated. While John McTiernan's 1999 remake is fun in its own right, it's hard to touch the pure effortless cool of the original.

9 The Town (2010)

What *Heat* was for Los Angeles, Ben Affleck's *The Town* is for Boston. Affleck clearly learned a lot of his tricks from Mann, but what's most striking about *The Town*—aside from its structural similarities to *Heat*—is the way that Affleck and company take that sensibility, then twist it to defy our expectations. What starts with a gloriously tense opening robbery set piece and builds to a big last job ultimately becomes a standoff not between a cop and a crook who respect each other, but between two best friends who are supposed to be on the same side, each longing for their own version of freedom.

10 Widows (2018)

Director Steve McQueen teamed up with *Gone Girl* author Gillian Flynn to tell the story of a group of women driven to desperation after the deaths of their criminal husbands. Together they hatch a plan to rob a corrupt politician based on an idea the husband of one of them left behind, and in so doing find their own power.

> # "I'm robbing a bank because they got money here. That's why I'm robbing it."
>
> **— Dog Day Afternoon**

HEDWIG AND THE ANGRY INCH (2001)

WRITTEN BY: John Cameron Mitchell and Stephen Trask

DIRECTED BY: John Cameron Mitchell

OTHER MOVIES DIRECTED BY JOHN CAMERON MITCHELL: *Shortbus* (2006); *Rabbit Hole* (2010); *How to Talk to Girls at Parties* (2017)

In the 1990s, after a chance meeting on an airplane sparked a friendship, writer-actor John Cameron Mitchell and musician-composer Stephen Trask began collaborating on what Mitchell hoped would become a new rock musical. Several twists and turns later, they had produced *Hedwig and the Angry Inch*, one of the greatest rock musicals ever made. Just a few years later, the rock musical became a rock musical *film*, giving even more people the opportunity to become "Hed-heads."

HEDWIG WAS BASED ON A REAL PERSON.

The character of Tommy Gnosis was largely inspired by Mitchell himself, a military kid who grew up in Kansas loving rock 'n' roll, but Hedwig Schmidt also grew out of a real person Mitchell knew from his childhood. As he and Trask began developing the show, Mitchell told his collaborator about a German woman who once babysat him named Helga; she had moved to America after marrying a soldier. Like Hedwig's, Helga's marriage eventually fell apart, and like her, she lived in a trailer in Kansas, where she carried herself with a certain regal quality.

"She knew she was the shit, but she didn't have anything," Mitchell later recalled. "But I was like, 'How can someone be so regal with nothing?'" Trask was so interested in Helga's story that he suggested Mitchell incorporate her character into their show, and Helga eventually became Hedwig.

THE SAME RESTAURANT PLAYED THE PART OF EVERY BILGEWATER'S LOCATION.

Though they had the backing of a major studio, *Hedwig* was still a relatively low-budget production and had to make efficient use of its locations. That meant that, while the story chronicles Hedwig's journey to various Bilgewater's restaurants around the country, the production could only use *one* restaurant to stand in for several. Production designer Thérèse DePrez redecorated what was once a Western-themed family pizza restaurant to stand in for the fictional seafood chain, even decorating the walls with murals of famous shipwrecks.

THE "WIG IN A BOX" TRAILER WAS REAL (AND SO WAS THE HAIR).

Though *Hedwig* was a small production, the filmmakers managed to make room for some very impressive musical sequences, thanks to a combination of ingenuity and luck. One key example was the "Wig in a Box" sequence, which featured a real trailer that the crew converted into a foldout stage in the midst of an actual trailer park outside of Toronto. Oh, and that wig suit Hedwig wears at the end of the song? According to Mitchell, it was made entirely of human hair.

DEBBY BOONE'S "YOU LIGHT UP MY LIFE" WAS ORIGINALLY USED TO CLOSE OUT THE SHOW.

Both the play and movie ended with the original song "Midnight Radio," which was only written about a week before *Hedwig*'s off-Broadway debut. They originally closed the show out with a German version of "You Light Up My Life," but couldn't secure the rights to it.

THERE'S A SEQUEL (SORT OF).

In the years following *Hedwig*'s cult success, Mitchell would occasionally talk publicly about the idea of a follow-up story, one that might pick up on Hedwig's adventures later in life. In 2019, he finally made good on all that talking with a project that could be considered a *Hedwig* sequel . . . sort of. Titled *Anthem: Homunculus*, the project debuted as a rock musical in podcast form, created by Mitchell and Bryan Weller, that followed the life of Ceann Mackay, who records a confessional podcast from a trailer in Kansas in an effort to crowdfund surgery for a brain tumor. The connective tissue to *Hedwig* is that Ceann is from the same town where Hedwig settled in America and lives in the same trailer she used to occupy. So it's not quite a sequel, but it is part of a shared universe, and Mitchell describes Ceann as "what I would have been like if I had never left my small town."

HEREDITARY

(2018)

WRITTEN BY: Ari Aster

DIRECTED BY: Ari Aster

OTHER MOVIES DIRECTED BY ARI ASTER:
Midsommar (2019);
Disappointment Blvd.
(2022)

*H*ereditary premiered in 2018, forever ruining treehouses, miniature art, and clucking sounds for everyone who saw it. Part occult horror and part domestic drama, the movie follows a family grappling with the traumatic death of its youngest member and the dark traditions that haunt its bloodline. The movie has been praised as an impressive debut from writer-director Ari Aster and a highlight of the new golden age of horror.

HEREDITARY WAS INSPIRED BY ANOTHER UNSETTLING MOVIE.

Aster's vision for *Hereditary* was inspired by a few horror staples including *Carrie* (1976) and *Rosemary's Baby* (1968). But there was another, more obscure source he drew from when crafting his movie. For those who are unfamiliar with Peter Greenaway's *The Cook, the Thief, His Wife & Her Lover*, the 1989 film starring Helen Mirren and Michael Gambon, it centers on a woman having an affair with a man at her abusive husband's restaurant. Like *Hereditary*, it's more than the straightforward drama it appears to be on the surface. The unrated film is noteworthy for a host of controversial elements including explicit sex, defecation, and cannibalism. As a guest on the CineFix Directors Series, Aster said that he snuck the movie out of his local video store around age twelve after learning that it had upset his stoic father. "I regretted watching it for many years," Aster said.

In spring of 2018, an Australian movie theater accidentally screened the *Hereditary* trailer before a showing of the family film *Peter Rabbit*. At least forty children were in the theater, and they were understandably upset. The cinema gave out free movie passes as an apology.

TONI COLLETTE WAS HESITANT TO TAKE THE LEAD ROLE.

Collette's performance as Annie is rightly lauded as a highlight of *Hereditary*. But the role almost went to someone else—not because that's what the director wanted, but because Collette was hesitant to sign on. She doesn't consider herself a horror fan, and at the time she was approached with the script, she was only interested in doing lighter films. "I realllllly wasn't looking to do anything this heavy," Collette told the Daily Beast. But after reading the script and realizing it wasn't a typical horror flick, she couldn't resist saying yes.

ASTER AVOIDED CALLING HEREDITARY A HORROR MOVIE.

Any movie that has as much demonism, decapitation, and creepy kid content as *Hereditary* does automatically falls into the horror genre. But when he was initially pitching the film, Aster was hesitant to use the label. "As I was pitching it, I was describing it as a family tragedy that curdles into a nightmare," Aster told NPR. "I wanted the film to function first as a vivid family drama before I even bothered attending to the horror elements." Aster's plan worked: The movie relies on classic horror tropes, but by bringing in elements from other genres, Aster convinced studios—and critics—to take it more seriously.

THE CAR ACCIDENT IS ASTER'S FAVORITE SCENE.

If you remember any part of *Hereditary*, it's likely the gut-wrenching car accident scene that sets the horrifying events of the second half in motion. Aster is well aware of how effective it is. "That's probably my favorite sequence in the film," he told *Vanity Fair*, "everything that's happening around those 15 minutes."

THE CULT'S SYMBOL IS HIDDEN THROUGHOUT THE MOVIE.

Observant viewers will notice many references to the film's ending sprinkled throughout *Hereditary*. One of these is the symbol of the cult that terrorizes the family. Annie's mother can be seen wearing it as a necklace at her funeral, but it also shows up in unexpected places, like on the telephone pole that decapitates Charlie.

HOME ALONE (1990)

WRITTEN BY: John Hughes

DIRECTED BY: Chris Columbus

OTHER MOVIES DIRECTED BY CHRIS COLUMBUS:
Mrs. Doubtfire (1993); *Stepmom* (1998);
Harry Potter and the Sorcerer's Stone (2001);
Harry Potter and the Chamber of Secrets (2002);
Rent (2005)

FREEZE-FRAME

No hit movie would be complete without a great little conspiracy theory. In the case of *Home Alone*, it's that Elvis Presley—who (allegedly?) died in 1977—makes a cameo in the film. (He apparently makes an appearance in the scene where Catherine O'Hara, who plays Kevin's mom, Kate McAllister, first meets John Candy's character.)

On November 16, 1990, what appeared to be a fun-filled little family yarn about a kid (Macaulay Culkin) left to his own devices at Christmastime turned into a surprisingly effective action flick when said kid is forced to fend off a couple of bungling burglars (Joe Pesci and Daniel Stern). Today, no holiday movie marathon is complete without a viewing of *Home Alone*, the movie that turned Culkin into one of the biggest kid stars of all time.

Between *Home Alone* and *National Lampoon's Christmas Vacation*, it's clear that John Hughes must have suffered some kind of yuletide-based trauma. For the Griswolds of *Christmas Vacation* it's living beyond their means and needing more lights. For Kevin McCallister, it's about neglect that should demand a call to Child Protective Services. The lesson of every elementary schooler's dream of independence is that it's okay to order your own cheese pizza—as long as you also buy more toothpaste and fight off violent robbers.

THE ROLE OF KEVIN MCCALLISTER WAS WRITTEN SPECIFICALLY FOR CULKIN.

But that didn't stop director Chris Columbus from auditioning more than a hundred other rascally kids for the part. Which really was all for naught, as Culkin nailed the audition and nabbed the role.

JOE PESCI REALLY WANTED CULKIN TO BE AFRAID OF HIM.

In order to get the most authentic performance possible, Pesci—who played Harry, one half of the so-called Wet Bandits—did his best to avoid Culkin on the set so that the young actor would indeed be afraid of him. And no one could blame the young actor for being petrified, as he still bears the physical scar from one accidental

altercation. "They hung me up on a coat hook, and Pesci says, 'I'm gonna bite all your fingers off, one at a time,'" Culkin recalled of a particular scene. "And during one of the rehearsals, he bit me, and it broke the skin."

THE TARANTULA ON DANIEL STERN'S FACE WAS REAL.

At one point, Kevin places a tarantula on Marv's face, and it was indeed a real spider. They had tried a prop, but the real thing was much better. And while legend states that Stern had to mime his scream so as not to upset the spiders, the actor maintains that he was really letting one out.

JOHN CANDY WRAPPED HIS FILMING IN ONE DAY.

But what a long day it was: Twenty-three hours, to be exact. Gus Polinski—the polka-playing nice guy he plays in *Home Alone*—was inspired by his character in *Planes, Trains & Automobiles*.

THE LYRIC OPERA OF CHICAGO BENEFITED FROM THE MOVIE'S SNOWFALL.

When filming of *Home Alone* wrapped, the production donated some of the artificial snow they had created to the Lyric Opera of Chicago. It was used in a number of their productions.

HOME ALONE HELD A GUINNESS WORLD RECORD FOR MORE THAN TWO DECADES.

In its opening weekend, *Home Alone* topped the box office, making $17,081,997 in 1,202 theaters. The movie maintained its no. 1 spot for a full twelve weeks and remained in the top ten until June of the following year. It became the highest-grossing film of 1990 and earned a Guinness World Record as the highest-grossing live-action comedy in a single territory. It held on to that title for quite some time—twenty-seven years, to be exact—until the Chinese blockbuster *Never Say Die* knocked it out of the top spot in 2017.

THE MOVIE'S UNPRECEDENTED SUCCESS LED TO ITS TITLE BECOMING A VERB.

In his book *Who Killed Hollywood? And Other Essays*, Oscar-winning screenwriter William Goldman admitted that the unexpected success of *Home Alone* contributed a new phrase to the Hollywood lexicon: "to be *Home Alone*d," meaning that other films suffered at the box office because of *Home Alone*'s long and successful run.

CLOSE-UP

Watching *Home Alone* with friends and family has become a Christmas tradition in Poland, where the film has aired on national television since the early 1990s. It is titled *Kevin Sam w Domu*, which literally translates to Kevin Alone at Home.

'TIS THE SEASON:
SPIRITED HOLIDAY(ISH) MOVIES

We all have our own lineup of movies—old and new—that instantly leaps to mind when you think of the holiday seasons. Movies that you watch on repeat without fail once the end of the year rolls around. Here are some of the best of them that capture the holiday spirit, even at its most dysfunctional. (Note: The exclusion of *Die Hard* is simply because it's featured on page 68. We most definitely consider it a Christmas movie!)

The Best Man Holiday (2013)

Just as *The Hangover II* is just *The Hangover* but in Thailand, and the sadly never-filmed *Beetlejuice 2: Beetlejuice Goes Hawaiian* would have been *Beetlejuice* but in Hawaii, *The Best Man Holiday* takes the characters we loved hanging out with from *The Best Man* and puts them all together for Christmas. It's got every emotion under the sun, including a lot of laughs and a lip sync dance number to "Can You Stand the Rain," and the rest of the soundtrack is smart enough to include a Christmas tune from Mary J. Blige. It's also further proof that Terrence Howard should be added to movies if only just to spout gruff one-liners, throw cell phones, and roll out.

Black Christmas (1974)

Fittingly, the same man who brought us *A Christmas Story* also brought us its twisted cousin. Before Bob Clark co-wrote and directed the 1983 saga of Ralphie Parker, he helmed *Black Christmas*. It concerns a group of sorority sisters who are systematically picked off by a man who keeps making threatening phone calls to their house. Oh, and it all happens during the holidays. *Black Christmas* is often considered the godfather of holiday horror, but it was also pretty early on the slasher scene, too.

Bridget Jones's Diary (2001)

The only thing that screams "Christmas movie!" louder than an image of Colin Firth in a Rudolph-themed knit sweater (aka jumper) is a final scene where the two romantic leads kiss amidst a backdrop of falling snow and twinkling Christmas lights. Renée Zellweger's classic rom-com *Bridget Jones's Diary* has both of those things. This adaptation of Helen Fielding's bestselling book is an updated take on Jane Austen's *Pride and Prejudice*, which sees the eponymous publishing industry professional (Zellweger) caught between her womanizing boss, Daniel Cleaver (Hugh Grant), and the often-grumpy but still irresistible barrister Mark Darcy (Colin Firth, in a role he perfected in the BBC's 1995 *Pride and Prejudice* miniseries), who loves Bridget "just as you are."

Carol (2015)

Todd Haynes's Oscar-nominated adaptation of Patricia Highsmith's romance takes some dark, personal turns while still reveling in Christmas cheer. In it, Cate Blanchett plays Carol, a woman who falls for the store clerk (Rooney Mara) who advises her to buy a train set for her daughter's Christmas present. The intensity of their budding romance is set against Carol's difficult divorce proceedings, creating a whirlwind story filmed with the lushness of a holiday department store display.

A Christmas Story (1983)

There's a reason TBS plays this on a loop for a full twenty-four hours heading into the big day. Endlessly quotable, the youthful memoir is stacked with iconic moments involving tongues on flagpoles, risqué leg lamps, a sadistic Santa, and a supersafe BB gun. Go ahead and shout out all your favorite lines right now. Just don't shoot your eye out.

Elf (2003)

There is no tamping down Buddy the Elf's enthusiasm. Like a retelling of *Big* with yellow tights and a green pointy hat, Will Ferrell navigates the big-city world of cynics to help them locate their inner child and believe in Christmas again. The main gag is how ridiculous Ferrell is as a giant elf, but the movie turns to magic because of its refusal to be even slightly mean-spirited. It's like taking a big bite out of spaghetti topped with M&Ms, marshmallows, sprinkles, and chocolate syrup.

Emmet Otter's Jug-Band Christmas (1977)

It's "The Gift of the Magi" with singing river otters. That's an automatic win on the adorability scale, but Jim Henson's tale of family togetherness glides by on sheer sweetness and joy, revealing that you don't have to have expensive equipment (or even a good band name) to create beautiful harmonies.

Fred Claus (2007)

While Mrs. Claus plays an integral role in many movies and stories about Santa, we don't know much about where St. Nick himself came from or what his family was like. In the case of this 2007 comedy, Santa has a brother named Fred, a down-on-his-luck repo man who is forced to come and help out at the North Pole after getting nabbed for impersonating a Salvation Army bell ringer and calling on his brother to bail him out. In many ways, the movie plays out like a typical dysfunctional family comedy—only in this case, the fate of Santa's Christmas Eve flight is at risk with only Fred able to step in to help.

Gremlins (1984)

The cackling, spawning, murderous demons make *Gremlins* a near-perfect contender for a Halloween horror classic—if it weren't for the fact that all the chaos ensues over the holidays, and the original gremlin was purchased as a Christmas gift, though Warner Bros. ultimately went with a summer release. Steven Spielberg actually considered Tim Burton—the man behind another confusing horror/holiday hybrid film, *The Nightmare Before Christmas* (1993)—to direct it.

The Holiday (2006)

The purity and heart are what make Nancy Meyers's Christmas-set house-swapping romantic comedy an annual must-watch. Cameron Diaz's and Kate Winslet's characters trade cities for the winter and both discover that new locations are exactly what they need to put them in the path of the right guy. It sticks to the formula, leaving its stars to swoon, act goofy, and proposition Jude Law for sex.

Joyeux Noël (2005)

A prestigious epic chronicling the famous World War I Christmas truce of 1914, wherein German, French, and British soldiers crossed into No Man's Land to stay the fighting and exchange gifts. The film is a sentimental melodrama that uses the perspectives of several different characters (Allied, Central Powers, and civilian) to celebrate peace's possible existence even in the hellish, frozen waste of war.

Love Actually (2003)

Richard Curtis's modern Christmas classic has everything you could want from a romantic comedy. Seriously: There are ten loosely interlocked story lines, from Mark's (Andrew Lincoln) unrequited love for his best friend's (Chiwetel Ejiofor) wife (Keira Knightley), to aging rocker Billy Mack's (Bill Nighy) newfound affection for his manager (Gregor Fisher). Hugh Grant dances to the Pointer Sisters—which he was initially reluctant to do—Emma Thompson sobs to Joni Mitchell, and, in the end, everyone learns that love actually is all around.

The Man Who Invented Christmas (2017)

Surprisingly deft and sweet, Scrooge meets his maker in this film about Charles Dickens and the apparent parallels of personality he shared with one of his most famous characters. *Downton Abbey* star Dan Stevens really shines as Dickens, slapping on a charming presence even in the midst of an existential breakdown and every writer's worst nightmare: a deadline. The strangest element is Christopher Plummer as Scrooge in direct communication with his author, but like a ghost of Christmas past, it works to stunning effect. The movie, the man, and the manuscript all hinge on whether Dickens can accept that people can change.

The Muppet Christmas Carol (1992)

Undoubtedly controversial, everyone has their personal favorite version of Charles Dickens's important treatise on humanity and self-inflicted loneliness. The 175-year-old story has been adapted more than a hundred times counting movies, TV, radio, and graphic novels. Maybe 1951's *Scrooge* is your favorite, maybe you like George C. Scott or Patrick Stewart best. The Muppets and Michael Caine, though, brought a fresh, playful flavor that allowed a rat to co-narrate.

National Lampoon's Christmas Vacation (1989)

The blessing! More outright embarrassing and less sardonic than *A Christmas Story*, the Griswold family's suburban misadventures lovingly devolve into the kind of chaos that requires a SWAT team. If you're hosting your whole family, a flaming, flying set of plastic reindeer may just be the best symbol for the season. Fun fact: Mae Questel (who stole scenes as Aunt Bethany) sounds familiar because she was the voice of Olive Oyl and Betty Boop.

The Nightmare Before Christmas (1993)

What's this? What's this? It's Henry Selick's perfect stop-motion celebration of Christmas cheer through a gothic lens. With so many Christmas movies, it's hard to stand out from the crowd, but *The Nightmare Before Christmas* is defiantly different—mostly because it has werewolves, a singing sack filled with bugs, and a ghost dog who saves the day. So many movies focus on Christmas getting canceled because Santa gets detained, so it's nice to see a movie about the ghouls who detain him.

Rare Exports: A Christmas Tale (2010)

Do you know the real origin of Santa Claus? If you said, "Giant goat beast buried a mile underground in Lapland," consider yourself on the Nice List. This Finnish flick starts as a horror film, but evolves into a winter adventure featuring a bunch of naked old men, naughty children stolen from their homes, and a standing-ovation-worthy explanation for how every mall in America gets its own Santa.

The Santa Clause (1994)

So many great Christmas movies follow Dickens's blueprint of transforming someone skeptical into a true believer, and this Tim Allen comedy goes one step further by converting the crank into Kris Kringle. It's ostensibly an argument against growing up too soon (or at all), and it established the *Highlander*-esque rule that if Santa dies from falling off your roof, you become Santa.

Scrooged (1988)

Another stellar adaptation of Dickens, Richard Donner's manic spree recasts Scrooge as a power-hungry television president played by a breathless Bill Murray. Beyond its intrinsic entertainment value and Carol Kane's national treasure status, it also gives us all a break from a season of sentimental stories. It's also a reminder that we should petition to make *Bob Goulet's Old Fashioned Cajun Christmas* a real thing.

THE HURT LOCKER

(2009)

WRITTEN BY: Mark Boal

DIRECTED BY: Kathryn Bigelow

OTHER MOVIES DIRECTED BY KATHRYN BIGELOW:
Near Dark (1987); *Point Break* (1991);
K-19: The Widowmaker (2002);
Zero Dark Thirty (2012); *Detroit* (2017)

K athryn Bigelow's *The Hurt Locker*, starring Jeremy Renner and Anthony Mackie, dramatized the life-or-death exploits of an elite Explosive Ordnance Disposal (EOD) unit in Baghdad during the Iraq War. Though the film didn't smash box office records, it shattered glass ceilings on the awards circuit and led critic Roger Ebert—who gave it four stars—to declare, "This movie embeds itself in a man's mind."

IT WAS INSPIRED BY SCREENWRITER MARK BOAL'S TIME IN IRAQ.

Boal, a journalist, spent two weeks embedded with a U.S. Army Explosives Ordnance Disposal (EOD) squad in 2004. When he recounted some of what he saw to Kathryn Bigelow, "we kind of arrived at this idea of making a bomb-squad movie," Boal told the *New Yorker*.

Their goal, Boal told the *Hollywood Reporter* shortly before filming began, was to make "the first movie about the Iraq War that purports to show the experience of the soldiers. We wanted to show the kinds of things that soldiers go through that you can't see on CNN."

JEREMY RENNER TRAINED HARD FOR HIS ROLE.

For Bigelow, it was essential that the cast and crew do their research and train extensively. The director herself spent time with EOD units stateside and in Kuwait, and military advisers were present on set.

Renner, who played Sergeant Will James, trained with the EOD unit at California's Fort Irwin, which entailed stepping into a real hundred-pound bomb suit and performing both physical and mental tests. It started with a stack of paper clips. "I had to get on the ground, pick one up, walk fifteen feet, get on the ground, and put it down. It seems so trivial, but that exhausted me," he told *Popular Mechanics*. "After all the physical tasks you do you take off the suit and you're drenched, and you do simple division . . . Doing the math is to see how mentally tough you are, because it'll push you to your limits."

IT WAS VERY HOT ON SET.

Many directors may have chosen to substitute a soundstage or a stateside desert for the Middle East, but not Bigelow. *The Hurt Locker* shot in Jordan, often mere miles from the Iraqi border.

The location added realism to the film—Renner told *Men's Journal*, "The heat conditions and the surroundings informed everything." But it also presented challenges. "Jeremy [Renner] is wearing something that weighs close to 100 pounds in well over 110-degree weather," Bigelow told the DGA. "That was one of the greatest challenges, to make sure that he was comfortable and drinking a lot of water to bring his core body temperature down."

CRITICS LOVED IT, BUT MANY VETERANS WERE CRITICAL.

The Hurt Locker opened in June 2009, and generally earned rave reviews . . . from movie critics, anyway. Soldiers were less enthused. Some members of the military criticized the film as "painfully inaccurate." Brian Makenhaupt, an Iraq War veteran, had issues with things like the risks taken by Renner's character and scenes of the unit driving solo through the war zone (which he said would never happen).

BIGELOW BECAME THE FIRST WOMAN TO WIN A BEST DIRECTOR OSCAR.

The Hurt Locker was nominated for nine Oscars and won six, including Best Picture and Best Original Screenplay. But the most groundbreaking win was for Best Director, which made Bigelow the first woman in Academy Awards history to take home that trophy (she even beat out her ex-husband, James Cameron, who was nominated for *Avatar*). "It's the moment of a lifetime," she said when accepting the award, which she dedicated to the members of the military fighting in Iraq and Afghanistan.

Another woman wouldn't take home Best Director until 2021, when Chloé Zhao won for *Nomadland*.

IRON MAN

WRITTEN BY: Mark Fergus, Hawk Ostby, Art Marcum, and Matt Holloway

DIRECTED BY: Jon Favreau

OTHER MOVIES DIRECTED BY JON FAVREAU:
Made (2001); *Elf* (2003); *Iron Man 2* (2010);
Chef (2014); *The Jungle Book* (2016);
The Lion King (2019)

In May 2008, Marvel Studios launched its inaugural feature film with *Iron Man*, and in the process launched what is now the most successful film franchise in cinematic history. Today, the Marvel Cinematic Universe is stronger than ever thanks to the massive box office success of *Black Panther* (2018), *Avengers: Endgame* (2019), and *Spider-Man: No Way Home* (2021)—and it shows no signs of slowing down.

IT WAS THE FIRST MARVEL STUDIOS MOVIE BECAUSE KIDS SAID SO.

One of the main goals of Marvel convening its own movie studio was to sell toys based on its characters, even more than selling the movies themselves. The initial plan was to kick the slate of films off with *Captain America*, but that changed after the company assembled its own very particular kind of focus group—one made up of children—to determine which character might move the most merchandise.. The kids were given a crash course in the characters Marvel had movie rights to, including their images and powers, and the winner was Iron Man. That put Tony Stark over the top in the race to be the first Marvel Cinematic Universe star.

TOM CRUISE WAS ONCE CONSIDERED FOR TONY STARK.

Before Robert Downey Jr. donned the famous suit of the Armored Avenger, several other stars were in contention for the role. The most famous of these was Tom Cruise, who took an interest in Tony Stark before the rights were back with Marvel. Another contender from those pre–Marvel Studios days was Nicolas Cage, but he too ultimately fell by the wayside. By the time the character made it back home to Marvel, the studio considered Colin Farrell and Patrick Dempsey for the part, but both director Jon Favreau and producer Kevin Feige believed Robert Downey Jr. was the right man for the role.

ROBERT DOWNEY JR. SHOWED UP FOR HIS SCREEN TEST WEARING A TUXEDO.

Before *Iron Man* hit, Downey was an acclaimed film and television actor whose career had dropped off considerably after very public struggles with addiction. Feige and Favreau fought for Downey, both because of his talent and because his personal demons could mirror those of Stark himself (who, in the comics, is an alcoholic). Downey, eager to land the role, agreed to do a screen test (something major stars with years of experience don't typically have to do) and showed up in true Tony Stark style, wearing a tuxedo. Downey impressed Marvel executives and was hired for $2.5 million plus a potential bonus if the film did well. If that sounds like a lot, consider that—due to *Iron Man*'s success—Downey was paid an estimated $50 million for *The Avengers* alone.

MUCH OF THE MOVIE WAS IMPROVISED.

Iron Man did more for Marvel Studios than generate a solid box office return and launch the ability to make sequel upon sequel. It also established a certain lighthearted tone that has continued through almost all of the company's films, even the darkest ones. That's thanks in part to the improvisation that took place on set. Downey in particular was apparently fond of interspersing comedy into the superhero drama, and Favreau encouraged it.

MARVEL WASN'T SURE ITS SHARED UNIVERSE IDEA WOULD WORK.

Marvel Studios has had many filmmakers come through its doors over the past decade-plus of movies, but there has been one constant force whom fans have grown to know and love: President Kevin Feige, who has long been credited as the architect of the Marvel Cinematic Universe. Feige is the guy who shepherded the studio through the long and complex journey that took them to *The Avengers* and beyond, but at first even he wasn't entirely sure if those lofty ambitions could be met. In fact, one of the reasons Nick Fury (Samuel L. Jackson) appears only in a teaser scene after the credits in *Iron Man* (which has since become a Marvel tradition) was Feige's desire to downplay expectations over what may or may not come next.

"We put it at the end of the credits so that it wouldn't distract from the movie," he later told *Vanity Fair*. "People going, 'What is Sam Jackson doing in this movie all of a sudden? What's going on?' I thought it would just begin the potential conversation of hard-core fans . . . That blew up much faster than I was anticipating."

CLOSE-UP

Though Robert Downey Jr. was always his first choice for Tony Stark, Jon Favreau later revealed he had a backup idea in mind if his first choice fell through: Sam Rockwell, who went on to play fellow billionaire industrialist and Iron Man nemesis Justin Hammer in *Iron Man 2* (2010).

JAWS
(1975)

WRITTEN BY: Carl Gottlieb and Peter Benchley (based on the book by Peter Benchley)

DIRECTED BY: Steven Spielberg

OTHER MOVIES DIRECTED BY STEVEN SPIELBERG: *Close Encounters of the Third Kind* (1977); *Raiders of the Lost Ark* (1981); *E. T. the Extra-Terrestrial* (1982); *Jurassic Park* (1993); *Schindler's List* (1993); *West Side Story* (2021)

Steven Spielberg invented the modern summer blockbuster with *Jaws*. When a rogue great white shark starts attacking beachgoers in the sleepy New England island town of Amity, police chief Martin Brody (Roy Scheider) takes it upon himself to stop it. Even after teaming up with an expert oceanographer (Richard Dreyfuss) and a grizzled shark hunter (Robert Shaw), his fishing expedition quickly turns into a fight for survival. With an estimated production budget of just $7 million, Spielberg—who was virtually unknown at the time—turned a horror movie disguised as beachy fun into a record-breaking box office sensation that grossed about half a billion dollars worldwide. What's most impressive about *Jaws* today is how gripping it still is, thanks to clever camerawork and editing, as well as Spielberg's innate understanding that what we don't see is always more unsettling than what we do (even if that tactic was mostly dictated by a temperamental mechanical shark).

FREEZE-FRAME

Jaws author Peter Benchley makes a cameo in the film as the news reporter who addresses the camera on the beach. Steven Spielberg also makes a cameo—sort of: He voiced the Amity Island dispatcher who calls the Orca with Sheriff Brody's wife on the line.

THE OPENING SCENE TOOK THREE DAYS TO SHOOT.

To achieve the jolting motions of the shark attacking a swimmer in the opening sequence, a harness with cables was attached to actress Susan Backlinie's legs and was pulled back and forth by crew members along the shoreline. Spielberg told the crew not to let Backlinie know when she would be yanked back and forth, so her terrified reaction is genuine.

THERE'S NOT A LOT OF JAWS IN JAWS.

The shark doesn't fully appear in a shot until eighty-one minutes into the two-hour film. Part of the reason is that the mechanical shark—which Spielberg nicknamed "Bruce" after his lawyer, Bruce Ramer—rarely worked, so the director had to create inventive ways (like Quint's yellow barrels) to shoot around the gigantic prop.

RICHARD DREYFUSS WASN'T THE FIRST CHOICE TO PLAY HOOPER.

Spielberg initially approached Jon Voight, Timothy Bottoms, and Jeff Bridges to play oceanographer Matt Hooper. When none of them could commit, George Lucas suggested Richard Dreyfuss, whom Lucas had directed in *American Graffiti*.

A MARTHA'S VINEYARD FISHERMAN WAS THE REAL QUINT.

Robert Shaw based his performance as grizzled shark hunter Quint on Martha's Vineyard native and fisherman Craig Kingsbury, a nonactor who appeared in the film as Ben Gardner. Kingsbury helped Shaw with his accent and reportedly told Shaw old sea stories that the actor incorporated into some improvised dialogue.

SOME OF WHAT YOU SEE IN JAWS IS REAL SHARK FOOTAGE.

Producer Richard Zanuck demanded that real shark footage be used in the movie, though Spielberg used it sparingly. He hired experts Ron and Valerie Taylor to shoot underwater footage of fourteen-foot-long sharks off the coast of Australia.

DESPITE ALL THE BLOODY SHARK ATTACKS, JAWS IS RATED PG.

Jaws was initially rated R by the MPAA. But after removal of some of the more gruesome frames of the shot showing the severed leg of the man attacked by the shark, the film was given a PG rating.

JAWS WAS THE BIGGEST HIT HOLLYWOOD HAD EVER SEEN.

Jaws was released in more than four hundred theaters in the U.S. and the first movie to gross more than $100 million at the box office. It was the highest-grossing movie of all time until *Star Wars* came along two years later.

THE ENDING YOU KNOW ISN'T HOW IT WAS ORIGINALLY WRITTEN.

The original ending in the script had the shark dying of harpoon injuries inflicted by Quint and Brody, but Spielberg thought the movie needed a crowd-pleasing finale and came up with the exploding tank as seen in the final film. The dialogue and foreshadowing of the tank were then dropped in as they shot the movie.

Chief Brody's famous

"You're gonna need a bigger boat"

line was improvised by Roy Scheider on the day of shooting.

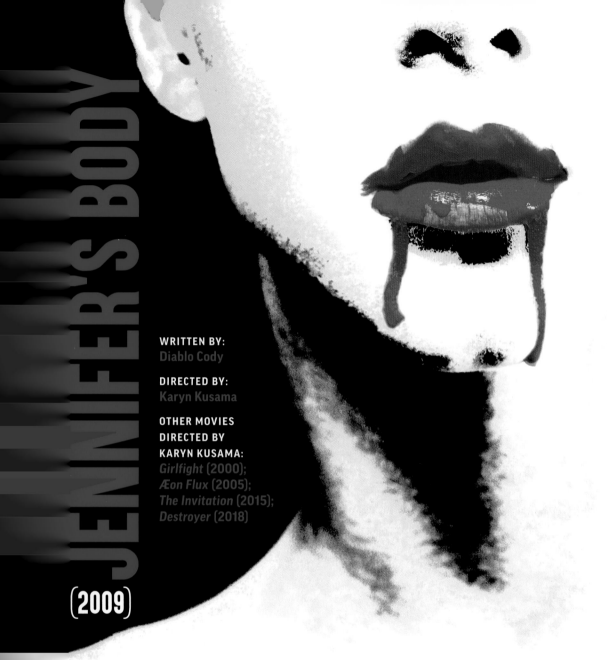

JENNIFER'S BODY

WRITTEN BY:
Diablo Cody

DIRECTED BY:
Karyn Kusama

**OTHER MOVIES
DIRECTED BY
KARYN KUSAMA:**
Girlfight (2000);
Æon Flux (2005);
The Invitation (2015);
Destroyer (2018)

(2009)

Since it was released to scathing reviews and box office embarrassment in September 2009, *Jennifer's Body* has enjoyed a dramatic reappraisal. The Diablo Cody–scripted horror-comedy about a teenage girl who goes on a boy-eating spree after she's possessed by a demon, and the best friend who tries to stop her, gained a cult following over the years. But something bigger happened around 2018, when the #MeToo movement coincided with the movie's impending tenth anniversary. The film's defenders finally went on the offensive, taking 20th Century Fox to task for the way it doomed *Jennifer's Body* by aiming it squarely at horny teenage boys rather than the young women Cody and director Karyn Kusama had in mind. "That movie was very much about the issues that women face and about the feeling of being powerless and . . . wanting to turn the tables," Cody told Vox in 2018.

DIABLO CODY WROTE *JENNIFER'S BODY* BEFORE *JUNO* MADE HER A SENSATION.

Cody's life changed dramatically in 2008, when *Juno* became distributor Fox Searchlight's first film to surpass $100 million at the box office and netted the first-time screenwriter an Oscar for Best Original Screenplay. While *Juno*'s success made it relatively easy to get *Jennifer's Body* made, Cody had actually written the screenplay in 2006—the year before *Juno* was filmed.

A NUMBER OF NOW-FAMOUS ACTRESSES WERE CONSIDERED FOR THE ROLE OF ANITA "NEEDY" LESNICKI.

While casting the role that eventually went to Amanda Seyfried, Kusama and Cody auditioned a number of then-up-and-coming actresses, including Emma Stone, Amanda Bynes, Lizzy Caplan, and Brie Larson. Kusama told *Variety* that the pair ultimately selected Seyfried because she "had this complete wide-eyed wonder about the world in her audition and it traveled through her whole performance."

KUSAMA SET THE TONE BY SCREENING *EVIL DEAD 2* FOR THE CAST.

Kusama and Cody, both lifelong horror fans, found inspiration in a variety of classic genre titles, from the gory 1970s films of Dario Argento to eighties fare such as *The Howling* and *An American Werewolf in London.* "They didn't have the gloss that horror films have today," Cody told *Variety* in 2019, "and I think we were trying to emulate that vintage feel." To set the mood for *Jennifer's Body,* Kusama invited cast members to her hotel room to watch Sam Raimi's 1987 splatter comedy *Evil Dead 2.*

FILMING THE SACRIFICE SCENE LEFT MEGAN FOX AND KUSAMA BADLY SHAKEN.

While much of *Jennifer's Body* is played for laughs, the pivotal scene where Fox's character is sacrificed to Satan by members of the indie rock band Low Shoulder in hope of boosting their careers is famously unsettling. "I remember being deeply upset by it," Kusama said at Beyond Fest in 2019. "I find it really difficult to watch."

Not only was the scene physically grueling for Fox—she spent take after take bound to a rock in a wintry Vancouver forest, at night—but it also had disturbingly personal connotations. "[T]hat scene represented my relationship with the movie studios at the time," she told the crowd at Beyond Fest. "I felt like I was being sacrificed for their gain with almost no concern for my physical well-being."

KUSAMA CUT TWO VERSIONS OF THE MOVIE.

Kusama ultimately produced two versions of *Jennifer's Body*: a 102-minute theatrical edit that she calls "the studio cut" and a 107-minute director's cut that included additional emotional beats and character development. "My original cut spent more time focusing on the fact that these boys were actually really people, and that their deaths were meaningful," Kusama told Australian film magazine *4:3* in 2018. But the studio reportedly thought her preferred version was "a little too sad; too emotionally real."

THE STUDIO WANTED FOX TO PROMOTE THE MOVIE ON AMATEUR ADULT ENTERTAINMENT SITES.

Jennifer's Body is well known as a movie-marketing horror story; though it's widely regarded as a feminist horror film, it was test-screened largely to young men, and the filmmakers were presented with focus group feedback such as "needs moar bewbs [*sic*]." Still, it's hard to overstate just how awful some of the studio's proposals were. According to Kusama, the marketing department suggested that Fox promote the movie by doing live chats on amateur porn sites—an idea that Kusama begged the studio not to broach with the actress.

The filmmakers have insisted that Megan Fox was always their Jennifer, but some sources report that Fox was offered the role after Blake Lively turned it down due to a scheduling conflict.

JURASSIC PARK
(1993)

WRITTEN BY: David Koepp
(based on the book by Michael Crichton)

DIRECTED BY: Steven Spielberg

OTHER MOVIES DIRECTED BY STEVEN SPIELBERG: *Jaws* (1975); *Close Encounters of the Third Kind* (1977); *Raiders of the Lost Ark* (1981); *The Color Purple* (1985); *Schindler's List* (1993); *Saving Private Ryan* (1998); *West Side Story* (2021)

In 1993, Steven Spielberg created a movie that was sixty-five million years in the making. Based on the novel by author Michael Crichton, *Jurassic Park* explores what would happen if scientists (and a theme park executive played by Richard Attenborough) used cloning technology to bring dinosaurs back to life. As paleontologist Alan Grant (Sam Neill), paleobotanist Ellie Sattler (Laura Dern), and mathematician Ian Malcolm (Jeff Goldblum) discover, nature doesn't like to be contained. With cutting-edge effects and the thrilling direction you'd expect from the blockbuster filmmaker behind *Jaws* and *Raiders of the Lost Ark*, *Jurassic Park* went on to become the highest-grossing film ever at the time. While the original movie spawned a massive franchise, the new and old characters came together in the summer of 2022 to reunite for *Jurassic World: Dominion*. In Hollywood, even nearly thirty years after its original release, it still doesn't get much bigger than *Jurassic Park*.

STEVEN SPIELBERG FOUND OUT ABOUT *JURASSIC PARK* WHILE WORKING ON *ER*.

When Spielberg and Crichton were working on a screenplay that would eventually become the television series *ER*, Spielberg asked the writer what he was planning for his next book. Crichton told him about *Jurassic Park*, and Spielberg immediately tapped Universal to buy the film rights—sparking a bit of a bidding war before the book was even published.

JURASSIC PARK ALMOST TOOK A BACKSEAT TO *SCHINDLER'S LIST*.

Though excited about *Jurassic Park*, Spielberg wanted to direct his dream project—*Schindler's List*—first. But MCA/Universal president Sid Sheinberg would only greenlight Spielberg's epic Holocaust drama if the director agreed to make his dinosaur picture first. Both films were released in 1993; *Jurassic Park* in June and *Schindler's List* at the end of the year.

THE MOVIE COAXED RICHARD ATTENBOROUGH OUT OF RETIREMENT.

Attenborough, who plays InGen CEO John Hammond, had been on a fifteen-year hiatus from acting when Spielberg approached him about appearing in *Jurassic Park*. Attenborough had been directing, but supposedly he agreed to make an exception because Spielberg had "the charm of the devil."

SPIELBERG HAD PALEONTOLOGISTS SERVE AS CONSULTANTS.

Famed paleontologist Jack Horner was used during production to ensure the dinosaurs exhibited scientifically accurate behavior, and Robert T. Bakker—also a paleontologist—gave animators information about the dinosaur's physical characteristics. Bakker had nothing but praise for the filmmakers; in 2012, he told *Popular Mechanics* that the dinosaur artists working on *Jurassic Park* were "better animal morphologists than most tenured professors."

IT TOOK MANY DIFFERENT ANIMALS TO CREATE THE *T. REX*'S ROAR.

The sound design of the *T. rex*'s roar was reportedly a composite of tiger, alligator, and baby elephant sounds. The deadly *Dilophosaurus* roar was created by combining hawk screeches and rattlesnake hisses.

ONE ICONIC MOMENT WAS INSPIRED BY LISTENING TO EARTH, WIND & FIRE.

The idea for the rippling water and rattling mirror in the tour vehicle caused by the approaching *Tyrannosaurus* was inspired by Spielberg listening to Earth, Wind & Fire with the bass blasting in his car. On set, special effects supervisor Michael Lantieri had an assistant pluck a guitar string underneath the cups to create the ripples; a vibrating motor above the windshield made the mirror shake.

AFTER FILMING WRAPPED, ANOTHER FAMOUS DIRECTOR TOOK THE REINS.

Spielberg and his crew completed filming on *Jurassic Park* on November 30, 1992—twelve days ahead of schedule—but he had to quickly shift gears and concentrate on shooting and completing his next film, *Schindler's List*, which went into production in March 1993. Because of the tight shooting schedule on that film and the extensive postproduction needed for *Jurassic Park*, he handed over some postproduction responsibilities to friend and frequent collaborator George Lucas, who owned ILM. Lucas was given a "Special Thanks" credit in the final film.

"Must go faster."

'90S

CAN'T-MISS NINETIES MOVIES

The last decade of the previous millennium was an exciting time for movies. Fueled by Sundance, independent films were on the rise, with new voices like Quentin Tarantino and Richard Linklater emerging. The Hollywood studios, having exercised too much control and churned out too many generic products in the 1980s, started giving filmmakers more leeway, and established directors like Martin Scorsese and Steven Spielberg continued to make great movies, as evidenced by these titles.

Before Sunrise (1995)

Richard Linklater came onto the scene with popular back-to-back movies about Gen-X slackers: *Slacker* (1991) and *Dazed and Confused* (1993)—but followed them up with this mature, minimalist romantic drama about two strangers (Ethan Hawke and Julie Delpy) meeting on a train and having only one evening to spend together. It's the first movie in what eventually became a trilogy.

Blade (1998)

Wesley Snipes seems practically born to play Blade, the titular half-human, half-vampire, all-badass hero of this superhero-horror flick. He absolutely slays it here, and it's hard to imagine anyone else donning the vampire hunter's signature black shades with as much verve.

Boogie Nights (1997)

Paul Thomas Anderson's first film, *Hard Eight* (1996), went largely unnoticed. But his sophomore effort—a sprawling, rags-to-riches story about L.A.'s pornography business in the 1970s—put him on the map permanently. Julianne Moore and Burt Reynolds were frequently singled out by awards-giving bodies for their supporting performances, but the amazing cast also included Mark Wahlberg, Don Cheadle, John C. Reilly, William H. Macy, Heather Graham, Philip Seymour Hoffman, and Alfred Molina.

Clerks (1994)

Kevin Smith was just twenty-three years old when he kick-started an indie moviemaking revolution—and launched thousands of imitators—with this micro-budget, black-and-white feature. The slacker comedy follows a day (and night) in the life of two pals who are left to ponder the lack of romantic or vocational direction in their lives as they do their best to just get through the tedium of life behind a cash register.

The Crow (1994)

Long before superheroes on the big screen became a part of shared universes and billion-dollar mega-franchises, *The Crow* became what is perhaps the ultimate Generation X comic book movie. It's the story of an aspiring rock star (Brandon Lee) who is murdered alongside his fiancée by thugs on Devil's Night, and returns from the dead one year later as a supernatural vigilante to seek his vengeance for her death. Director Alex Proyas's visuals are gothic perfection, and the film's soundtrack alone is worth the price of admission. Of course, *The Crow*'s real legacy lies in an on-set tragedy: Lee, the twenty-eight-year-old son of superstar Bruce Lee, was fatally wounded by a prop gun when filming one of his final scenes, which required the filmmakers to have to change the story (and eliminate one character, the Skull Cowboy, entirely).

Daughters of the Dust (1991)

You can single out director Julie Dash's *Daughters of the Dust* for being the first film directed by a Black woman to get a major theatrical release in the U.S., but reducing it to a footnote does it a disservice. Shot mostly in Gullah, the film is a mesmerizing immersion into a family of islanders off the Georgia coast who strike out for the mainland in 1902. The result is a story free of gawking outsiders, explanations, or even subtitles. It's the viewer that's acclimated to the Gullah Islanders' way of life, not the other way around. Beyoncé is a noted fan of the film, and referenced it in the visuals of the hour-long film that accompanied her 2016 *Lemonade* album (which led to a twenty-fifth anniversary re-release in theaters).

Dumb and Dumber (1994)

Jim Carrey had a legendary year in 1994, moving from television's *In Living Color* to the success of *Ace Ventura: Pet Detective* and *The Mask*. He finished the year alongside Jeff Daniels in this physical, farcical buddy comedy that sees two clueless friends cross the country to pursue Carrey's crush (Lauren Holly). Carrey is the human equivalent of Silly Putty; Daniels excels in one of the greatest laxative scenes in the history of cinema.

Eyes Wide Shut (1999)

There are so many Christmas trees in Stanley Kubrick's erotic thriller that, if you ignore everything else in the film, it could pass for a really festive, albeit R-rated, game of I Spy. In addition to the heavy-handed Christmas imagery, Kubrick opens the film with a ritzy holiday party and closes it with a feel-good (at least, relative to the other scenes) shopping trip to Manhattan's FAO Schwarz. Interestingly enough, the characters in the source material, Arthur Schnitzler's 1926 novella *Traumnovelle*, were Jewish.

Fargo (1996)

For their sixth movie, brothers Joel and Ethan Coen returned to a favorite subject—bumbling criminals—and introduced a new one: the singsong Minnesota accents of their homeland. People went around talking like Marge Gunderson (Frances McDormand) and Jerry Lundegaard (William H. Macy) for months after its release, but the film's dark comedy, righteous heroes, and pathetic wrongdoers made it resonate even longer.

Fear and Loathing in Las Vegas (1998)

Johnny Depp is gonzo journalist Hunter S. Thompson in director Terry Gilliam's cinematic depiction of a psychedelic trip through Las Vegas. Based on Thompson's book of the same name, the film is a feverish fantasy and likely not for all tastes, though those who don't mind a meandering narrative will find an enthusiastic performance by Depp and the kind of hallucinatory imagery Gilliam has become known for.

The Fifth Element (1997)

Director Luc Besson delivers a sumptuous future in this marvel of production design, with Bruce Willis once again playing an everyman thrust into the middle of a grand-scale conflict. Here, he's a cabbie in the twenty-third century who runs afoul of aliens looking to destroy Earth.

Gattaca (1997)

High school biology students have this Ethan Hawke and Uma Thurman sci-fi thriller to thank for helping them learn the four bases that make up the double helix of DNA. In addition to teaching viewers some basic science, the movie is also a lesson on the dangers of eugenics, as the "valid"— babies created based on biometrics— are prioritized over "in-valids," or kids conceived the old-fashioned way. But the film's anti-eugenic themes may have been lost on some people: To promote *Gattaca*, a full-page ad for "children made to order" ran in major newspapers. Thousands of people reportedly called the listed number, wishing to design their own kid.

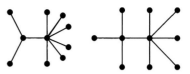

Good Will Hunting (1997)

Tired of being passed up for substantial roles, Ben Affleck and Matt Damon wrote this Horatio Alger story about a janitor (Damon) whose surly demeanor hides both an impressive intellect and a reservoir of emotional pain. Robin Williams won an Academy Award for his portrayal of Damon's gentle but challenging therapist.

Howards End (1992)

James Ivory's adaptation of E. M. Forster's 1910 novel tells the story of free-spirited Londoner Margaret Schlegel (Emma Thompson) who befriends a dying woman, Ruth Wilcox (Vanessa Redgrave), who ends up bequeathing Margaret her beloved country home, Howards End. It's a stroke of luck for Margaret, who is about to be ousted from the home she has leased for years, but the Wilcox family feels that something is amiss. As Ruth's widower (Anthony Hopkins) attempts to investigate the situation, he finds himself falling under Margaret's spell.

Raise the Red Lantern (1992)

Director Zhang Yimou established himself as a master of intimate and emotionally beautiful art with this sumptuous, colorful drama about a rich man's young concubine in the 1920s. The exotic location, time period, and customs make it a "foreign" film, but Gong Li's lead performance drives home the universality of its themes.

Schindler's List (1993)

In 1993, Steven Spielberg brought all his filmmaking skills to bear in what was his most personal project to date. *Schindler's List* tells the true story of Oskar Schindler (Liam Neeson), a Nazi party member who spared the lives of more than one thousand Jewish factory workers by employing them so they would not be sent to concentration camps. Though Spielberg was already twenty years into a storied career when the film was released, it marked the first time he would collect a Best Director Academy Award.

The Silence of the Lambs (1991)

Serial killer perfection. Jonathan Demme managed to create an incredible thriller, detective yarn, and horror film all in one. Of course, Jodie Foster's performance as Clarice Starling is a quiet tornado at the dark center of this murder mystery, even if Anthony Hopkins gets to chew more scenery.

To Sleep with Anger (1990)

Dismissed with lukewarm reviews on first release, this independent drama by Charles Burnett (whose underground *Killer of Sheep* was one of the indie high points of the seventies) came to be better appreciated with time. Now it's held up as yet another example of a great filmmaker never getting his due in the mainstream, with a sizzling performance by Danny Glover as a devilish visitor who upsets a group of distant relatives.

Smoke Signals (1998)

Authenticity often eludes the Native American experience in Hollywood, which has long contorted that culture into villainy for western heroics. In *Smoke Signals*, Victor Joseph (Adam Beach) and Thomas Builds-the-Fire (Evan Adams) never suffer from a filmmaker's myopic viewpoint. They're road trippers, en route to picking up the ashes of Victor's father. Along the way, they talk—about their heritage, about how their culture is often distorted, and about life.

Strictly Ballroom (1992)

Baz Luhrmann made his big-screen debut with this delightfully campy film, which was expanded from a short play Luhrmann had previously written based on his own childhood experiences. The movie also kicked off Luhrmann's "Red Curtain Trilogy," which also includes *Romeo + Juliet* and *Moulin Rouge!*. *Strictly Ballroom* stars Paul Mercurio as Scott Hastings and Tara Morice as Fran, two mismatched dancers determined to find their way in Australia's fussy competitive ballroom scene.

The Sweet Hereafter (1997)

Canadian filmmaker Atom Egoyan's adaptation of Russell Banks's novel about the aftermath of a deadly school bus accident in a small town is a somber fairy tale about the various ways people respond to tragedy and our human tendency to avoid responsibility. It's rapturous, agonizing, and complex, and while Egoyan has continued to make quality movies, he's never regained this level of subtle mastery.

The Thin Red Line (1998)

Coming on the heels of *Saving Private Ryan*, this other World War II epic from 1998 might have gotten lost in the shuffle if it hadn't been outstanding in its own right (not to mention director Terrence Malick's first movie in twenty years). Rambling, messy, bloody, mournful, and vexing, it's the mad counterpart to Spielberg's more staid view of the war.

Unforgiven (1992)

Clint Eastwood, an actor since the 1950s and director since 1971, made good (if not great) movies in the seventies and eighties, then reached the pinnacle of his filmmaking career with this violent anti-violence Best Picture winner. With weighty performances by Eastwood, Gene Hackman, and Morgan Freeman, it also won Oscars for Eastwood as Best Director and Best Picture (plus one for Hackman and another for Best Editing) and proved there was still life left in cinema's oldest genre: the western.

WRITTEN BY: Greta Gerwig
(based on the book by Louisa May Alcott)

DIRECTED BY: Greta Gerwig

OTHER MOVIES DIRECTED BY GRETA GERWIG:
Nights and Weekends (2008); *Lady Bird* (2017)

LITTLE WOMEN
(2019)

I n 2019's *Little Women*, writer-director Greta Gerwig preserves the warm glow of nostalgia so often associated with Louisa May Alcott's semi-autobiographical 1868 coming-of-age novel about the March sisters (doting Meg, fiery aspiring writer Jo, shy and gentle Beth, and "regular snow-maiden" Amy) finding their way in a world in which women are expected to aspire only toward marriage and motherhood, but also gives it a new twist. In Gerwig's version, Jo March actually pens and publishes *Little Women* in the movie, mirroring Alcott's trajectory as a writer more closely.

The film's focus on female agency, specifically as it pertains to the pursuit of art, was reflected off-screen, too. Gerwig pitched herself as screenwriter as soon as she heard Columbia Pictures was considering a *Little Women* remake; Saoirse Ronan and Meryl Streep both volunteered—or, perhaps more accurately, simply claimed—their respective roles as Jo and Aunt March.

LITTLE WOMEN FEATURES A LOT OF THE ACTORS' OWN IDEAS.

Gerwig fostered collaboration and used many of the actors' suggestions about costumes, blocking, and dialogue. For example, it was Florence Pugh's idea to wear fairy wings when her character, Amy, burns Jo's manuscript, and Timothée Chalamet proposed standing on a chair during Laurie's Latin lesson. One of Marmee's lines to Jo, "There are some natures too noble to curb and too lofty to bend," is straight from a letter that Alcott's mother wrote to her, which Laura Dern came across and passed along to Gerwig.

Streep told Gerwig it was important to her that the film convey Victorian women's utter powerlessness in their marriages: Everything, including their children, belonged to their husbands. Gerwig said she used Streep's words "basically verbatim" for Amy's poignant monologue about how marriage, to women, is an economic proposition.

IT WAS FILMED IN AND AROUND LOUISA MAY ALCOTT'S HOMETOWN.

Alcott wrote and set *Little Women* in her family home, Orchard House, in Concord, Massachusetts. A full-scale replica was constructed in Concord for exterior shots; and the interior was reproduced on a soundstage in nearby Franklin. Everything else was filmed in Massachusetts, too. The Crane Estate in Ipswich and Harvard University's Arnold Arboretum were used for the Paris scenes; Laurie's proposal to Jo took place on Groton's Gibbet Hill; and Boston's Gibson House Museum brought Jo's New York City boardinghouse to life.

GERWIG CONSIDERS THE MOVIE "NERDILY FOOTNOTABLE."

Little Women is rife with references to real-life inspirations, making it, in Gerwig's words, a "nerdily footnotable" film. Jo reads to Beth from *A Mill on the Floss* by George Eliot because Gerwig noticed Alcott's collection of Eliot works during a visit to Orchard House. The beach scene emulates Winslow Homer's 1870 painting, *Eagle Head, Manchester, Massachusetts (High Tide)*; and costume designer Jacqueline Durran modeled Jo's post-haircut hat on one in another Homer artwork, *Crossing the Pasture*. The short, shaggy hair obscured by said hat is styled after Amelia Earhart.

SAOIRSE RONAN HAD AN ALTER EGO ON SET NAMED "PAM."

When Pugh saw Ronan knitting on set in her short-haired wig, she thought her co-star looked more like a Pam than a Saoirse. "Pam" became Ronan's alter ego: a persnickety Australian woman who's very outspoken at town meetings and might leave negative reviews on Tripadvisor. Her catchphrases included "I'm very frustrated right now" and "I don't like this."

THEY BLASTED DAVID BOWIE WHILE FILMING THE FINAL SCENE.

The film ends with Jo March watching through the window as printers create copies of her novel, *Little Women*. Gerwig suggested a few songs to play on set during the scene—which was also the last one they shot—and Ronan chose David Bowie's "Moonage Daydream." It was a fitting selection, as Gerwig had asked composer Alexandre Desplat to make the actual movie score "Mozart meets David Bowie." After they wrapped, Ronan and Gerwig each took home one of the books created in that final scene.

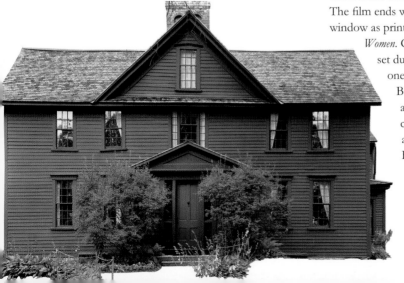

10 ENCHANTING PERIOD PIECES

Like any great period piece, *Little Women* manages to nail all the historical minutiae without sacrificing substance. Here are ten other movies that have transported us back in time.

1 The Age of Innocence (1993)

Martin Scorsese's adaptation of Edith Wharton's 1920 novel depicts 1870s New York City in all its Gilded Age glory. But one publicity image printed in *Us* magazine looked a little more modern: Michelle Pfeiffer, ardently embracing Daniel Day-Lewis, was accidentally clutching a roll of Certs mints. "Oops!" said Columbia Pictures executive Sidney Ganis.

2 Atonement (2007)

To translate Ian McEwan's World War II romantic drama *Atonement* for the screen, director Joe Wright bucked convention by casting Saoirse Ronan as the youngest iteration of Briony Tallis before choosing the two actors who'd play the character at older ages (Romola Garai and Vanessa Redgrave). During joint rehearsals, Garai and Redgrave worked to match Ronan's mannerisms, rather than the other way around.

3 Belle (2013)

Belle is based on the true story of Dido Elizabeth Belle, the daughter of a British naval officer and an enslaved African woman, who was raised as a British aristocrat in the eighteenth century. The portrait that Dido (Gugu Mbatha-Raw) and her white cousin, Elizabeth Murray (Sarah Gadon), sit for in the film is a re-creation of a real portrait—one that inspired Misan Sagay to write the initial screenplay and director Amma Asante to sign on to the project.

4 Bright Star (2009)

Based on the John Keats poem "Bright star, would I were steadfast as thou art," this 2009 film—directed by Academy Award–winning filmmaker Jane Campion—followed the last three years of the poet's (Ben Whishaw) life and his steamy relationship with Fanny Brawne (Abbie Cornish). *Bright Star* premiered at the sixty-second Cannes Film Festival, with some critics dubbing it Campion's best work since 1993's *The Piano*.

5 Elizabeth (1998)

Elizabeth, director Shekhar Kapur's first English language feature, chronicles Queen Elizabeth I's early years on the throne. Cate Blanchett received a Best Actress Oscar nomination for portraying the ruler, but lost to Gwyneth Paltrow for *Shakespeare in Love*. Ironically, Dame Judi Dench won the Best Supporting Actress Oscar that year for playing a much older Elizabeth I in . . . *Shakespeare in Love*.

6 The Favourite (2018)

The Favourite recounts (with artistic liberties) the historical rivalry between the two closest companions of Queen Anne (Olivia Colman), who ruled from 1702 to 1714. To help the actors absorb the story's comedy, director Yorgos Lanthimos padded rehearsals with whimsical tasks, like trying to avoid collisions while walking backward, and interlocking arms to create what Rachel Weisz called "a human pretzel."

7 Gosford Park (2001)

Robert Altman was kicking around the idea of directing an Agatha Christie–style whodunit when his friend Bob Balaban suggested a screenwriter: Julian Fellowes, who was still years away from creating *Downton Abbey*. Fellowes took the offer, and Balaban co-produced (and co-starred in) what became one of the most entertaining portrayals of 1930s British high society in film history. Despite the movie's massive ensemble cast, Altman didn't let the actors swoop in for a few days to shoot only their scenes—everyone had to sign on for all ten weeks.

8 Neruda (2016)

Because director Pablo Larraín considers Chilean poet/politician Pablo Neruda "impossible to put in a box," he instead developed an "anti-bio" that fictionalizes Neruda's (Luis Gnecco) 1949 escape from Chile—adding a made-up inspector who pursues him (played by Gael García Bernal). To give the film its distinctly vintage feel, Larraín combined red and blue to create a faint purple filter.

9 Portrait of a Lady on Fire (2019)

Céline Sciamma's evocative romance follows the illicit relationship between an eighteenth-century French artist (played by Noémie Merlant) and the high-born young woman (Adèle Haenel) she's been commissioned to paint. Oil painter Hélène Delmaire created nearly all the art in the film, clocking roughly three months' worth of sixteen-hour days.

10 A Room with a View (1985)

Merchant Ivory Productions' *A Room with a View*, based on E. M. Forster's 1908 coming-of-age novel, was a star vehicle for two now–household names—Helena Bonham Carter and Daniel Day-Lewis. The film also contains a Forster Easter egg: The gossip Eleanor Lavish (Dame Judi Dench) shares with Charlotte Bartlett (Dame Maggie Smith) during their picnic echoes the plot of Forster's novel *Where Angels Fear to Tread*. Bonham Carter went on to star in the 1991 adaptation of that book, too.

WRITTEN BY: Fran Walsh, Philippa Boyens, Peter Jackson, and Stephen Sinclair (based on the books by J. R. R. Tolkien)

DIRECTED BY: Peter Jackson

OTHER MOVIES DIRECTED BY PETER JACKSON:
Bad Taste (1987); *Heavenly Creatures* (1994); *The Frighteners* (1996); *King Kong* (2005); *The Hobbit* Trilogy (2012–2014)

THE LORD OF THE RINGS TRILOGY

(2001–2003)

Between on-set injuries, extensive script changes, and one whopper of a casting process, at various points in the life of *The Lord of the Rings* trilogy it seemed as if director Peter Jackson might have bitten off more than he could chew. In all fairness, translating J. R. R. Tolkien's classic fantasy epic was no small ask: The story begins with a somewhat whimsical quest to destroy a potentially world-ending ring of power and quickly escalates into an all-out war of good versus evil. The makeup, costumes, and special effects used to bring Middle-earth's magical places and faces to life influenced future filmmaking, just as Tolkien's original work had influenced the entire fantasy genre.

IT WENT THROUGH A TON OF SCRIPT REVISIONS.

When *The Lord of the Rings* started out, it was originally going to be two movies. Later, concerned about the ballooning budget, producers tried to persuade Jackson to condense the movie into a single film. At various points in the scripting process, it was suggested to cut Saruman or make him a "Darth Vader to Sauron's Emperor" character; and Rohan and Gondor were combined into one kingdom. Ultimately, *The Lord of the Rings* ended up as a trilogy.

THE PRODUCER REALLY WANTED TO KILL A HOBBIT.

Before it found its eventual home at New Line Cinema, *The Lord of the Rings* trilogy was being made at Miramax. As Jackson would later recall, Bob Weinstein really, *really* thought one of the four main Hobbits should die: "'Well, we can't have [all of them surviving],' he said, 'we've got to kill a Hobbit! I don't care which one; you can pick—I'm not telling you who it should be: you pick out who you want to kill, but we've really got to kill one of those Hobbits!'" Jackson recalled. "In situations like that, you just nod and smile and say, 'Well, that's something we can consider.'"

SEAN CONNERY DIDN'T UNDERSTAND THE SCRIPT.

The filmmakers wanted Sean Connery to play Gandalf but after reading the script, the actor admitted, "I never understood it. I read the book. I read the script. I saw the movie. I still don't understand it . . . I would be interested in doing something that I didn't fully understand, but not for 18 months." Connery's deal, if he had taken the role, would have been for a small fee plus up to 15 percent of the films' profits. Incidentally, the entire trilogy went on to earn just shy of $3 billion worldwide (though due to the nebulous process that is Hollywood Accounting, according to New Line the trilogy made "horrendous losses").

ARAGORN WAS AN EXTREMELY DIFFICULT ROLE TO CAST.

Nicolas Cage was offered the role of Aragorn, which he turned down due to "family obligations." Famously, the role then went to up-and-coming Irish actor Stuart Townsend, who spent two months on the set training and rehearsing, but was fired just before shooting was set to begin. While different reasons have been given for that move, Jackson was reportedly worried that Townsend wasn't ready for the role and was doubting his own abilities. In need of an older actor, Jackson went to Viggo Mortensen; he took the role at the urging of his son Henry, who was a fan of the books.

JAKE GYLLENHAAL AUDITIONED TO PLAY FRODO. IT DIDN'T GO WELL.

"I remember auditioning for *The Lord of the Rings* and going in and not being told that I needed a British accent. I really do remember Peter Jackson saying to me, 'You know that you have to do this in a British accent?'" Gyllenhaal later recalled. "We heard back it was literally one of the worst auditions." The role went to Elijah Wood.

FREEZE-FRAME

Jackson and his co-writers Fran Walsh and Philippa Boyens were constantly revising the scripts, even during production. As such, the actors would often get new dialogue to memorize the night before shooting a particular scene. That was the case with Boromir's famous speech in *The Fellowship of the Ring*'s Council of Elrond scene. Look closely and you'll notice Sean Bean occasionally lowering his eyes to look at the new script page, which was taped to his knee.

VIGGO MORTENSEN TOOK SEVERAL BEATINGS.

A variety of injuries beset the cast during production, but Mortensen had it particularly hard: In *The Two Towers*, that scream he let out upon kicking a helmet after discovering the burnt corpses of the Orcs who abducted Merry and Pippin might have had something to do with the fact that he had just broken two of his toes. "Normally, an actor would yell 'Ow!' if they hurt themselves," noted Jackson. "Viggo turned a broken toe into a performance." Elijah Wood remembered Mortensen "getting half of his tooth knocked out during a fight sequence, and his insistence on applying superglue to put it back in to keep working."

AN ENTIRE ACTION SCENE WAS DESTROYED BY A FLOOD.

The end of *The Fellowship of the Ring* originally featured a scene where the heroes are ambushed by a band of Orcs as they row through rapids on the Anduin river. "We had all kinds of action planned with boats flipping over . . . and Legolas's boat afloat as it bucks and tosses, while the Elf—standing with a foot on each of the gunwales—would be firing arrows at the attackers," Jackson shared. But Mother Nature had other ideas, and a massive flood—in addition to causing a state of emergency in Queenstown, New Zealand—washed the entire ambush set down the river.

WOMEN IN BEARDS WERE USED AS EXTRAS.

A good chunk of the Riders of Rohan in *The Two Towers* and *The Return of the King* were actually women outfitted with fake beards. Why? "There are some very good women riders in New Zealand, and it'd be silly not to take advantage of them," Mortensen said.

CLOSE-UP

The Lord of the Rings trilogy marked a return to the Shire for Bilbo actor Ian Holm, who played Frodo in a 1981 radio dramatization of *The Lord of the Rings* on a BBC Radio 4 broadcast. His performance in that factored into Jackson's decision to offer him the Bilbo role.

A SCENE WHERE ARAGORN FIGHTS SAURON IS IN *THE RETURN OF THE KING* . . . SORT OF.

Jackson filmed a scene for the end of *The Return of the King* where Aragorn goes toe-to-toe with the physical version of Sauron, in a sort of updated version of the Sauron-Isildur battle from the prologue of *The Fellowship of the Ring*. "By the time we had got to postproduction," Jackson remembered, the scene "no longer felt right," so they cut it. But they did still use the footage: In the final battle, Aragorn can be seen battling a giant cave troll that was digitally superimposed over what was originally meant to be Sauron.

ONE OF THE MOST EMOTIONAL SCENES WAS SHOT OVER THE SPAN OF ONE YEAR.

All three *The Lord of the Rings* movies were shot in one long stretch. As with most movies, the shoot wasn't consecutive, meaning on any given day the schedule included scenes from all over the trilogy. Possibly the most extreme example of this has to do with the scene in *The Return of the King* where Frodo, urged by Gollum to think Sam has betrayed him, orders his loyal sidekick to go home. First Sam's part was filmed, then Frodo's—one year later. "Every time we cut to and fro between Frodo and Sam we are actually jumping back and forth across a year-long gap," Jackson explained.

FRODO ORIGINALLY "STRAIGHT-OUT" MURDERED GOLLUM.

The final confrontation between Frodo and Gollum in *The Return of the King* was originally going to end with Frodo pushing Gollum off the ledge into Mount Doom; "straight-out murder," Jackson admitted, "but at the time we were OK with it because we felt everyone *wanted* Frodo to kill Gollum. But, of course, it was very un-Tolkien." Years later, the scene was reshot, and that's what you see in the movie.

15

EXPLOSIVE ACTION MOVIES

Combining the precision of the best stunt and visual effects work with the emotional resonance of the best dramas and comedy, a truly great action film feels like something that really does have it all, even when the focus is tight and the set pieces are unquestionably over-the-top. There are plenty of masterpieces in the genre, but these are some of the very best.

1 The Bourne Ultimatum (2007)

When director Paul Greengrass stepped in to helm Matt Damon's *Bourne Identity* sequels in the 2000s, he perhaps unknowingly launched an action movie style trend that persists to this day. While the first Bourne film was unquestionably action-packed, Greengrass's entries into the series dialed the visceral nature of Jason Bourne's adventures up to eleven with a handheld, seat-of-your-pants style that influenced everything from superhero movies to Bond films in the years that followed.

2 Drunken Master II (1994)

Drunken Master II takes all the joy and comedic invention of the original 1978 film and adds everything Jackie Chan learned about action comedy filmmaking in the ensuing sixteen years for a movie experience that's both joyous and jaw-dropping. Whether he's fighting while squatted down under a train or setting himself on fire in the incredible final sequence, it's one of the world's greatest action stars in absolute top form.

3 Enter the Dragon (1973)

Enter the Dragon, which arrived in theaters just one month after Bruce Lee's sudden death at the age of thirty-two, is the movie that made the martial artist a legend. Steeped in classic Hong Kong kung fu movie style with layers of emerging Western action sensibilities creeping in, Lee's final completed film still plays not just as a showcase for his tremendous talent but as a testament to his abilities as a visual and physical storyteller.

4 *First Blood* **(1982)**
Though the subsequent *Rambo* sequels became increasingly bloody exercises in absolute machismo, Ted Kotcheff's original film remains the best in the series because it is much more fascinated with interior pain than exterior. Sylvester Stallone gives us a weary searcher wandering through an America that doesn't seem to want him anymore and charts the course of John Rambo's descent back into violence with real vulnerability.

5 *The Fugitive* **(1993)**
Though it's based on the earlier TV series of the same name, it's nearly impossible to imagine *The Fugitive* now without the dueling personalities of Harrison Ford and Tommy Lee Jones at its center. Andrew Davis's lean, mean, blisteringly paced thriller is best remembered now for that iconic dam sequence, but every minute of this film stands as a showcase of star-driven nineties action power.

6 *Hard Boiled* **(1992)**
John Woo's *Hard Boiled* perfected the gun fu subgenre with an all-out extravaganza of shoot-outs, motorcycle stunts, explosions, and an unforgettable climax in a terror-stricken hospital. In a career full of all-timers, this is perhaps the purest expression of Woo's natural style.

7 *John Wick* **(2014)**
Keanu Reeves has managed to carry, or help carry, an action spectacle in just about every phase of his career. But even he likely couldn't have predicted just how well *John Wick* would work. Featuring Keanu in peak brooding vengeance mode, Chad Stahelski's film combined furious gun fu fighting with neon noir visuals and a killer ensemble to make an action classic that's been imitated by action and crime filmmakers around the world in the years since its release.

8 *Kill Bill: Vol. 1 and 2* **(2003–2004)**
Uma Thurman turns in an absolutely thunderous performance as the Bride, a trained assassin hell-bent on the former colleagues who betrayed her, in Quentin Tarantino's homage to the revenge cinema of Japan, the kung fu epics of Hong Kong, and beyond. Two decades later, the whole bloody affair that is *Kill Bill* still works as a modern action showcase.

9 *Léon: The Professional* **(1994)**
In a decade packed with grand-scale action showcases, there's something both refreshing and instantly compelling about the relatively small-scale clashes in Luc Besson's intimate master class in tension and personal violence. Jean Reno and Natalie Portman are perfect together; Gary Oldman is in top form as the unhinged villain; and Besson's restrained, often emotional action sequences both cement and threaten the heart that beats at the center of the narrative.

10 **The Matrix (1999)** Perhaps the greatest testament to the power of *The Matrix* is the fact that so much of it should feel dated, but it doesn't. In the late '90s, as blockbuster filmmaking moved into a new age of computer-generated wizardry, the Wachowskis created a sci-fi spectacle that combined cyberpunk and bondage aesthetics with wire fu fight choreography and anime-inspired visuals, and somehow it all just . . . worked. More than 20 years on, Bullet Time, Agent Smith, and Trinity and Neo shooting up the place still rules.

> **"Those of you lucky enough to still have your lives, take them with you. However, leave the limbs you've lost. They belong to me now."**
>
> *— Kill Bill*

11 **Ong-Bak: The Thai Warrior (2003)** There are quite a few action films out in the world that are pretty transparently crafted as a showcase for a gifted martial artist who wants to leap and kick across the screen for two hours, and few films have ever worked that format quite as well as *Ong-Bak*. The incredible Tony Jaa performs one jaw-dropping display of physical prowess after another, from fighting off crowds of opponents to leaping through the streets like a parkour legend.

12 **Point Break (1991)** Kathryn Bigelow directs *Point Break*'s many stunt-centric set pieces—from bank robberies to foot chases to the iconic skydiving scene—with flair and visceral intensity, but it's the core relationship between Johnny Utah (Keanu Reeves) and Bodhi (Patrick Swayze) that makes the film so memorable. The tension between the FBI agent and the surfer–bank robber carries the film through all of its action bravado, and Bigelow's understanding of that is what makes the movie.

13 **The Raid: Redemption (2011)** On the surface, *The Raid*'s story seems almost puzzlingly simple: A group of cops have to infiltrate a building in Jakarta and take down the crime lord who lives at the top. That's the entire setup, and yet as Gareth Evans's film progresses through fight scene after blistering fight scene, the emotional stakes keep rising.

14 **Speed (1994)** *Speed* is one of those action films that makes you wonder as soon as you hear the premise—there's a bomb on a bus, and if the bus drops below a certain speed it explodes—exactly how the story can possibly sustain itself for a feature-length runtime. The answer? Keanu Reeves and Sandra Bullock's incredible chemistry, Dennis Hopper's indulgent villainy, and a whole lot of amazing bus-based set pieces.

15 **Terminator 2: Judgment Day (1991)** An all-star cast, a bigger budget, and a lot of technological ambition allowed James Cameron and *T2* co-writer William Wisher to flip the script on what made the first film work so well, turn the bad guy into a good guy, and deliver a sequel that retained the sci-fi horror feel of the original while topping it in terms of scale, emotional stakes, and wild set pieces.

THE LOST BOYS

(1987)

WRITTEN BY: Jan Fischer, James Jeremias, and Jeffrey Boam

DIRECTED BY: Joel Schumacher

OTHER MOVIES DIRECTED BY JOEL SCHUMACHER: *St. Elmo's Fire* (1985); *Falling Down* (1993); *Batman Forever* (1995); *Tigerland* (2000); *The Phantom of the Opera* (2004)

The 1980s were chock-full of vampire movies, from *The Hunger* (1983) and *Fright Night* (1985) to *Once Bitten* (1985) and *Near Dark* (1987). But very few of those features have stood the test of time quite like *The Lost Boys*. The dark teen-vamp horror-comedy became a cult classic and consistently ranks high among the greatest vampire films of all time. Plus, it introduced eighties audiences to the phenomenon that would become "the Two Coreys."

THE TOWN OF SANTA CARLA DOES NOT EXIST.

Landmarks shown throughout *The Lost Boys* reveal its real-world location as being close to Santa Cruz, home to the Santa Cruz Beach Boardwalk, California's oldest surviving amusement park. The Giant Dipper roller coaster opened there in 1924 and is still in operation today.

THE VAMPIRES WERE SUPPOSED TO BE MUCH YOUNGER.

The title of the film is a reference to *Peter Pan*'s Neverland clique of eternally young boys, and that influence was reflected in the screenplay. Executive producer Richard Donner brought Joel Schumacher on board to direct, but Schumacher was not into the idea of making a "*Goonies* go vampire" film, so the vampires grew into older model types (including Billy Wirth, who was working as a model when he auditioned and was cast as a vampire named Dwayne).

IT WAS THE BIRTH OF "THE TWO COREYS."

Actors Corey Haim (Sam Emerson) and Corey Feldman (Edgar Frog) ruled the eighties as teen idols. *The Lost Boys* was the first of many films that they would appear in together before ultimately landing a reality show called *The Two Coreys*, which aired on A&E for two seasons beginning in 2007. Both former child stars had troubled careers, and Haim struggled publicly with drug addiction before dying of pneumonia in 2010 at the age of thirty-eight.

"I've worked with a lot of great people through the years," Feldman told Larry King about his friendship with Haim in 2010. "And with Corey, you know, you set us in front of a camera and tell us to go and it just happens. And there's really no explaining that."

FELDMAN'S CHARACTER WAS INSPIRED BY THE ACTION STARS OF THE DAY.

In a special features interview, Feldman talked about getting the part and the direction he was given by Schumacher to help find the character of Edgar Frog. "Basically he gave me an order to go out and rent all of the Stallone movies and all the Chuck Norris movies, like *Rambo* and *First Blood* and *Missing in Action* . . . [Schumacher] said 'That is your character. I want you to meld all of these guys together and make something out of it.' So that's what I did."

THE "SEXY SAX MAN" IS A TRAINED COMPOSER AND MULTI-INSTRUMENTALIST.

During a random but memorable beach scene, teens are shown head-banging to a live concert by an oiled-up muscle man pretending to play the saxophone. The actor—credited as "Beach Concert Star," but commonly referred to as "Sexy Sax Man"— is Timmy Cappello, a musician who trained at the New England Conservatory of Music after dropping out of school at the age of fifteen. Cappello also trained under jazz pianist Lennie Tristano before going on to perform with numerous musicians in the 1980s, including Peter Gabriel, Carly Simon, and Tina Turner, with whom he toured for fifteen years. The two-hour acting gig became a lasting part of Cappello's life and place in pop culture, to the point that it was parodied in one of *Saturday Night Live*'s Digital Shorts in 2010.

WRITTEN BY: George Miller, Brendan McCarthy, Nick Lathouris

DIRECTED BY: George Miller

OTHER MOVIES DIRECTED BY GEORGE MILLER:
Mad Max (1979); *The Road Warrior* (1981);
The Witches of Eastwick (1987); *Babe: Pig in the City* (1998)

MAD MAX: FURY ROAD

(2015)

I n an age of decades-later sequels, one desert-baked car chase defied all logic by being utterly, fantastically good. *Mad Max: Fury Road* will be remembered for decades to come for its beauty, intensity, and a story that came together perfectly.

Nearly forty years after first introducing "Mad" Max Rockatansky to audiences, director George Miller returned to that post-apocalyptic world to continue the legacy of one iconic character and the wasteland he calls home. In *Mad Max: Fury Road*, Max (Tom Hardy, taking on a role previously played by Mel Gibson) reluctantly aids Imperator Furiosa (Charlize Theron) as she tries to help a harem of "wives" (Rosie Huntington-Whiteley, Riley Keough, Zoë Kravitz, Abbey Lee, and Courtney Eaton) escape the violent dictator Immortan Joe (Hugh Keays-Byrne). From the simplest of plots comes one of the most emotional action films ever made.

IT WAS SUPPOSED TO BE MADE IN 2003 WITH HEATH LEDGER.

Fury Road spent decades in development hell. Miller had been thinking of a feature-length chase scene for the fourth film since 1987, but the concept didn't fully coalesce until 1998, when he came up with the idea to make people (versus oil) the object of the chase. Plans to shoot in 2001 were scrapped after 9/11 and the subsequent collapse of the American dollar against the Australian dollar. Had that production moved forward, Max would have been played by Heath Ledger—and it still might have been had Miller begun shooting the movie before Ledger's death in 2008.

RAIN DELAYED FILMING FOR AN ENTIRE YEAR.

Shooting was all set to begin in the Australian desert in 2010 until a once-in-a-century rain turned the area into a slightly lusher green space than the film required. Miller postponed shooting for a year to see if the desert would dry back up; when it didn't, he hauled hundreds of people and vehicles to Namibia.

IT SET A MAJOR OSCAR RECORD.

We usually think of something like *The Godfather Part II* when considering Oscar-worthy sequels, but it's a genuine rarity that a sequel would be nominated for a Best Picture Academy Award without the original film first paving the way. Before *Fury Road*, *Toy Story 3* was the only movie to be nominated for Best Picture without previous films in the series earning nominations.

THE FLAMING GUITAR WEIGHED 132 POUNDS.

To heighten the film's intensity, Miller insisted on a ton of practical effects versus using CGI. As a result, the flame-throwing guitar the Doof Warrior (iOTA) rocks out with is totally real. The musical monstrosity weighed 132 pounds and used the whammy bar to control the flames.

THE AUTHOR OF *THE VAGINA MONOLOGUES* WAS A CONSULTANT.

Miller invited *The Vagina Monologues* writer Eve Ensler to visit the set in Namibia for a week to share her insights and expertise. She gave the cast (particularly the Wives) some reality checks about violence targeted at women in war zones.

TOM HARDY AND CHARLIZE THERON DID *NOT* GET ALONG.

While *Fury Road* was shooting, a number of stories leaked from the set that Hardy and Theron were having a hard time getting along. Both actors opened up about the tension in Kyle Buchanan's oral history *Blood, Sweat & Chrome: The Wild and True Story of Mad Max: Fury Road*. In the book, camera operator Mark Goellnicht talked about one particularly heated argument, and noted that Hardy "was quite aggressive. [Charlize] really felt threatened, and that was the turning point." Theron requested that producer Denise Di Novi remain on the set, as she believed that "sending a woman producer down could maybe equalize some of it, because I didn't feel safe."

Ultimately, Theron realized that they were both reacting to the real world around them as their characters might. "Because of my own fear, we were putting up walls to protect ourselves instead of saying to each other, 'Fuck, this is scary for you and it's scary for me, too. Let's be nice to each other.' We were functioning, in a weird way, like our characters: Everything was about survival."

IT ALMOST DIDN'T HAVE A BEGINNING—OR END.

Unhappy at the production going over budget, then-president of Warner Bros. Jeff Robinov flew to Namibia to deliver an ultimatum: Cameras stop shooting December 8 no matter what. The problem was that they hadn't even started to film the bookending moments in the Citadel, and when production stopped, they faced the prospect of cutting together a movie that had no real beginning or end. Editor Margaret Sixel (who won the Best Editing Oscar in 2015) spent a year assembling a movie from 480 hours of footage that was all one big middle. When Robinov was replaced by Kevin Tsujihara, he reversed the decision and gave Miller an extra month to finish shooting.

WRITTEN BY: David Lynch

DIRECTED BY: David Lynch

OTHER MOVIES DIRECTED BY DAVID LYNCH:
Eraserhead (1977); *The Elephant Man* (1980); *Dune* (1984); *Blue Velvet* (1986); *The Straight Story* (1999); *Inland Empire* (2006)

David Lynch's surrealist movies may follow dream logic, but that doesn't mean their plots can't be readily discerned. *Mulholland Drive* is his most striking work precisely because, in spite of its more bizarre moments, it adds up to a coherent, tragic story. The mystery starts innocently enough with the dark-haired Rita (Laura Elena Harring) waking up with amnesia following a car accident in Los Angeles and piecing together her identity alongside the plucky aspiring actress Betty (Naomi Watts). It takes a blue box to unlock the secret that Betty is in fact Diane, who is in love with and envious of Camilla (also played by Harring) and has concocted a fantasy version of their lives. The real Diane arranges for Camilla to be killed, leading to her intense guilt and suicide. Only Lynch can go from Nancy Drew to nihilism so swiftly and deftly.

MULHOLLAND DRIVE

(2001)

MOST OF THE IDEAS FOR *MULHOLLAND DRIVE* CAME FROM LYNCH'S TRANSCENDENTAL MEDITATION.

Lynch practices transcendental meditation, which he describes as a way to "expand consciousness." When the film version of *Mulholland Drive* was finally green-lit, he had no ideas and hadn't even been thinking about it. The day that he needed to put ideas on pages, he meditated and that's when "all the ideas came, all at once."

LYNCH DIDN'T AUDITION ANY OF HIS ACTORS.

Before being cast, Naomi Watts merely had a thirty-minute conversation with Lynch, which is similar to how all the leads were chosen. "I never make anyone read a scene, because then I want to start rehearsing—no matter who it is," Lynch said of his casting process in 2001. "I just get a feeling based on a conversation. It's something in the eyes. It's some sort of feeling in the air. And I know that this person can do that role."

HARRING GOT INTO A CAR ACCIDENT WHILE DRIVING TO HER MEETING WITH LYNCH.

Harring was very excited to finally be at a point in her career where someone like Lynch's casting agent would call her. That excitement distracted her and she rear-ended another car. Luckily for Harring, it was the car of another actor on the way to an audition. So they left the scene of the accident. She learned at the meeting that her character, Rita, gets into a car accident in one of the first scenes.

LYNCH CALLS IT A LOVE STORY.

"It's strange how films unfold as they go," Lynch said. "There may be a noir element in *Mulholland Drive*, and a couple of genres swimming around in there together. For me, it's a love story."

ROGER EBERT DIDN'T KNOW WHAT TO CALL IT.

To many, the film is undoubtedly a mystery. But Roger Ebert denied that idea shortly after the film was released. He wrote that "*Mulholland Drive* isn't like *Memento*, where if you watch closely enough you can hope to explain the mystery. There is no explanation. There may not even be a mystery."

FREEZE-FRAME

Sunset Boulevard is one of Lynch's favorite films. In *Mulholland Drive*, a *Sunset Boulevard* street sign can be seen in addition to a very similar shot of the Paramount Gates that's in *Sunset Boulevard*. Lynch even tracked down the same car from *Sunset Boulevard* to include in the shot of the Paramount Gates.

PLOT TWISTS

WILD MOVIE

An ending often makes or breaks a movie. There's nothing quite as satisfying as having the rug pulled out from under you, particularly in a thriller. But too many flicks that try to shock can't stick the landing—they're outlandish and illogical, or signal where the plot is headed. Not all of these films are entirely successful, but they have one important attribute in common: From the classic to the cultishly beloved, they involve hard-to-predict twists that really do blow viewers' minds, then linger there for days, if not for life. (Warning: Massive spoilers follow.)

Deep Red (1975)

It's not rare for a horror movie to flip the script when it comes to unmasking its killer, but it's much rarer that such a film causes a viewer to question their own perception of the world around them. Such is the case for *Deep Red*, Italian director Dario Argento's (*Suspiria*) slasher masterpiece. A pianist living in Rome (David Hemmings) comes upon the murder of a woman in her apartment and teams up with a female reporter to find the person responsible. Argento's whodunit is filled to the brim with gorgeous photography, ghastly sights, and delirious twists. But best of all is the final sequence, in which the pianist retraces his steps to discover that the killer has been hiding in plain sight all along. Rewind to the beginning and you'll discover that you caught an unknowing glimpse, too.

Fight Club (1999)

Edward Norton is no stranger to taking on extremely disparate personalities in his roles. The unassuming actor can quickly turn vicious, which led to ideal casting for *Fight Club*, director David Fincher's adaptation of the Chuck Palahniuk novel. Fincher cleverly keeps the audience in the dark about the connections between Norton's timid, unnamed narrator and Brad Pitt's hunky, aggressive Tyler Durden. After the two start the bruising group of the title, the plot significantly increases the stakes, with the club turning into a sort of anarchist terrorist organization. The narrator eventually comes to grips with the fact that he is Tyler and has caused all the destruction around him.

> "The first rule of Fight Club is: You do not talk about Fight Club. The second rule of Fight Club is: You do not talk about Fight Club."
>
> — *Fight Club*

Oldboy (2003)

For months, and then years, poor Oh Dae-su (Choi Min-sik) pounds the walls of a plain hotel room he finds himself trapped in. Dae-su doesn't know he's angered Lee Woo-jin (Yoo Ji-tae), a wealthy and vengeful former classmate who believes Dae-su is responsible for his sister's death. After being released, Dae-su seeks answers and, with an open and wounded heart, falls for the plucky Mi-do (Kang Hye-jung). In the movie's emotionally brutal finale, Woo-jin reveals Mi-do is Dae-su's now-grown daughter, whom he left behind as a child after being kidnapped—and who has now become his lover. Viewers were further tormented when Spike Lee opted to remake *Oldboy* in 2013.

The Others (2001)

Nicole Kidman gives a superb performance in the elegantly styled film from the Spanish writer-director Alejandro Amenábar, playing a mother in a country house after World War II protecting her photosensitive children from light and, eventually, dead spirits occupying the place. Only by the end does it become clear that she's in denial about the fact that she's a ghost, having killed her children in a psychotic break before taking her own life. It's a bleak capper to a genuinely haunting yarn.

Primal Fear (1996)

No courtroom movie can surpass *Primal Fear*'s discombobulating effect. Defense attorney Martin Vail (Richard Gere) becomes strongly convinced that his altar-boy client Aaron (Edward Norton) didn't kill the archbishop he's charged with murdering. The meek, stuttering Aaron has sudden violent outbursts in which he becomes "Roy" and is diagnosed with dissociative identity disorder, leading to a not-guilty ruling. Gere's lawyer visits Aaron about the news, and as he's leaving, a wonderfully maniacal Norton reveals that he faked the multiple personalities.

The Sixth Sense (1999)

Early in his career, M. Night Shyamalan was frequently (perhaps a little too frequently) compared to Alfred Hitchcock for his ability to ratchet up tension while misdirecting his audience. He hasn't always earned stellar reviews since, but *The Sixth Sense* remains deservedly legendary for its final twist. At the end of the ghost story, in which young Cole Sear (Haley Joel Osment) can see dead people, it turns out that the psychologist (Bruce Willis) who's been working with the boy is no longer living himself—the result of a gunshot wound witnessed in the opening sequence.

"I see dead people!"

— *The Sixth Sense*

The Usual Suspects (1995)

The Usual Suspects has left virtually everyone who watches it breathless by the time they get to the fake-out conclusion. Roger "Verbal" Kint (Kevin Spacey), a criminal with cerebral palsy, regales an interrogator with stories of his exploits with a band of fellow crooks, seen in flashback. Hovering over this is the mysterious, villainous figure Keyser Söze. It's not until Verbal leaves and jumps into a car that customs agent David Kujan (Chazz Palminteri) realizes that the man fabricated details, tricking the law and the viewer into his fake reality, and is in fact the fabled Söze.

"People say I talk too much."

— *The Usual Suspects*

THE MUPPET MOVIE

(1979)

WRITTEN BY: Jerry Juhl and Jack Burns

DIRECTED BY: James Frawley

OTHER MOVIES DIRECTED BY JAMES FRAWLEY:
The Christian Licorice Store (1971);
Kid Blue (1973); *The Big Bus* (1976);
Fraternity Vacation (1985)

When the Muppets made their feature film debut in *The Muppet Movie*, it finally answered the question fans had been asking: How did this crew of charming characters come together? By Kermit beginning his cross-country to Hollywood, of course, and the result was pure magic. The dreamy songs, innovative special effects, and bubbly characters all catapulted the flick to box office gold and widespread critical acclaim. (It also kicked off a beloved movie franchise that's still chugging along today.) But pulling it off wasn't easy, as Muppets creator Jim Henson, director Jim Frawley, and the never-ending lineup of A-list stars who made cameos soon discovered.

"THE RAINBOW CONNECTION" REQUIRED A DIVING BELL.

For the movie's adored opening song, Henson had to find a way to operate Kermit while completely hiding himself in a swamp set. His solution was to fold himself into a custom-made diving bell placed in a water tank—and we do mean *fold*. Because the tank was only four feet deep, the diving bell was correspondingly short; so Henson, who was six foot three, had to contort himself into the bell with his monitor. Then he would stick his arm through a rubber tube to control Kermit. The whole scenario was so strange that it actually scared Henson's thirteen-year-old son John when he visited the set.

FOUR PUPPETEERS AND A LITTLE PERSON DROVE THE STUDEBAKER.

The sequences where Fozzie, Kermit, Miss Piggy, and the gang cruise around in that old Studebaker seem effortless, but they were a logistical nightmare. Kermit and Piggy each required a puppeteer, Fozzie required two, they all needed video monitors, and none of them could appear in the shot. So four men squeezed underneath the dashboard of the car with their video monitors to accomplish this movie magic—but the engineering didn't stop there. Frawley told SFGATE that they also "had a little person in the back of the car, steering and driving. We had a video camera on the nose of the car so he could see where he was going."

ORSON WELLES'S CHARACTER IS NAMED FOR THE MOVIE'S PRODUCER.

Welles appears briefly in the movie as producer Lew Lord, and that moniker was no accident. It was a nod to British producer Lew Grade, who got *The Muppet Show* on the air when all the American networks passed and executive-produced *The Muppet Movie*. Also, he was an actual lord.

THE MUPPET MOVIE BY THE NUMBERS

The finale featured
250 puppets.

Henson had a vision for the musical finale of *The Muppet Movie*, and that vision involved 250 puppets. He wasn't content to fill the screen with placeholders, either; Henson wanted every single puppet actively participating in the number. To accomplish this feat, the production had to hire almost 150 extra performers through the Los Angeles Guild of Puppeteers of America. On the day of filming, everyone took their marks on the floor of an enormous pit, and when Frawley shouted, "Muppets up!" each person raised their Muppet(s) for the ambitious final number.

THE CREW HAD TO BUILD A SIXTY-FOOT ANIMAL.

When Animal accidentally eats Dr. Bunsen Honeydew's Insta-Grow pills, he memorably balloons through the roof. Henson refused to use a normal puppet on a miniature set to accomplish this effect, so the crew constructed a sixty-foot-tall Animal head.

THE PUPPETEERS INCLUDED JOHN LANDIS AND TIM BURTON.

Director John Landis revealed to the *New York Times* that he was one of the many extras involved in the closing song. Frank Oz, who was busy handling Miss Piggy, asked him to fill in for Grover. But he wasn't the only famous director in the pit. As Landis recalled, "Thirty years later, I was in a restaurant in Beverly Hills and got introduced to Tim Burton. Tim said: 'We met before. I used to be in the animator/puppeteers union, and I'm in the pit on *The Muppet Movie*. And everyone was saying, 'That's the guy that made *Animal House*!'"

MY OWN PRIVATE IDAHO (1991)

WRITTEN BY: Gus Van Sant

DIRECTED BY: Gus Van Sant

OTHER MOVIES DIRECTED BY GUS VAN SANT:
Drugstore Cowboy (1989); *To Die For* (1995);
Good Will Hunting (1997); *Gerry* (2002);
Milk (2008); *Promised Land* (2012)

Before *Good Will Hunting* and *Finding Forrester*; before the ill-advised *Psycho* remake and the experimental *Gerry*; before the movies about Harvey Milk and Kurt Cobain, Portland-based indie auteur Gus Van Sant made *My Own Private Idaho*, an avant-garde drama about Mikey Waters (River Phoenix), a narcoleptic gay hustler and Scott Favor (Keanu Reeves), his friend and co-worker.

The film was part of a new wave of gay cinema, and it added to Phoenix's burgeoning reputation as a sensitive, brooding actor—made all the more tragic by his sudden death two years later. It changed Van Sant's life, too, putting him on the path that would lead to high-profile hits like *Good Will Hunting*.

IT'S A COMBINATION OF THREE STORIES, INCLUDING ONE BASED ON SHAKESPEARE.

Van Sant had three ideas rolling around his head that he smushed into one movie. One was a screenplay about street kids in Portland and was based on William Shakespeare's *Henry IV*. Much of Keanu Reeves's character's story comes from this part, complete with occasional Bard-like dialogue. Another source (which Van Sant had already titled *My Own Private Idaho*) was another screenplay about street hustlers, one older and one younger, who travel to Spain looking for one's mother. The third element was a short story Van Sant wrote called "In a Blue Funk," about the River Phoenix character being picked up by a German man and kept in a house.

GUS VAN SANT'S SCREENPLAY WAS ... PROBLEMATIC.

Van Sant's script was only seventy pages long, which would translate to a seventy-minute movie. (He intended the actors to flesh it out with improvisation, which they did.) For another thing, he wrote it in a poetic, non-standard typographical format—words down the middle of the page, random capitalization, etc.—making it challenging for some people to decipher.

VAN SANT LEARNED SECONDHAND THAT THE FILM WAS BEING MADE.

Any would-be filmmaker can tell you how nerve-racking it is to meet with potential producers and then wait to hear back about whether they're going to make your movie. Van Sant said he found out his producers had committed to making *My Own Private Idaho* when other filmmakers told him, "Congratulations, they're skipping our film to make yours."

ONE KEY SCENE WAS WRITTEN ALMOST ENTIRELY BY RIVER PHOENIX.

The way Van Sant wrote it, the scene where Mike and Scott sit around a campfire in the desert and Mike confesses his love for Scott was a three-page scene with no such declaration. Van Sant was leaving it ambiguous whether either of the hustlers was actually gay. But according to Van Sant, Phoenix really wanted to beef up the impact of the scene. "He had decided that that scene was his character's main scene and, with Keanu's permission, he wrote it out to say something that it wasn't already saying." As a result, the film became, at least in part, about unrequited love, adding another tragic element to it.

IT WOULD HAVE BEEN VAN SANT'S SECOND MOVIE INSTEAD OF HIS THIRD, BUT IT WASN'T COMMERCIAL ENOUGH.

After getting some attention with his micro-budget debut, *Mala Noche* (1986), Van Sant wanted to make *My Own Private Idaho* next. But everyone in Hollywood told him a story about gay hustlers was too "niche" to get any traction. So instead he made *Drugstore Cowboy* (1989), about a roving band of drug addicts who rob pharmacies—a premise with more mainstream appeal, apparently.

THE FILM HAS SOME DOCUMENTARY ELEMENTS.

Those brief snippets where anonymous Portland street kids talk about their experiences aren't just meant to look like a documentary—they *are* a documentary. Van Sant knew some of the local street kids and had them on set as advisers and extras. One day, Van Sant turned the camera on these guys and interviewed them, hoping to inspire the cast with some authenticity. The result was so intriguing that he put some of that footage into the film.

"I love you, and you don't pay me."

ESSENTIAL LGBTQ MOVIES

Queer cinema—or, as it was endearingly branded in the nineties, New Queer Cinema—has afforded directors of all sexual identities and orientations from around the world an opportunity to showcase distinctive, nuanced, personal stories of what it means to be a member of the LGBTQ community.

1 ***Bad Education*** **(2004)**
After a three-year break from directing, Oscar-winning Spanish auteur Pedro Almodóvar came back into the spotlight in 2019 with his semi-autobiographical *Pain and Glory*. But his criminally underrated *Bad Education* touches on gay youth and abuse in a fascinating, brutally straightforward fashion. It might be the best performance of Gael García Bernal's career.

2 ***Blue Is the Warmest Color*** **(2013)**
It's perhaps less than an authentic portrayal of first lesbian love, but Cannes winner *Blue Is the Warmest Color* works so well because the beats of a fluttering romance turned hurtful are universal.

3 ***Bound*** **(1996)**
The Wachowskis were way ahead of their time with this tight, noirish crime thriller in which Jennifer Tilly and Gina Gershon can't resist each other in a mob-filled Art Deco apartment building.

4 ***The Crying Game*** **(1992)**
If you lived through the nineties, you probably know the shot: the mid-film reveal that Dil (Jaye Davidson), the mysterious young woman IRA terrorist Fergus (Stephen Rea) finds himself falling for, is actually a man. But while too many of us focused on the sexual dynamics of *The Crying Game*, Neil Jordan's masterwork sensitively weaves a queer romance into a tapestry covering fascinating corners of Irish life. It's also one of the rare instances where full frontal male nudity is absolutely essential to the plot.

5 Far from Heaven (2002)

From the 1990s on, Todd Haynes has been the towering director behind some of cinema's greatest queer movies, including *Safe* (1995) and *Carol* (2015). Haynes's best film, *Far from Heaven*, may not appear queer at first, but the slick update of mid-century melodramas then known as "women's pictures" masterfully queers up its source material. Cathy (Julianne Moore) is a love-deprived housewife flirting with her Black gardener (Dennis Haysbert), while her husband, Frank (Dennis Quaid), is a suit with a closeted affection for men. But everyone here is painfully inching their way to a full expression of their sexual and romantic selves—something any LGBTQ person knows well.

6 Happy Together (1997)

If you haven't dabbled in Chinese cinema, here's a gorgeous place to start. Hong Kong director Wong Kar-wai trains his eye on two men feeling the heady push and pull of mutual lust and dissatisfaction. The photography alone, from noisy urban Hong Kong streets to the swirling waterfalls of Buenos Aires, is swoon-worthy.

7 In a Year with 13 Moons (1978)

Watch this movie only if you're up for a profoundly disturbing (albeit beautifully rendered) experience. German filmmaking legend Rainer Werner Fassbinder is at his most stark here, unraveling the tale of a trans woman taking account of lost love and her current identity. Hard as it is to watch, it's a vital window into the still all-too-real problems and violence the trans community faces.

8 Laurence Anyways (2012)

In more recent years, we've gotten fresh cinematic portraits of trans life. *Laurence Anyways* from French Canadian indie darling Xavier Dolan is on the florid side, as with all of Dolan's films, but it's oh so pretty. He films the blossoming of a trans woman in a difficult relationship like a glossy music video simmering with heartbreak.

9 Paris Is Burning (1990)

At the time it came out, *Paris Is Burning* was a surprising commercial success and a curiosity. Director Jennie Livingston spent careful time observing the world of Harlem-based voguing balls (which inspired Madonna's hit "Vogue" as well as the groundbreaking TV series *Pose*, which ran from 2018 to 2021) and the wildly talented, frequently catty, fabulous but downtrodden dancers who inhabited them. That many of those performers have died from HIV/AIDS complications makes it that much more essential a documentary.

10 Tangerine (2015)

This low-tech black comedy from Sean Baker (*The Florida Project*) doesn't look like it was shot on an iPhone, but it was. *Tangerine* is a bleary, saturated fever dream that touches on corners of trans sex work in L.A., but it also illuminates the deep abiding hope of people who just want to be recognized as the humans they are.

THE NEVERENDING STORY (1984)

WRITTEN BY: Wolfgang Petersen and Herman Weigel
(based on the book by Michael Ende)

DIRECTED BY: Wolfgang Petersen

OTHER MOVIES DIRECTED BY WOLFGANG PETERSEN:
Das Boot (1981); *In the Line of Fire* (1993); *Outbreak* (1995);
The Perfect Storm (2000); *Poseidon* (2006)

The movie adaptation of German writer Michael Ende's 1979 fantasy novel was released during that special era in the 1980s when a PG rating almost certainly meant nightmares for children.

Ten-year-old Bastian (Barret Oliver) locks himself in his school attic to begin reading what he's been told is a magical storybook. He's immediately entranced by a magical land known as Fantasia, where a brave young warrior named Atreyu (Noah Hathaway) has been tasked with saving the land's young Empress (Tami Stronach) before it is destroyed forever. Ultimately, Bastian becomes an intricate part of the plot and learns that while he's been reading about Atreyu's adventures, other readers have been reading about Bastian witnessing Atreyu's adventures—and so on. Hence, the *NeverEnding* of the title.

IT WAS THE MOST EXPENSIVE MOVIE IN GERMANY'S HISTORY.

With a price tag of about $27 million, the project supplanted 1981's Oscar-nominated *Das Boot*—also directed by Wolfgang Petersen—as the country's priciest film at the time of its release.

THE BOOK'S AUTHOR CALLED THE MOVIE "REVOLTING."

Despite having worked with Petersen on the script, *The NeverEnding Story* author Michael Ende publicly bashed the finished product. He referred to the film as "the revolting movie" and demanded that his name not appear in the credits, claiming that the filmmakers "did not understand the book at all."

PETERSEN WAS A PERFECTIONIST.

In a 2015 interview with the *News Tribune* of Tacoma, Washington, Noah Hathaway (who played Atreyu) said that Petersen, whose English was limited, was a perfectionist who sometimes required up to forty takes before he was satisfied with a single scene. "A three-month movie turned into a year," Hathaway said. "It was a lot of work."

IT TOOK A WHILE TO TRAIN A HORSE TO "DROWN."

There's a reason why the Swamp of Sadness scene took so long to shoot. The short version is that most horses won't walk into deep pools of mud if they have a choice. It took two trainers seven weeks to teach the horses

The U.S. version of *The NeverEnding Story* is about seven minutes shorter than the German version. The pacing needed to be a little quicker for American audiences, Petersen told MTV News, so he asked his friend Steven Spielberg for help. "It was just a polish kind of thing," Petersen said, "a few seconds here, a few things here." As a thank-you for his help, Petersen gave Spielberg the Auryn—the Empress's medallion, which protects those who wear it.

playing Artax to stand still on a hydraulic platform in the swamp with mud up to their chins without trying to swim or run away.

FALKOR IS A LUCKDRAGON— AND ALSO PART AIRPLANE.

The forty-three-foot-long luckdragon's face looks a lot like a dog's, but according to the source material, his official breed is 0 percent canine. While even the special effects director referred to the creature as a "golden retriever/dragon," Falkor's appearance was simply the director's interpretation. At least two Falkor models were constructed; the first, built by Giuseppe Tortora, used airplane steel for the frames, and the head alone weighed more than two hundred pounds.

THE STORY DOESN'T END WITH THE CREDITS.

If you're the type of moviegoer who avoids sequels, you may want to rethink that policy in this case—or at least pick up a copy of Ende's book. Because the film version of *The NeverEnding Story* ends at around the halfway point of the book, audiences never find out what happens to the beloved characters. George T. Miller's 1990 sequel includes plot points from Ende's novel, but also adds new elements to the story line. There is a third film (1994's *The NeverEnding Story III*), but it is an extended adventure that wasn't part of the book.

NO COUNTRY FOR OLD MEN (2007)

WRITTEN BY: Joel and Ethan Coen
(based on the book by Cormac McCarthy)

DIRECTED BY: Joel and Ethan Coen

OTHER MOVIES DIRECTED BY JOEL AND ETHAN COEN:
Raising Arizona (1987); *Miller's Crossing* (1990);
Fargo (1996); *The Big Lebowski* (1998);
A Serious Man (2009); *Inside Llewyn Davis* (2013);
The Ballad of Buster Scruggs (2018)

Though they're best known for their quirky takes on everything from murder (*Fargo*) to stoner life (*The Big Lebowski*), Joel and Ethan Coen scored one of the biggest box office hits of their careers in 2007 with the deadly serious *No Country for Old Men*—which won four of the eight Oscars it was nominated for, including Best Picture.

The film is an adaptation of Cormac McCarthy's 2005 novel, which follows the intersecting paths of Llewelyn Moss (Josh Brolin), a Vietnam vet who stumbles upon a drug deal gone bad in the West Texas desert plus $2 million in cash that's seemingly there for the taking; Anton Chigurh (Javier Bardem), a dead-eyed, cattle stun gun–wielding sociopath who's intent on finding that missing money; and Ed Tom Bell (Tommy Lee Jones), the soon-to-be-retired sheriff who is trying to track the both of them down before he officially retires.

GARRET DILLAHUNT AUDITIONED FOR THE ROLE OF LLEWELYN—FIVE TIMES.

Dillahunt plays the lovably naïve Deputy Wendell, but he originally auditioned for the role of Llewelyn—on more than one occasion. "I auditioned for Moss about five times, every time a star fell out," Dillahunt told the A.V. Club. "That happens to me a lot when stars fall out—they go to me, or I have a shot."

QUENTIN TARANTINO AND ROBERT RODRIGUEZ FILMED JOSH BROLIN'S AUDITION.

Though Brolin wasn't quite a marquee name when he eventually landed the role of Moss, he had some powerful friends on his side. The actor learned of *No Country for Old Men* while he was filming *Grindhouse* with Robert Rodriguez and Quentin Tarantino, so he asked if he could borrow a camera to shoot a quick audition. The duo did him one better: Tarantino directed it and Rodriguez shot it.

ANTON CHIGURH'S HAIRCUT WAS ITS OWN CHARACTER.

When asked about the 'do, Bardem told the *Los Angeles Times*, "You don't have to act the haircut; the haircut is acting by itself . . . so you don't have to act weird if you have that weird haircut."

THE MOVIE USED A LOT OF FAKE BLOOD, AND IT DIDN'T COME CHEAP.

A lot of blood is shed, and visible, in *No Country for Old Men*. While filmmakers can normally mix together sugar-based fake blood, shooting in the desert meant that the extras would have been covered in insects while trying to play dead. So the Coens had to special-order a unique kind of fake blood that wouldn't seem like a snack to all those creepy-crawly things. They ended up ordering it from England at a cost of about $800 a gallon.

THE FINAL SCENE WAS FILMED IN ONE TAKE.

The Coens have described *No Country for Old Men* as the closest they'll likely ever come to making an action movie, yet it ends on a much quieter note—with Jones delivering an extended monologue about a dream he had about his late father, and it's pitch-perfect. When asked by *W* magazine how many takes it took, Jones simply answered: "One." When asked whether it was a tough scene to film, his answer was just as succinct: "Naw. I'd been practicin'."

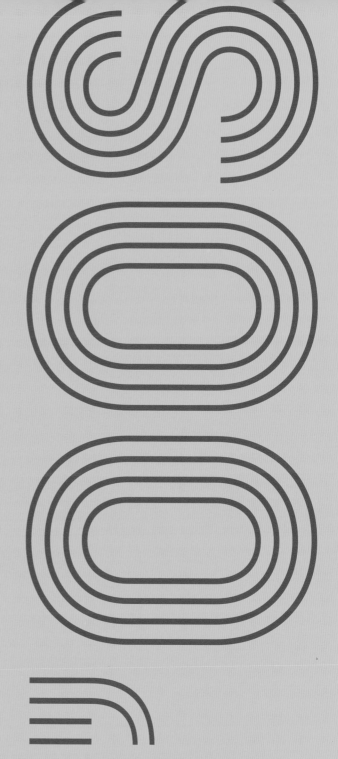

TERRIFIC MOVIES FROM THE 2000s

The world changed in the 2000s, and not just because the years started with "2" now (although that was huge). In movies, the spread of digital technology made filmmaking less expensive than before, resulting in a new batch of young directors entering the playing field.

About a Boy (2002)

There are movies on this list that are more hoity-toity, but few are as breezy, charming, and heartfelt as this comedy about Hugh Grant becoming friends with a bullied kid (Nicholas Hoult) and his mom (Toni Collette). Deceptively simple, it turns rom-com and other clichés on their heads while delivering a frankly beautiful story about connecting with others.

American Splendor (2003)

Paul Giamatti is at his rumpled best as Harvey Pekar, the real-life comics author whose musings on the human condition on paper and in person earned him accolades (and several appearances on David Letterman). When a health crisis arrives, it's Pekar's art that helps him endure. The real Pekar appears in segments, as does animation, giving the entire film a quilted quality that echoes Pekar's singular work.

Avatar (2009)

Say what you will about the plot of James Cameron's *Avatar*, but there's no denying that the film revolutionized 3D moviemaking. Using a version of the 3D Fusion camera system that Cameron and inventor Vince Pace developed for the 3D documentary *Ghosts of the Abyss*, augmented reality, the director was able to see his actors as their digital characters in their computer-generated environments on the set in real time. In doing so, Cameron elevated 3D from shlocky schtick mostly used for cheap jump scares to an immersive experience the likes of which hadn't been seen before, and has yet to be repeated.

Batman Begins (2005)

Following the tepid response to 1997's *Batman and Robin*, the Batman franchise returned to its gritty roots with this story of Bruce Wayne's arduous training and early activities as Gotham City's Dark Knight. Opposing his brand of law and order is the Scarecrow (Cillian Murphy) and Ra's al Ghul (Liam Neeson), a specter from Wayne's past. *Batman Begins* spawned a trilogy from Christian Bale and director Christopher Nolan.

Borat (2006)

When *Borat: Cultural Learnings of America for Make Benefit Glorious Nation of Kazakhstan* was released in 2006, a whole new audience was exposed to Borat Sagdiyev, a "journalist" portrayed by Sacha Baron Cohen who had made frequent appearances on the comedian's *Da Ali G Show*. In addition to becoming a box office smash, it also caused a bit of an uproar—especially among those unsuspecting "co-stars" whose patience had been tested by Cohen's anti-Semitic Kazakh character. Lawsuits were filed, box office records were broken, and hidden-camera cringe comedy would never be the same.

Brick (2005)

High school meets noir in director Rian Johnson's feature directorial debut. Joseph Gordon-Levitt plays Brendan, an outcast who gets a frantic phone call from ex-girlfriend Emily (Emile de Ravin) that sends him through a labyrinth of criminals, characters, and hard-boiled confrontations.

Brokeback Mountain (2005)

In an alternate universe, Ang Lee's beautifully rendered adaptation of Annie Proulx's short story about love between two cowboys won the Oscar for Best Picture, and *Crash* was never spoken of again. In our universe, we have Heath Ledger and Jake Gyllenhaal's emotional, taciturn performances centering a powerful film that taps into the universal aspects of falling in love.

Brooklyn's Finest (2009)

An ensemble cast (Richard Gere, Don Cheadle, Ethan Hawke, and Wesley Snipes) navigates the temptations and pitfalls inherent in police work in this drama from director Antoine Fuqua (and produced by *Cops* creator John Langley).

City of God (2002)

The lives of Brazil's criminal class are examined in this moving and often harrowing film from co-directors Fernando Meirelles and Kátia Lund about a group of friends looking to escape the poverty-stricken favelas of their youth. The striking authenticity comes in part from the performers, most of whom were amateurs who had never before appeared on camera.

Crouching Tiger, Hidden Dragon (2000)

It remains the highest-grossing foreign-language movie in U.S. box office history, and even adjusting for inflation, the highest since at least 1980. Such is the power of Ang Lee's masterful, breathtaking action epic that changed martial arts movies forever and was most Westerners' first introduction to Michelle Yeoh. Timeless romance and flying warriors never blended so well.

Eternal Sunshine of the Spotless Mind (2004)

A twenty-first-century love story from the brilliantly sad mind of Charlie Kaufman, directed by the visionary Michel Gondry, in which Jim Carrey seeks to erase his memories of a lost love (Kate Winslet). Visually, it's ingenious; thematically, it's melancholy and insightful (not to mention funny) in its exploration of true love and the persistence of memory.

A History of Violence (2005)

Long before *John Wick* rewrote the stealth-assassin trope, director David Cronenberg presented this collision of normalcy and bloodshed. Modest diner owner Tom Stall (Viggo Mortensen) stops a robbery, inviting the attention of rough characters from a past even his family doesn't know about. When his former life begins to bleed into his new one, Stall reveals he can do more than just make coffee.

The Hours (2002)

Stephen Daldry's film about three women in different eras each influenced by Virginia Woolf's novel *Mrs. Dalloway* offered brilliant performances by a trio of Hollywood's best actresses: Meryl Streep, Julianne Moore, and Nicole Kidman (who played Woolf herself and won an Oscar for it).

In the Loop (2009)

An extension of the British TV series *The Thick of It* and predating *Veep*, this profanely scabrous political satire directed and co-written by Armando Iannucci depicts both English and American politicians as cynical, petty, conniving opportunists. It's a dismally accurate view but a hilarious one, and the film features the decade's best, most creative swearing.

In the Mood for Love (2000)

Director Wong Kar-wai's love story cares little for the manufactured clichés of romance on film. Instead, it's a look at how guilt and cultural norms can pollute the heart. Apartment neighbors in 1962 Hong Kong, Chow (Tony Leung) and Su (Maggie Cheung) are married—to other people—and hardly looking for a scandal. But the two connect, and their feelings endure even as geographic and philosophical rifts keep them apart. In most love stories, the destination is the point. Here, it's that the timing of love matters as much as the feelings themselves.

Kiss Kiss Bang Bang (2005)

After writing *Lethal Weapon* and a handful of other noisy, ludicrous buddy-cop movies, Shane Black made his directorial debut skewering the genre, mocking the very conventions that Black helped create. A pulpy detective story à la Raymond Chandler, *Kiss Kiss Bang Bang* has a pre–*Iron Man* Robert Downey Jr. and a post-*Batman* Val Kilmer yukking it up with a Hollywood mystery and a screenplay full of screwy one-liners.

Lost in Translation (2003)

On the surface, *Lost in Translation* seems prepared to perpetuate the tired movie exercise of an influential older man attracting the gaze of a young woman. But the power dynamics of *Lost in Translation* are something else. As Bob Harris, an American movie star fading from the spotlight and hiding from a strained marriage in Tokyo, Bill Murray is subdued; as Charlotte, a married college grad, Scarlett Johansson grows to like Bob in spite of his work, not because of it. Their connection isn't quite romantic and isn't quite friendship. Instead, it's an abstract chemistry that director Sofia Coppola mines for emotion rather than titillation—less a love story and more a story about love.

Memento (2001)

Christopher Nolan collaborated with his brother Jonathan to make *Memento*, an ingeniously constructed neo-noir about a man with short-term memory loss trying to find his wife's killer—where two strands, one going backward and one forward, interact in an amazing way. More than a twisty thriller, it's about the tricks our memories play on us and the lies we tell ourselves.

Monsoon Wedding (2001)

Too often, popular culture uses the "other" of the unfamiliar for ridicule. In *Monsoon Wedding*, it's not a culture clash that divides the Verma family of Delhi, but a generational gap. Aditi (Vasundhara Das) is to be wed via arranged marriage to computer programmer Hemant (Parvin Dabas), as per the wishes of her traditional parents. While Aditi has questions about this, it's not the source of the humor or heart of the film, which spirals out into a series of mini-dramas surrounding their nuptials. *Monsoon* doesn't look to point out cultural differences. Instead, it's content to point out that families have problems no matter their background.

Napoleon Dynamite (2004)

ChapStick, llamas, and tots are just a few things worth talking about in *Napoleon Dynamite*, a cult film shot for a mere $400,000 that went on to gross more than $46 million worldwide. Director Jared Hess used his real-life upbringing in Preston, Idaho (he had six brothers and his mom owned llamas), to form the basis of the movie, about a nerdy teenager named Napoleon (Jon Heder) who encourages his friend Pedro (Efren Ramirez) to run for class president.

One Hour Photo (2002)

Robin Williams made several winning excursions into drama, but none proved as unsettling as Seymour Parrish, a photo lab technician who becomes obsessed with a family he knows only through their images. What could be a standard stalker thriller is elevated by Williams, who captures a desperately lonely man seduced by family photos—a pre-Instagram portrait of the perils of extreme social envy.

The Royal Tenenbaums (2001)

Wes Anderson firmly established his quirky, literary, vaguely French cinematic style with *The Royal Tenenbaums*, which chronicles the fraught reunion of the Tenenbaums, whose three children (played by Gwyneth Paltrow, Luke Wilson, and Ben Stiller) went from being early prodigies to aimless adults. The story, co-written with Owen Wilson (who also plays the Tenenbaums' neighbor, Eli Cash), was loosely inspired by the divorce of Anderson's own parents. Like Etheline Tenenbaum, his mother was an archaeologist.

Spirited Away (2002)

The fervor with which people love Hayao Miyazaki's imaginative animated films—particularly this one, about a girl who travels to the world of spirits—rivals the passion felt for Disney and Pixar (albeit without the same level of box office success). The inspired, magical weirdness of *Spirited Away* offers a glimpse at worlds most other animated films never even thought of.

Superbad (2007)

As teen movies go, most revolve around two things: getting the girl (or boy) and finally making it to that one incredible party. Millennials deserved their own version of this, and they got it with 2007's *Superbad*. Written by Seth Rogen and Evan Goldberg, this comedy still manages to skew the formula a bit, because underneath all the sex jokes and increasingly futile attempts to score booze, it's really a bromance between leads Evan (played by Michael Cera) and Seth (played by a scene-stealing Jonah Hill), who are both anxious about what college will mean for their friendship come fall. Producer Judd Apatow's signature style—the ability to deliver gross-out humor with touching earnestness—is all over this banger of a flick, and that's a big part of its charm. That, and one utterly epic scene set to Van Halen's "Panama"—because hey, if you could end the night of your life doing doughnuts in a cop car, why wouldn't you?

Synecdoche, New York (2008)

After scoring with screenplays for loopy, melancholy comedies like *Being John Malkovich*, *Adaptation*, and *Eternal Sunshine of the Spotless Mind*, Charlie Kaufman directed this one himself and out-weirded everything he'd done before, with Philip Seymour Hoffman as a theater director who creates a massive stage production based on his own life. Surrounded by whimsical, surreal details, it's an unforgettable piece of art about how life can slip away while you're not looking.

Training Day (2001)

Sometimes movie villains are formidable due to their physicality. Other times, it's their ability to remain a step ahead that prompts dread. As crooked cop Alonzo Harris in *Training Day*, Denzel Washington reigns as the king of the streets—a man who enforces the law when it happens to coincide with his own interests. Partnered with rookie Jake Hoyt (Ethan Hawke), he's a malicious Obi-Wan, teaching Hoyt not through his wisdom but through the perils of trying to follow his example. No one needs reminding that Washington is a terrific actor, but it's something else entirely to drape a character's presence over a film so soundly you feel it even when they're off-screen. *Training Day* refers to Hoyt's trial by fire, but it might as well double for Washington's master class in how to be a movie star.

The Triplets of Belleville (2003)

It wasn't Disney, Pixar, Studio Ghibli, or even DreamWorks that made one of the decade's most visually hilarious animated films, but Frenchman Sylvain Chomet. His gentle yet wild, almost dialogue-free adventure has something amusing or wonderful to look at in every frame—everything from surrealism to caricatures to Looney Tunes–style anarchy.

V for Vendetta (2005)

An Orwellian dystopia collides with costumed heroics in this politically fueled adaptation of the graphic novel by famed comic book writer Alan Moore and artist David Lloyd.

Valkyrie (2008)

Tom Cruise took a leap in deciding to portray German officer Claus von Stauffenberg, a man looking to sabotage the Nazi regime and assassinate Adolf Hitler. Based on a true story, you can guess he does not succeed, but that doesn't impede a genuinely suspenseful and well-crafted war sabotage thriller written by Nathan Alexander and Christopher McQuarrie. (Cruise and McQuarrie would later collaborate on the *Mission: Impossible* franchise.)

Wet Hot American Summer (2001)

The raunchy teen comedies of the 1980s get spoofed in this dry comedy from David Wain and Michael Showalter. Camp counselors (Janeane Garofalo, Paul Rudd, Showalter) juggle their crushes with the surreal intrusions of NASA debris and a cook (Christopher Meloni) who takes advice from a talking can of vegetables.

Y Tu Mamá También (2001)

The controversially sensual road movie that put Gael García Bernal and Diego Luna on the international map scored an Oscar nomination for writer-director Alfonso Cuarón. It's hard to believe he followed up this drug-and-sex-filled coming-of-age trip with a *Harry Potter* movie.

"Life is like the foam of the sea. You must dive into it."

— Y Tu Mamá También

ONCE (2007)

WRITTEN BY: John Carney

DIRECTED BY: John Carney

OTHER MOVIES DIRECTED BY JOHN CARNEY:
Begin Again (2013); *Sing Street* (2016)

In the mid-2000s, writer-director John Carney gathered up a handful of his musician (read: nonactor) friends and spent seventeen days and $150,000 filming *Once*. The indie musical dramedy tells the story of an aspiring musician (Glen Hansard) who, when he's not fixing vacuum cleaners, is busking for loose change in the streets of Dublin. One evening, his music catches the attention of a female flower-seller (Markéta Irglová) who has a vacuum in need of fixing and some musical chops of her own. The two form a fast friendship that flirts with possible romance, and their relationship plays out via the film's music, which acts as a narrator. Carney's film reinvigorated the movie musical and turned Hansard and Irglová into Oscar winners. Not bad for a movie that opted to forgo filming permits for the most part and grab shots when and where they could, infusing the movie with the kind of raw honesty that inspired the work of indie pioneers like John Cassavetes.

JOHN CARNEY OUTLINED THE FILM IN FIVE MINUTES.

In 2004, Carney—who was a bassist for the Frames, Hansard's band, from 1990 to 1993—was sitting in a café and missing his girlfriend, an actress who was living in London after landing a role that required her to relocate. In just five minutes, he wrote the outline for what would become *Once*, some of which was admittedly autobiographical.

IT WAS WRITTEN AS A VEHICLE FOR CILLIAN MURPHY.

Though Hansard's music was always going to provide the narrative of *Once*, Carney developed the project for Irish actor Cillian Murphy, with whom he had worked on 2001's *On the Edge*, and knew to be "quite a good singer." According to some sources, including Hansard, Murphy was reluctant to sign on partly because he wasn't sure he could pull off Hansard's songs.

HANSARD WASN'T INTERESTED IN STARRING IN THE FILM.

Though Hansard had a small role in Alan Parker's *The Commitments* (1991), he didn't consider himself an actor and wasn't particularly interested in becoming one. But *Once* would be full of his music and, as Carney told the *New York Times*, "He sells the songs better than anybody."

Still, as Hansard told CHUD.com, "I was terrified, for a few reasons. I didn't want to suck for [John's] sake, and I didn't want to suck for my own." Eventually, he relented—on one condition: If he did suck, Carney would immediately fire him.

MUCH OF IT WAS SHOT WITHOUT PERMITS.

Once was an indie film in the truest sense of the word. The *Washington Post* wrote, "The movie was shot guerrilla-style on the Dublin streets: no permits, no lighting, no production designers, no wardrobe, no paid extras, no location scouts, no production trailers—just a tiny crew using natural light, a couple of Sony-HD cameras and real places and people, including Hansard's friends and mother."

CARNEY PREDICTED THE MOVIE'S OSCAR WIN.

After filming the scene where Hansard and Irglová sing "Falling Slowly" in a music store, Hansard recalled that, "John said, joking, 'And the Oscar for Best Song goes to . . .' and we all started laughing because of the ridiculousness of the budget we were working on and the way we were shooting this film." On February 24, 2008, Hansard and Irglová did indeed take home the Oscar for Best Original Song.

HANSARD AND IRGLOVÁ WERE SUPPOSED TO DO THE DEED.

According to the *New York Times*, the film's title originally referred to a scene in which Hansard and Irglová's characters would sleep together—but only once. Though Carney wrote the scene, the actors didn't think it rang true to the unique nature of the characters' relationship (Irglová called it "so predictable"), so Carney scrapped it.

FREEZE-FRAME

One of *Once*'s most remarkable achievements is its intimacy; the way the film is acted and shot makes the viewer feel like part of the action. One way Carney extended the relatability of these characters was by never giving them names; they're simply known as Guy and Girl in the credits.

WRITTEN BY: Paul King and Hamish McColl
(based on the stories by Michael Bond)

DIRECTED BY: Paul King

OTHER MOVIES BY PAUL KING:
Bunny and the Bull (2009); *Paddington 2* (2017)

PADDINGTON

(2014)

Before his first screening of *Paddington* (2014), Michael Bond, the bear's creator, was anxious that the experience would wreck his night's sleep. "I was worrying that I'd be lying awake thinking: 'I've let Paddington down,'" he told the *Sunday Telegraph*. After seeing the film, he slept soundly. "There's so much in it that's magical," he said. "I'd give it full marks."

As the author of the Paddington Bear books, beginning with 1958's *A Bear Called Paddington*, Bond had more reason than most people to be apprehensive about the character's portrayal. But his feelings were shared by those who grew up with the beloved bear—and so was his glowing review. StudioCanal's live-action family flick, which follows the cub's intrepid quest to find a home in London, was a critical and commercial success (as was its 2017 sequel).

COLIN FIRTH WAS SUPPOSED TO VOICE PADDINGTON.
Just over five months before *Paddington*'s initial U.K. release in November 2014, Colin Firth relinquished his role as the voice of its eponymous character. "After a period of denial, we've chosen 'conscious uncoupling,'" the Oscar-winning actor told *Entertainment Weekly*. By all accounts Firth had already worked hard on the project and gotten along well with the rest of the team. But as director Paul King explained, they realized that Paddington was a "young, fluffy creature" who just didn't have "the voice of a very handsome older man." The more whimsical stylings of Ben Whishaw were a better match.

THE CREATOR OF PADDINGTON BEAR MAKES A CAMEO IN THE FILM.
When the Browns take Paddington home with them, their taxi passes a restaurant where a grandfatherly figure is seated alone. He raises his wineglass to Paddington, who doffs his hat in return. That man is Michael Bond.

HUGH BONNEVILLE'S DRAG SCENE CAUSED A RATINGS CONTROVERSY.
The British Board of Film Classification gave Paddington a PG rating partially due to "mild sex references," citing the scene in which Mr. Brown (Hugh Bonneville) dresses as a cleaning woman and charms a security guard after smuggling Paddington into the Geographers' Guild. Studio executives asked the board to revisit its assessment, prompting it to revise the phrasing to "innuendo." The BBFC also clarified that the "mild bad language" in its rating breakdown alluded to "a single mumbled use of 'bloody.'" It updated the warning to "infrequent mild bad language."

NICOLE KIDMAN PICKED UP SOME KNIFE TRICKS FOR HER ROLE.
To play the dastardly taxidermist Millicent Clyde, Kidman trained zealously to throw and twirl knives. Most of the evidence of those skills ended up on the cutting room floor, as they were deemed too scary for young viewers. "I just remember [producer David Heyman] going, 'It's a children's movie!'" she said.

THERE'S A REASON PADDINGTON IS MISSING HIS TRADEMARK WELLINGTONS.
It wasn't Bond who first put Wellington boots on Paddington, but Shirley Clarkson, who designed the first stuffed Paddington toys. Clarkson wanted her bears to be able to stand on their own, so she outfitted them in sturdy children's Wellies—size four—purchased from a nearby shoe store. In his 1976 book *Paddington Goes to the Sales*, Bond gave the boots a formal origin story: Paddington earns them as a reward for unwittingly helping a store manager sell some ugly pajamas. But since the film focuses on Paddington's early days, his paws were kept bare.

THE MOVIE HELPED BOOST MARMALADE SALES.
In the week following *Paddington*'s debut in U.K. theaters, sales of Robertson's brand marmalades increased by more than 20 percent, which manufacturers directly attributed to Paddington's penchant for the spread. This so-called "Paddington effect" appears to have popularized homemade marmalade, too: U.K. food distributor RH Amar later reported an unusually large spike in sales of liquid pectin, the ingredient that gives some marmalades their gel-like texture.

SEQUELS THAT WERE BETTER THAN THE ORIGINAL MOVIE

It's a widely shared opinion that movie sequels often fail to recapture the magic of the original cinematic masterpieces from which they sprang. But sometimes, a movie is merely a launching pad for greater films to follow, as these titles prove.

The Dark Knight (2008)
The second film in Christopher Nolan's *The Dark Knight* Trilogy is one of the most critically acclaimed superhero movies of all time. Heath Ledger's iconic version of the Joker cemented his place as one of cinema's greatest villains, and made Ledger the first (and so far only) person to posthumously win a Best Supporting Actor Oscar.

The Lord of the Rings: The Return of the King (2003)
The Return of the King was an epic ending to an epic trilogy. The third and final *Lord of the Rings* film won a staggering eleven Oscars at the 2004 Academy Awards, making it one of the most decorated films of all time.

Paddington 2 (2017)
Paddington (2014) was a hit, but its sequel took its success one step further. In the spring of 2021, it became the highest-reviewed movie on Rotten Tomatoes—that is, until one negative review dropped its rating from a perfect 100 percent to a still-very-impressive 99 percent.

Shrek 2 (2004)
The original *Shrek* made quite a splash when it hit theaters in 2001. Things only continued to go uphill for everyone's favorite ogre-donkey duo, with the 2004 sequel featuring improved animation, a larger cast, and a delightfully bonkers plot.

Star Wars: Episode V—The Empire Strikes Back (1980)
The Empire Strikes Back came out three years after 1977's *Star Wars*. Though viewers were initially unsure about its darker tone, it's now considered the star of the whole franchise (it probably helps that the film included Yoda's big debut). Despite the initial trepidation, *The Empire Strikes Back* was 1980's highest-grossing film, and it snagged multiple awards, including two Oscars and two Grammys.

Thor: Ragnarok (2017)
Though the second *Thor* film is one of the lowest-rated films in the Marvel Cinematic Universe, *Thor: Ragnarok* managed to turn things around for the character. Thanks to its abundance of zany humor and unexpected antics, the Marvel hero's third standalone movie, which was directed by Taika Waititi, is touted as one of the best in the franchise.

Toy Story 2 (1999)
When *Toy Story 2* hit theaters, fans of the original were even more impressed by its improved animation and tender plot. The fact that the beloved sequel even made its big debut is practically a miracle: The movie almost never saw the light of day, thanks to a technical error that nearly deleted the whole thing. Even more amazing? The two sequels that followed got even higher ratings from viewers.

PAN'S LABYRINTH

(2006)

WRITTEN BY: Guillermo del Toro

DIRECTED BY: Guillermo del Toro

OTHER MOVIES DIRECTED BY GUILLERMO DEL TORO: *The Devil's Backbone* (2001); *Hellboy* (2004); *The Shape of Water* (2017); *Nightmare Alley* (2021); *Pinocchio* (2022)

Between his modest comic book hits *Hellboy* and *Hellboy II: The Golden Army*, imaginative Mexican filmmaker Guillermo del Toro made a Spanish-language film that was considerably darker: *Pan's Labyrinth*, a horror-tinged fairy tale set in 1944 Spain, with the country under fascist rule. Young Ofelia (Ivana Baquero) begins exploring the countryside and encounters a mystical landscape, complete with creatures that act as both friend and foe. As Ofelia grows more enchanted, her twin realities threaten to collide.

Like many of del Toro's films, *Pan's Labyrinth* is as much a political allegory as it is a gothic fantasy. The heady mix of whimsy and violence wasn't everyone's cup of tea, but it won enough fans to make $83.25 million worldwide and receive six Oscar nominations (it won three).

IT'S A COMPANION PIECE TO *THE DEVIL'S BACKBONE*.

Del Toro intended *Pan's Labyrinth* to be a thematic complement to *The Devil's Backbone*, his 2001 film set in Spain in 1939. The movies have a lot of similarities in their structure and setup, but del Toro says that the events of September 11, 2001—which occurred five months after *The Devil's Backbone* opened in Spain, and two months before it opened in the U.S.—changed his perspective. "The world changed," del Toro said. "Everything I had to say about brutality and innocence changed."

IT CEMENTED DEL TORO'S HATRED OF HORSES.

The director is fond of all manner of strange, terrifying monsters, but real live horses? He hates 'em. "They are absolutely nasty motherfuckers," he said on the DVD commentary. His antipathy toward our equine friends predated *Pan's Labyrinth*, but the particular horses he worked with here—ill-tempered and difficult, apparently—intensified those feelings. "I never liked horses," he says, "but after this, I hate them."

THE PLOT WAS ORIGINALLY EVEN DARKER.

In del Toro's first conception of the story, it was about a married pregnant woman who meets the Faun in the labyrinth, falls in love with him, and lets him sacrifice her baby on faith that she, the baby, and the Faun will all be together in the afterlife and the labyrinth will thrive again. "It was a shocking tale," del Toro said.

THE SHAPES AND COLORS ARE THEMATICALLY RELEVANT.

Del Toro pointed out that scenes with Ofelia tend to have circles and curves and use warm colors, while scenes with Vidal and the war have more straight lines and use cold colors. Over the course of the film, the two opposites gradually intrude on each other.

DEL TORO WROTE THE ENGLISH SUBTITLES HIMSELF.

After being disappointed by the way the translators handled *The Devil's Backbone* ("subtitles for the thinking impaired"), the Mexican filmmaker, who speaks fluent English, did the job himself for *Pan's Labyrinth*. "I took about a month with a friend and an assistant working on them, measuring them, so that it doesn't feel like you're watching a subtitled film," he said.

IT APPARENTLY MADE STEPHEN KING SQUIRM.

Del Toro reports that he had the pleasure of sitting next to the esteemed horror novelist at a screening in New England, and that King squirmed mightily during the Pale Man scene.

FREEZE-FRAME

If you look closely at the banister in the Captain's mansion, you'll see the Faun's head in the design. It's a subtle reinforcement of the idea that the fantasy world is bleeding into the real one.

PARASITE

(2019)

WRITTEN BY: Bong Joon Ho and Han Jin-won

DIRECTED BY: Bong Joon Ho

OTHER MOVIES DIRECTED BY BONG JOON HO:
The Host (2006); *Mother* (2009);
Snowpiercer (2013); *Okja* (2017)

Parasite was both the first non–English language film to win the Academy Award for Best Picture and one of only three films in history to win both that and the Palme d'Or, Cannes's highest honor. The movie dazzled audiences with its hilarious, terrifying, genre-straddling social commentary and moral ambiguity. The South Korean movie follows a poor family who con their way into working for a rich one, posing as unrelated tutors and household staff to take what they can. However, they aren't the only ones hiding the truth.

BONG JOON-HO'S EXPERIENCE AS A TUTOR INSPIRED PART OF *PARASITE*.

While a lot of *Parasite* was informed by Bong Joon Ho's own experience working as a tutor for a wealthy family, he was also inspired by the story of Christine and Léa Papin, French sisters who worked as live-in maids in the 1930s. On February 2, 1933, the sisters killed the wife and daughter of their employer in Le Mans, France. While both sisters were found guilty of murder, their case became symbolic of class struggle and the put-upon, oppressed working classes rising up.

THERE'S MORE CGI IN THE MOVIE THAN MANY VIEWERS EVEN NOTICED.

Of the approximately 960 shots in the film, 400 contain visual effects. While the ground floor and garden of the house featured in the film were built on an outdoor movie lot, the second floor is entirely a CGI construct when seen from outside. Bong also had a 3D version of the whole mansion on his iPad, which he would use to meticulously plan camera placements and actors' positions. "He was able to control the camera and the actors, as if it was a video game," editor Jinmo Yang told Frame.io.

SOME OF THE MOVIE'S DETAILS WERE CHANGED FOR INTERNATIONAL AUDIENCES.

In the international version of the film, Ki-woo Kim's faked diploma is from Oxford University; in the Korean release, it comes from Yonsei University. Yonsei is one of the most prestigious universities in South Korea, but the filmmakers needed an institution that mass audiences would immediately recognize. Similarly, they changed references to the Korean messaging app KakaoTalk to WhatsApp.

THE STUDIO WORRIED THAT AUDIENCES MIGHT BE OFFENDED BY THE MOVIE'S COMMENTARY.

When presented with the final cut of the film, marketers were worried that audiences would be offended by the idea that they themselves were the parasites. As Bong told *Rolling Stone*, "There was concern around a particular line that Mr. Park says . . . about subway riders having 'a particular smell.' Most people would be coming out of the movie and getting on the subway to go home, they told me, 'You're going to offend most of the audience!'" The purpose of the line is to show how absurd the Parks' life is—of Seoul's 9.7 million people, 7 million ride the subway every day, so it's a particularly ridiculous piece of snobbery—but there might have been a murmur or two.

BONG FELT THAT A "CRUEL AND SAD" ENDING WAS THE ONLY WAY TO GO.

While the ending is almost left ambiguous, even optimistic, with Ki-woo outlining his "plan," Bong opted for the final shot of the film to destroy that ambiguity and make it clear he was destined for failure, showing the inescapable nature of his situation—broke, subterranean, hopeless. "It's quite cruel and sad," he told Vulture, "but I thought it was being real and honest with the audience. You know and I know—we all know that this kid isn't going to be able to buy that house. I just felt that frankness was right for the film, even though it's sad."

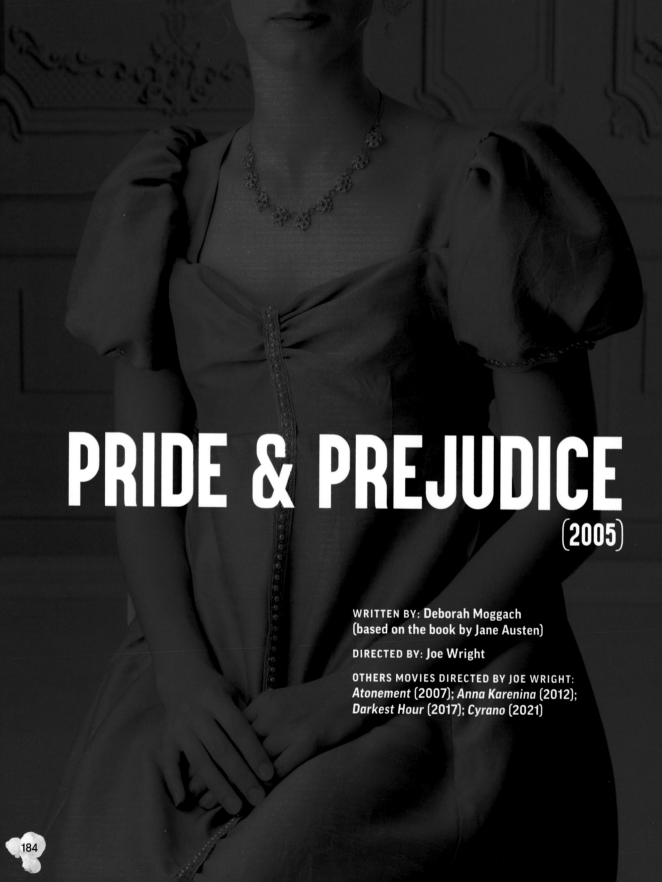

PRIDE & PREJUDICE

(2005)

WRITTEN BY: Deborah Moggach
(based on the book by Jane Austen)

DIRECTED BY: Joe Wright

OTHERS MOVIES DIRECTED BY JOE WRIGHT:
Atonement (2007); *Anna Karenina* (2012);
Darkest Hour (2017); *Cyrano* (2021)

Unless you've been living under a rock for the past two hundred years, you likely know the main plot of Jane Austen's *Pride and Prejudice*: Elizabeth Bennet is a strong-willed young woman with no inheritance but big ideas and isn't interested in being married off and losing her independence (she has four sisters who are more than happy to play that role). Then along comes the snobbish, and very rich, Mr. Darcy, who offends and repels, then slowly begins to beguile Lizzy. Despite various passionate feelings and many obstacles, the two eventually find their happily ever after.

For centuries, Mr. Darcy has been held up as a kind of romantic ideal—which makes casting a real, live human to play him a tricky business. But while shooting the scene in *Pride & Prejudice* in which Darcy (Matthew Macfadyen) makes his way across a foggy field and proposes to Elizabeth (Keira Knightley) in the dawn light, director Joe Wright reportedly heard a makeup artist whisper, "I wish that was my life."

Soon after *Pride & Prejudice* arrived in theaters in 2005, it became clear that she wasn't alone. Sure, some people still prefer the Colin Firth–starring miniseries from 1995, and Jane Austen purists like to wail about the omission of certain details from the book. But Wright's adaptation birthed a whole new generation of fans, and it also caused plenty of longtime Austen aficionados to fall in love with what screenwriter Deborah Moggach considers the "muddy-hem version" of Austen's classic novel.

JOE WRIGHT HAD NEVER READ JANE AUSTEN'S *PRIDE AND PREJUDICE*.

When Wright was offered the director's chair for *Pride & Prejudice*—his first feature film—he'd never read Jane Austen's book. And the only adaptation he had watched was the 1940 movie starring Laurence Olivier and Greer Garson. He didn't think he'd care much for the story but, as he told the *Harvard Crimson*, "I took the script to the pub and by about page 60, I was weeping into my pint of lager."

WRIGHT WORRIED THAT KEIRA KNIGHTLEY WAS TOO BEAUTIFUL TO PLAY ELIZABETH BENNET.

Knightley was both the right age to play Elizabeth—and famous enough to satisfy producers' desire to cast someone with name recognition. Wright, however, worried that Knightley's beauty might overshadow Elizabeth's more important characteristics. When they met, however, Wright realized Knightley's "scruffy independent spirit" was much like Elizabeth's. "[She] was not going to say what she thought you wanted her to say," Wright told *Film Journal International*. "She was going to say exactly what she thought."

MATTHEW MACFADYEN WAS THE FIRST CHOICE TO PLAY MR. DARCY.

Wright was a "huge fan" of Matthew Macfadyen, who was just the type of "great big hunk of a guy" the director envisioned playing Fitzwilliam Darcy. "He was our first choice," producer Paul Webster told the *New York Times*. However, knowing the studio would be keener on a bigger name, they conducted a full search anyway. "It was exhausting and pointless, as we came full circle back to Matthew," Wright told Script Factory.

EMMA THOMPSON DID SOME UNCREDITED SCRIPT DOCTORING.

Wright connected with Emma Thompson, who won a Best Adapted Screenplay Oscar for writing *Sense and Sensibility* (1995), for advice on adapting Austen. She suggested they travel to Hampstead Heath. "She acted bits out for me," Wright recounted. She edited the script, too; Thompson wrote all the dialogue where Charlotte tells Elizabeth she's engaged to Mr. Collins.

PROFANITY PERSUADED JUDI DENCH TO PLAY LADY CATHERINE DE BOURGH.

Wright didn't try to downplay Lady Catherine de Bourgh's general unpleasantness when offering the role to Judi Dench—in fact, he used it to his advantage. "I love it when you play a bitch," he wrote her. The tactic worked.

AMERICAN AUDIENCES SAW A DIFFERENT ENDING THAN BRITISH VIEWERS.

American test audiences reacted more positively to what Moggach called the "rather sickly scene" where the "incandescently happy" Darcys kiss on a bench at Pemberley, so it was only released in the U.S., which caused some controversy.

Many members of the Jane Austen Society of North America abhorred the mawkish ending, which society president Elsa Solender griped "insults the audience with its banality, and ought to be cut before release." Meanwhile, British fans launched a petition to have the scene added back in. "What did us poor Austen aficionados . . . do to deserve such injustice?" it read. Fortunately for all sappy romantics, the contentious scene is now freely watchable on YouTube.

PERFECTLY WONDERFUL CASTING DECISIONS THAT UNNECESSARILY INFURIATED FANS

Joe Wright's *Pride & Prejudice* was criticized from the get-go as stars Keira Knightley and Matthew Macfadyen committed the unforgivable sins of not being Jennifer Ehle and Colin Firth, who starred as Elizabeth Bennet and Mr. Darcy in the beloved BBC miniseries. Shocking!

Fannish enthusiasm can be a wonderful thing, but sometimes it can go a bit too far—as these actors discovered.

Daniel Craig // *Casino Royale* (2006)

In 2005, people couldn't handle a blond guy being cast as James Bond. Daniel Craig's general appearance was also an issue—the site DanielCraigIsNotBond.com wondered how "a short, blonde actor with the rough face of a professional boxer . . . [could] pull off the role of a tall, dark, handsome and suave secret agent." An actor "with his looks," the site suggested, should instead star in a *Caddyshack* prequel. Most of the world left the "James Blonde" hatred behind when *Casino Royale* proved Craig's critics wrong. The actor went on to have the longest tenure of any Bond—fifteen years—concluding with 2021's *No Time to Die*.

Robert Pattinson // *Twilight* (2008)

The *Twilight* Saga launched Robert Pattinson to the heights of teen heartthrob-dom, but it's easy to forget that when he was cast, many people were not pleased. French actor Gaspard Ulliel was a fan favorite choice to fill the role, a fact referenced by author Stephenie Meyer in a blog post where she named future Superman Henry Cavill as her preferred actor. Pattinson described the fan reaction as "unanimous unhappiness" to MTV. He told *Entertainment Weekly* that he "stopped reading [blogs] after I saw the signatures saying 'Please, anyone else.'"

Jennifer Lawrence // *The Hunger Games* (2012)

The biggest complaint against Jennifer Lawrence being cast as *The Hunger Games*' heroine Katniss Everdeen, who comes from the impoverished District 12? She wasn't skinny enough. Her hair color was also a point of contention, with some fans dismissing Lawrence as a "beach bunny blonde." In an interview with *Teen Vogue*, Lawrence said she understood the casting backlash: "The cool thing about Katniss is that every fan has such a personal relationship with her, and they understand and know her in a singular way. I'm a massive fan too, so I get it." The *Hunger Games* franchise went on to earn close to $3 billion globally.

Heath Ledger // *The Dark Knight* (2008)

Heath Ledger being cast as the Joker has become the litmus test for fans overreacting to a casting decision. Much of the backlash against Ledger stemmed from his roles in teen-centric comedies like *10 Things I Hate About You*. One Redditor reacted to the news by saying, "Heath Ledger has the charisma of a lettuce leaf." Another plainly called it "probably the worst casting of all time." The Academy, however, had the final say when they awarded Ledger a posthumous Best Supporting Actor Oscar for the part.

Michael Keaton // *Batman* (1989)

Ledger wasn't the first Batman actor to suffer the rage of fanboys: When Michael Keaton was cast as the Caped Crusader back in the late eighties, fans sent physical complaint letters (oh, pre-web days) to the studio—by one account, more than fifty thousand of them. The primary complaints: Keaton was a comedian, and he wasn't physically intimidating enough. A 1988 article in the *Toronto Star* noted that Batman "may turn out to be a wimp," as Keaton was "no Sylvester Stallone." Director Tim Burton explained that "I met with a number of very good, square-jawed actors, but the bottom line was that I just couldn't see any of them putting on a bat suit."

Renée Zellweger // *Bridget Jones's Diary* (2001)

Bridget Jones's Diary fans couldn't imagine the Texas-born Renée Zellweger playing Bridget Jones, a modern-day version of *Pride and Prejudice*'s Elizabeth Bennet. "The criticism has been hurtful," noted Zellweger in a 2000 interview with the *Guardian*. Co-star Hugh Grant came to Zellweger's defense, telling *Entertainment Weekly*, "She's very funny, and she's been living in England a long time now, mastering the accent. It'll be a triumph." The time with a vocal coach—Barbara Berkeley, who worked with Gwyneth Paltrow for *Shakespeare in Love*—paid off, and *Bridget Jones's Diary* became a modern rom-com classic.

THE PRINCESS BRIDE (1987)

WRITTEN BY: William Goldman
(Based on the book by William Goldman)

DIRECTED BY: Rob Reiner

OTHER MOVIES DIRECTED BY ROB REINER:
This Is Spınal Tap (1984); *Stand by Me* (1986);
When Harry Met Sally . . . (1989);
Misery (1990); *A Few Good Men* (1992);
The American President (1995)

William Goldman wrote a fairy tale for the ages with *The Princess Bride*, which Rob Reiner mounted for the big screen in 1987. The family adventure-comedy tells the story of a beautiful young woman named Buttercup (Robin Wright) who is madly in love with a lowly farmhand named Westley (Cary Elwes). So that he can ask for her hand, Westley sets sail for a faraway land in order to build his fortune so that they can be together. Alas, his ship is attacked by pirates (it happens), and Westley is presumed dead. Buttercup, meanwhile, is set to marry Prince Humperdinck (Chris Sarandon), but is kidnapped just days before the wedding. What follows is a mad dash for the best man to save Buttercup—and win her love.

FOR YEARS, PEOPLE TRIED—AND FAILED—TO MAKE THE MOVIE.

At one point or another, Robert Redford, Norman Jewison, John Boorman, and François Truffaut all tried to get William Goldman's book made into a movie, but due to a series of unrelated incidents—"green-lighters" getting fired, production houses closing—it languished for years. (In one of these proto–*Princess Brides*, a then-unknown Arnold Schwarzenegger was supposed to play Fezzik.) After several false starts, Goldman bought back the rights to the book so that he could control the process.

ANDRÉ THE GIANT HAD AN UNCONVENTIONAL METHOD FOR LEARNING HIS LINES.

Reiner and Goldman met André the Giant, then a famous wrestler, at a bar in Paris to discuss the role of Fezzik.. "I brought him up to the hotel room to audition him. He read this three-page scene, and I couldn't understand one word he said," Reiner recalled. "I go, 'Oh my God, what am I going to do? He's perfect physically for the part, but I can't understand him!' So I recorded his entire part on tape, exactly how I wanted him to do it, and he studied the tape. He got pretty good!"

WILLIAM GOLDMAN WAS INCREDIBLY NERVOUS ON THE SET.

Of all the projects he'd written and worked on—which included the Academy Award–winning *Butch Cassidy and the Sundance Kid*—Goldman loved *The Princess Bride* best of all. This manifested itself as extreme nervousness about the project. Reiner invited Goldman to be on set for the duration of the filming, which Goldman normally didn't like to do, but made an exception here. From the get-go, he proved to be a bit of a nuisance. The first couple takes were plagued by a barely audible chanting, which turned out to be Goldman praying things would go well. And when Robin Wright's character's dress (intentionally) caught on fire, he panicked, yelling, "Oh my god! Her dress is on fire!"—even though he had written that into the script.

WALLACE SHAWN WAS BRILLIANT, BUT ALWAYS ON EDGE.

After learning from his agent that Reiner had originally wanted Danny DeVito for the role of Vizzini the Sicilian, Shawn was racked with insecurity, perpetually convinced that he was going to be fired after every bad take. "Danny is inimitable," Shawn said. "Each scene we did, I pictured how he would have done it and I knew I could never possibly have done it the way he could have done it."

THE DUEL BETWEEN WESTLEY AND INIGO WAS EXCRUCIATINGLY RESEARCHED AND REHEARSED.

Goldman spent months researching seventeenth-century sword-fighting manuals to craft Westley and Inigo's duel; all the references the characters make to specific moves and styles are completely accurate. Elwes and Mandy Patinkin, who played Inigo Montoya—neither of whom had much fencing experience (Patinkin had learned while at Juilliard, but that was ten years earlier)—spent more months training to perfect the sport, both right- and left-handed.

ONE ON-SCREEN INJURY WASN'T FAKED.

As soon as Westley recognizes Count Rugen as the six-fingered man, the script calls for the count to knock our hero unconscious with the butt of his sword. Christopher Guest, who played Rugen, was naturally reluctant to really hit Elwes for fear of hurting him. Unfortunately, this reticence was reading on-screen. Finally, Elwes suggested Guest just go for it, at least tapping him on the head to get the reaction timing right. The tap came a little too hard, however, and Elwes was knocked unconscious; he later awoke in the ER. It's that take, with Elwes actually passing out, that appears in the film.

CLOSE-UP

In an alternate ending that was eventually cut, Fred Savage—who plays the initially reluctant audience to Peter Falk's reading of *The Princess Bride*—goes to his window after his grandfather has left and sees Fezzik, Inigo, Westley, and Buttercup all on their white horses.

189

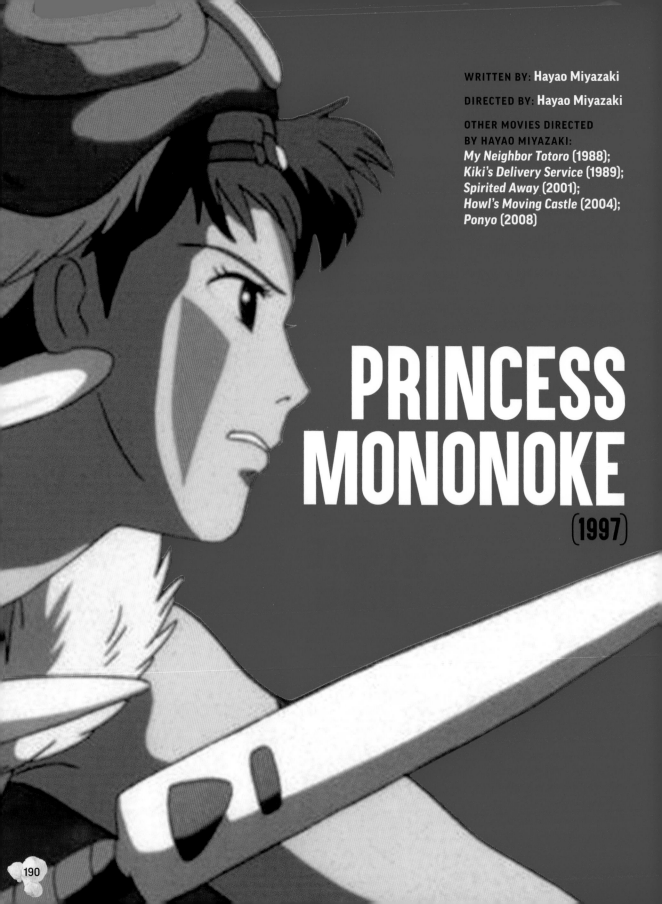

WRITTEN BY: **Hayao Miyazaki**

DIRECTED BY: **Hayao Miyazaki**

OTHER MOVIES DIRECTED
BY HAYAO MIYAZAKI:
My Neighbor Totoro (1988);
Kiki's Delivery Service (1989);
Spirited Away (2001);
Howl's Moving Castle (2004);
Ponyo (2008)

PRINCESS MONONOKE

(1997)

*P*rincess Mononoke sounds like a charming foreign family film. And that would be a fair assumption, if you were going off director Hayao Miyazaki's previous animated hits like *Kiki's Delivery Service* and *My Neighbor Totoro*. But *Princess Mononoke* was neither cuddly nor innocent. The movie's violent tale of Ashitaka, an exiled prince trying to keep the peace between warring animals and humans, was a stark departure from Miyazaki's previous work. It was also his most commercially and critically successful movie to date when it opened in 1997.

The film's phenomenal profits in Japan helped carry it over to America, where Miyazaki was known only among hard-core animation geeks. Today he enjoys a more established international reputation, and it's all largely thanks to *Princess Mononoke* and *Spirited Away*, which was released four years later.

HAYAO MIYAZAKI WAS INSPIRED BY JOHN FORD WESTERNS.

The movie's production notes reveal that Miyazaki wanted his frontier community of Tatara Ba (or "Iron Town") to look like it "could be at the edge of any wilderness" in the world. So he turned to one of his favorite directors: John Ford. Miyazaki used classic Ford westerns like *My Darling Clementine* to inform the look and feel of Tatara Ba, a town full of "characters from outcast groups and oppressed minorities who rarely, if ever, appear in Japanese films."

THE MOVIE WAS ONLY 10 PERCENT COMPUTER GENERATED.

Despite the success of *Toy Story* in 1995, Miyazaki remained wary of computer-generated animation. "Computers are really just an electronic pen or pencil, and I like regular pencils better," the director told Hollywood.com. As a result, just 10 percent of *Princess Mononoke* is CGI. The vast majority of the movie is composed of hand-drawn cels—approximately 144,000 of them in total.

IT BROKE BOX OFFICE RECORDS IN JAPAN.

When *Princess Mononoke* hit theaters, *E. T.* had been the reigning champion of the Japanese box office for more than a decade. But Miyazaki's animated epic set a new record with its 18.25 billion yen, or about $134 million, haul. Unfortunately, the movie didn't stay on the throne for long. *Titanic* arrived mere months later and reset the bar yet again.

NEIL GAIMAN TWEAKED THE SCRIPT FOR AMERICAN AUDIENCES.

Once the movie was picked up for U.S. distribution, the studio hired British fantasy writer Neil Gaiman to adapt the script for English-speaking audiences. Gaiman had to add dialogue explaining Japanese cultural references that likely wouldn't register with audiences, such as the significance of Ashitaka cutting his hair. He also altered characters so they translated better abroad. For instance, in the original Japanese script, Jigo complains that a bowl of soup tastes like "water," which is a cutting insult in Japan. That's hardly a burn by American standards, though, so Gaiman made it "donkey piss."

THE MOVIE IS SECRETLY ABOUT LEPROSY.

Princess Mononoke fans have long touted a theory about the workers in Iron Town. When Ashitaka first meets them, they explain that they fled brothels for the Iron Town factory, because it's one of the few places where they are accepted. Several are covered from head to toe in bandages. Although the Japanese script says they suffer from *gyobyo* or "an incurable disease," the fan theory claims they're actually afflicted with leprosy. Miyazaki finally responded to this idea in 2016. His verdict? It's all true.

"While making *Princess Mononoke*, I thought I had to depict people who are ill with what's clearly called an incurable disease, but who are living as best they can," he explained. He apparently even visited a sanatorium in Tokyo to talk with patients about their experiences.

PULP FICTION

(1994)

WRITTEN BY: Quentin Tarantino and Roger Avary

DIRECTED BY: Quentin Tarantino

OTHER MOVIES DIRECTED BY QUENTIN TARANTINO:
Reservoir Dogs (1992); *Jackie Brown* (1997);
Kill Bill: Vol. 1 and 2 (2003, 2004); *Inglourious
Basterds* (2009); *Django Unchained* (2012);
Once Upon a Time . . . in Hollywood (2019)

Quentin Tarantino synthesized all the genres he watched and rewatched endlessly as a video store clerk at Video Archives, from crime sagas to Hong Kong thrillers, then dropped the bloody and brash *Pulp Fiction* in a year when Hollywood studios were obsessed with the likes of more traditional fare like *Forrest Gump*. In the process, he managed to change movies forever.

The film is a twist-laden account of various hoods in and around Los Angeles, from hit-men odd couple Jules (Samuel L. Jackson) and Vincent (John Travolta) to crooked boxer Butch (Bruce Willis) to a terrifying basement dweller known only as the Gimp (Steve Hibbert). *Pulp Fiction* is a cinematic contradiction—a carefully executed ode to the cheap and quickly written crime paperbacks that once filled drugstores. In the process, Tarantino launched a new genre of his own and had studio execs desperate for a voice "like Tarantino's." As the endless copycats proved, there's only one.

THE FILM WAS RELEASED IN SOUTH KOREA, JAPAN, AND EVEN SLOVAKIA BEFORE IT ARRIVED IN AMERICA.

Pulp Fiction played at the Cannes Film Festival in May 1994. It was shown at other festivals around the world, from Munich to Locarno, before hitting American shores on September 23, 1994, at the New York Film Festival. The film was released in South Korea, Japan, and Slovakia before it officially opened in the U.S. The feature rolled out across Asia and Europe throughout 1994 and 1995.

THE MOVIE MADE MORE THAN $100 MILLION, BUT IT TOOK A WHILE.

Pulp Fiction ended up being a monster hit, but it took some time to get there. The film was in release for approximately 190 days before it finally pulled in $100 million in the U.S. For comparison, it took *Forrest Gump*, which was released just a few months prior to *Pulp Fiction*, a little over two weeks to hit the same milestone.

VINCENT VEGA'S 1964 CHEVY CHEVELLE MALIBU WAS STOLEN.

Travolta's character had a sweet ride—which, in real life, belonged to Tarantino—and it was such a hot rod that it was stolen soon after the film's release. It wasn't found for nearly two decades, when cops happened upon some men stripping a Malibu. An investigation determined the vehicle belonged to them, but also that there was a cloned VIN on a Malibu in the wild. When that was hunted down, they learned it was Tarantino's.

UMA THURMAN WASN'T TARANTINO'S FIRST PICK FOR MIA WALLACE.

Virginia Madsen, Marisa Tomei, Patricia Arquette, Jennifer Beals, Alfre Woodard, Phoebe Cates, and Robin Wright were all reportedly in the mix—with Tarantino's original favorite supposedly being Michelle Pfeiffer.

HONEY BUNNY WAS NAMED AFTER AN ACTUAL RABBIT.

Honey Bunny belonged to Linda Chen, who typed up Tarantino's handwritten script for *Pulp Fiction*. In lieu of payment, she asked Tarantino to watch her rabbit when she went on location; Tarantino wouldn't do it, and when the rabbit later died, he named Amanda Plummer's character after Chen's pet.

JULES WAS WRITTEN FOR SAMUEL L. JACKSON, BUT HE ALMOST LOST THE PART.

Tarantino very much had Jackson in mind for the role of Jules, but when he auditioned Paul Calderón, he was so struck by the actor's performance that he very nearly hired him. But studio executives urged Tarantino to reconsider, so he had both Calderón and Jackson read again. Calderón was great, but Jackson killed it and got the part. (Calderón played a smaller role.)

ROBERT RODRIGUEZ DIRECTED PARTS OF THE FILM.

When Tarantino is on-screen as Jimmie, someone else had to be behind the camera—and that someone was Robert Rodriguez. The pair later teamed up for a number of other projects, including *From Dusk till Dawn* (1996) and *Grindhouse* (2007).

PULP FICTION BY THE NUMBERS

The film contains 265 F-bombs.

Even that hefty number isn't Tarantino's highest (*Reservoir Dogs* used the expletive 269 times). Still, the film was the big "F-word" winner of 1994, as no other film released that year even came close to that amount of profanity.

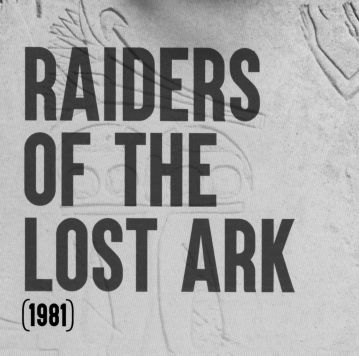

RAIDERS OF THE LOST ARK

(1981)

WRITTEN BY: Lawrence Kasdan, George Lucas, and Philip Kaufman

DIRECTED BY: Steven Spielberg

OTHER MOVIES DIRECTED BY STEVEN SPIELBERG:
Jaws (1975); *The Color Purple* (1985); *Hook* (1991); *Jurassic Park*
(1993); *Schindler's List* (1993); *Saving Private Ryan* (1998);
Lincoln (2012); *West Side Story* (2021)

With George Lucas and Steven Spielberg ushering in the summer blockbuster with *Star Wars* and *Jaws*, respectively, anticipation ran high for their first collaboration. Released in 1981, *Raiders of the Lost Ark* didn't disappoint: Led by Harrison Ford as whip-cracking and whip-smart archaeologist Indiana Jones racing to beat the Nazis to the Ark of the Covenant, the action classic offered cliff-hangers, lost treasures, and cutting-edge filmmaking—all of it an homage to the adventure serials of the 1940s Spielberg and Lucas consumed like candy. In the decades to follow, countless movies would pay tribute of their own to *Raiders'* action formula, though few have ever done it better.

ONE DOG INSPIRED BOTH INDIANA JONES AND CHEWBACCA.

While developing the film with Spielberg and screenwriter Lawrence Kasdan, Lucas named the main character "Indiana Smith." But Spielberg protested that it was too similar to the 1966 Steve McQueen western *Nevada Smith* and requested a change. The three agreed that the last name should be as universal and nondescript as "Smith," so Lucas threw out "Jones" as a possibility. Indiana came from Lucas's dog, an Alaskan Malamute named Indiana. The big, hairy pup was also the inspiration for Chewbacca from *Star Wars*.

THE BOULDER SCENE ALMOST WASN'T A SCENE AT ALL.

A boulder nearly crushing Indy as he escaped from the temple with the idol in the opening was always part of the script, but it was originally only supposed to be a minor detail. When production designer Norman Reynolds brought the fiberglass boulder onto set, Spielberg fell in love with it so much that he decided to extend the rolling boulder another fifty feet to make it a major part at the end of the thrilling scene.

SPIELBERG DIDN'T HAVE ENOUGH SNAKES IN THE WELL OF SOULS.

Indy is famously afraid of snakes, but Spielberg was most definitely not. When shooting the scene where Indy and Sallah descend into the Well of Souls to uncover the Ark—only to find it completely covered in slithering asps (though really it was a combination of boa constrictors, pythons, and cobras)—the production originally had about two thousand snakes on set at their disposal. But that didn't satisfy the director, because the two thousand snakes didn't cover the entire set. Spielberg then estimated they would need at least seven thousand *more* snakes to make it believably scary, so he had the producers raid all the pet shops in London (where they were shooting the film at Elstree Studios) and elsewhere around Europe to get enough of the slithering reptiles.

IT TOOK DAYS TO GET THE MONKEY TO DELIVER A NAZI SALUTE.

The insert scene where the small capuchin monkey gives the Nazi salute to the German spies was part of the film's postproduction pickup schedule—an allotted time to reshoot or tweak scenes from the principal production shoot—supervised by Lucas at Elstree Studios in London. Despite the animal trainers training the monkey to perform the move prior to the shoot, they couldn't get him to do it during a take. At first, the trainers tried tapping on the animal's head to get a reaction, but days dragged on and the monkey didn't do the proper salute. Finally, the filmmakers resorted to dangling grapes with fishing line just off camera to provoke the little guy, and that was how they finally got a useable take.

10

OBVIOUS MOVIE ANACHRONISMS

Whether by choice, by laziness on the part of those on research duty, or a genuine mistake, cinema is rife with historical anachronisms. Case in point: A map illustrating Indiana Jones's travels in *Raiders of the Lost Ark* sees the intrepid archaeologist passing near Thailand on his way to Nepal—which is a bit odd, considering the movie is set in 1936, and Thailand was called "Siam" until 1939. Here are some others.

1 The Aviator (2004)

Chocolate chip cookies were invented by Ruth Graves Wakefield in the 1930s. Which means that Howard Hughes—who ordered "ten chocolate chip cookies, medium chips, not too close to the outside" in a scene from Martin Scorsese's *The Aviator*, which takes place in 1928—will have to wait a while.

2 Back to the Future (1985)

Back to the Future's Marty McFly, stuck in 1955, probably didn't fix the DeLorean and hop forward to 1958 so he could pick up a Gibson ES-345 guitar (introduced that year) to use for his rockin' rendition of "Johnny B. Goode" at Hill Valley High's Enchantment Under the Sea dance.

3 Braveheart (1995)

Though it's one of the best-known movies about Scottish history, *Braveheart* director-star Mel Gibson probably should have ditched Scotland's most iconic piece of clothing, the kilt. The modern-day kilt, according to Hugh Trevor-Roper's *The Highland Tradition of Scotland*, "is unknown before the 18th century . . . Far from being a traditional Highland dress, it was invented by an Englishman after the Union of 1707; and the differentiated 'clan tartans' are an even later invention." Needless to say, thirteenth-century freedom fighter William Wallace would not have been wearing one.

4 Forrest Gump (1994)

Forrest Gump's galumphing through twentieth-century history took him to the Vietnam War, into President Kennedy's White House, and into the orbit of Apple. Lieutenant Dan (Gary Sinese) invested Gump's shrimping money into the future tech behemoth, which would make Gump a millionaire if he still had the stock today. Except it looks like Lieutenant Dan might have gotten got; the letter Gump received from Apple thanking him for his investment is dated 1975, but Apple didn't go public until 1980. (Also, the company didn't start using the logo seen at the top of the letter until 1977.)

5 Gladiator (2000)

In the big battle scene that kicks off *Gladiator*, one of Maximus's soldiers is of the canine variety—specifically, a German Shepherd. In our non-movie world, German shepherds didn't come into existence as a breed until the late 1800s.

6 The Godfather (1972)

Per Francis Ford Coppola on the DVD commentary for *The Godfather*, it was insufficient attention paid during second unit shots that allowed this late 1940s–early 1950s crime drama to suffer an accidental invasion of the hippies. In a scene where Michael Corleone goes to Vegas, you can see a few distinctly out-of-place men hanging out in the background.

7 The Green Mile (1999)

Though set in 1935, Frank Darabont's *The Green Mile* has death by electric chair as Louisiana's preferred method of execution. The chair would not replace the gallows in that state until the early 1940s.

8 The Hurt Locker (2009)

Early on in Kathryn Bigelow's Oscar-winning war drama *The Hurt Locker*, Specialist Owen Eldridge (Brian Geraghty) comments that a local man filming him is "getting ready to put me on YouTube." Not unless that man is a time traveler: *The Hurt Locker* is set in 2004, and YouTube didn't get its start until 2005.

9 Marie Antoinette (2006)

In a scene from Sofia Coppola's *Marie Antoinette*, the writer-director intentionally left a pair of Converse sneakers next to more period-appropriate shoes. "I didn't want [the film] to be a history lesson, I wanted it to be more impressionist," Coppola said.

10 The Untouchables (1987)

The Canadian flag design painted on the side of some wooden crates in Brian De Palma's *The Untouchables* has only been in use since 1965. Before then—say, in the thirties, when *The Untouchables* was set—the flag was a mash-up of the Coat of Arms of Canada and the Union Jack.

ROBOCOP

(1987)

WRITTEN BY: Edward Neumeier and Michael Miner

DIRECTED BY: Paul Verhoeven

OTHER MOVIES DIRECTED BY PAUL VERHOEVEN:
Spetters (1980): Total Recall (1990); Basic Instinct
(1992); Starship Troopers (1997); Black Book
(2006); Benedetta (2021)

On its surface, the idea behind *RoboCop* was so ludicrous that studios, directors, and actors dismissed it out of hand: a story of a police officer killed in the line of duty, then resurrected as a cyborg. But in the hands of Paul Verhoeven, *RoboCop* became one of the sharpest satires of the eighties, using its high-concept sci-fi premise to ridicule the perils of industrialization, consumerism, and big business.

As slain Officer Murphy, Peter Weller does the impossible, using his body language and the lower half of his face (the only part visible) to communicate the pain of a man trapped in a purgatory between artificial life and death. Murphy's struggle for humanity isn't relegated to his cybernetic body: it's also desperately needed in Verhoeven's vision of a future dazed and confused by tyrannical tech overlords—one that seems less like satire and more like reality every day.

STAN LEE TURNED IT DOWN.

In 1984, Neumeier decided to see if he could spin the *RoboCop* script into a comic book to use as a launching pad for a feature. He ran the idea by Stan Lee; before Lee could commit one way or the other, he and Neumeier attended an early screening of *The Terminator*, which also had a humanoid as the main character. An impressed Lee told the writer, "Boy, you're never going to top that!" and passed.

PETER WELLER BECAME A MIME FOR THE ROLE.

Knowing the RoboCop suit (which was still being fabricated) would limit his facial expressions, Orion Pictures head Mike Medavoy suggested to Peter Weller that he seek out a mime coach in order to become more physically expressive. After interviewing several in what amounted to a mime-off, Weller settled on Moni Yakim, a performer who taught at Juilliard. The two worked for months on fluid, balletic movements that incorporated dance training; Weller even suited up in football gear and walked around Central Park to get a feel for moving with added bulk.

WELLER COULD BARELY MOVE IN THE ROBOCOP SUIT.

After protracted design debates with Verhoeven, effects artist Rob Bottin was unable to deliver the suit until the day they were to begin shooting with it. It took Weller nearly eleven hours to squeeze himself into it, at which point he spent an hour trying to catch a set of car keys for a fleeting shot. Cumbersome beyond his expectations, all of Weller's mime work had gone out the window; Yakim took the frustrated actor aside and told him to begin thinking of himself as a "beast." Production was halted for several days so that Weller could grow comfortable with his movements.

WELLER REFUSED TO ANSWER TO HIS REAL NAME.

According to co-star Miguel Ferrer, Weller instructed the producers to issue a memo to the cast and crew advising that no one should refer to him by his real name; he preferred to be called by his character's name, Murphy, or "Robo."

CLOSE-UP

While he may not actually possess a stomach, there's just no killing RoboCop's appetite for chicken: RoboCop shilled for a Korean frozen food company in the 1980s, terrorizing a housewife before making off with the entire refrigerator.

IT RECEIVED AN X RATING— EIGHT TIMES.

Verhoeven thought he had sensationalized the violence to a comedic degree, particularly in a scene where an office executive is the victim of a "glitch" in law enforcement machine ED-209. The robot essentially tears him to shreds by firing high-caliber ballistics, at which point someone asks for a medic. The MPAA did not find this as amusing as Verhoeven did and asked him to cut down the scene, as well as the murder of Weller's Officer Murphy. In all, Verhoeven submitted the film eight times before finally receiving an R rating.

A PROVOCATIVE HISTORY OF THE X RATING

When the Motion Picture Association of America (MPAA) introduced the modern movie ratings system in 1968, they couldn't have known that one of their classifications would become the calling card of pornography. The X rating, intended to denote films not suitable for anyone under the age of sixteen (later seventeen), went from being attached to Oscar contenders to filling video store spaces located behind saloon doors. More than fifty years after its debut, take a look at the most infamous letter in moviegoing history.

ACCEPTING THE RATING WAS VOLUNTARY (KIND OF).

In 1968, the MPAA introduced a four-tier system to classify films: G was suitable for all audiences; M was the equivalent of PG, indicating that juveniles should consult with a parent before attending; R was intended for adults, or children only with a guardian; X marked films that shouldn't be seen by adolescent eyes. But the MPAA never forced a film studio to submit to its decision. It could release a film with no rating at all. The problem? The MPAA's arrangement with the National Association of Theater Owners meant that an unrated film would almost certainly have difficulty finding a theater to screen it.

A ROBERT DE NIRO MOVIE WAS THE FIRST TO GET SLAPPED WITH AN X.

In 1968, immediately after the introduction of the ratings system, the advisory board got its first bona fide sample of an X-rated submission: Brian De Palma's *Greetings*, starring Robert De Niro as a man confronting the possibility of being drafted, garnered the rating due to its sexually explicit content.

FILMMAKERS COULD GIVE THEMSELVES THE RATING.

Though it didn't last long, there was a time when an X rating for a mainstream film was a badge of honor and an effective marketing tool that signaled a film was being made for discerning moviegoers. It's been suggested that Arthur Krim, the head of United Artists, willingly gave John Schlesinger's *Midnight Cowboy* (1969) an X of his own volition even after he realized the MPAA would give it an R.

PORN TOOK OVER THE RATING DUE TO AN MPAA OVERSIGHT.

An X rating in 1969 was no big deal. By the mid-1970s, it signaled to audiences that they were about to watch an anatomy lesson. That's because the burgeoning adult film industry was screening films in theaters and blared advertisements with promises of "XXX" salaciousness. The MPAA never reviewed these films, and never bothered to copyright X as it applies to film ratings, so titles like 1972's *Deep Throat* used the mark freely. In short order, the X rating became synonymous with pornography and grew into a scarlet letter for films. No reputable theaters would book such movies, and few newspapers would take ads for them.

IN 1990, THE RATINGS SYSTEM GOT AN OVERHAUL.

In 1990, a year that saw ten movies get slapped with an X, the MPAA dropped the X in favor of NC-17, which it hoped would distance films with artistic merit from pornographic material. And this time, the pornography industry couldn't co-opt it: Learning from its past mistake, the MPAA trademarked the designation.

ROCKY

(1976)

WRITTEN BY:
Sylvester Stallone

DIRECTED BY:
John G. Avildsen

**OTHER MOVIES DIRECTED
BY JOHN G. AVILDSEN:**
The Karate Kid (1984);
The Karate Kid Part II (1986);
Lean on Me (1989); *Rocky V* (1990)

Sylvester Stallone's underdog story about a streetwise boxer from Philadelphia who gets his shot at the big-time mirrors Stallone's own torturous path to success. The actor, who was often chastised for his unconventional looks and rumbling voice, was perceived as little more than a background thug in films before he decided to take control of his own destiny and write a script about a disrespected prizefighter. Both underdogs won—Rocky got a moral victory, while the film took home an Academy Award for Best Picture. Countless bombastic sequels later, it's the home-brewed original that shows Rocky at his most charming, vulnerable, and real.

STALLONE BASED *ROCKY* ON A REAL MUHAMMAD ALI FIGHT.

When Stallone was still an aspiring actor, broke and living in New York City, he caught a broadcast of a 1975 boxing match between heavyweight legend Muhammad Ali and underdog challenger Chuck Wepner, who was expected to crumble under Ali's offense. But to everyone's surprise, Wepner hung in there and even put Ali on the canvas before Ali knocked him out. Inspired by the sight of a man counted out but up for a fight, Stallone started writing.

HE WROTE THE ORIGINAL DRAFT OF *ROCKY* IN JUST UNDER A WEEK.

In a creative outburst, Stallone wrote the first draft of *Rocky* in three and a half days using pen and paper. (Computers were rare then, yo.) While Stallone admitted the story underwent significant changes— Rocky originally threw the fight—the bones were there.

PRODUCERS HAD TO MAKE THE MOVIE ON A TIGHT BUDGET.

With Stallone an unknown in Hollywood, United Artists flinched at allocating any kind of real budget to *Rocky*. Boxing pictures rarely did well, and without a star like Burt Reynolds or James Caan, they feared they'd lose their shirts. Producers Irwin Winkler and Robert Chartoff agreed to make the movie for less than $1 million and cover any cost overruns themselves. That's one reason the ice-skating scene between Rocky and Adrian (Talia Shire) was shot in an empty rink: The movie couldn't afford any extras.

"Yo, Adrian!"

THE BIG FIGHT BETWEEN ROCKY AND APOLLO WAS HEAVILY REHEARSED.

While athletic, neither Stallone nor Carl Weathers (who played Apollo Creed) had ever boxed before. Director John G. Avildsen told Stallone to write out each punch of their climatic bout, which the two actors then rehearsed for a week straight to nail it. They looked like professionals, but ironically, it was Burt Young (Paulie) who had actually fought: He was reportedly 14–0 as a pro.

ROCKY WAS ALMOST A G.I. JOE TOY.

Millions of dollars and many years later, Rocky Balboa became a pop culture icon—one worthy of being named an honorary G.I. Joe. The toymakers at Hasbro tried to license Stallone's likeness so Rocky could be enlisted in the toy line as the Joes' combat trainer. Because Stallone already had a Rambo toy deal wrapped up, it never happened.

STALLONE NEVER PLANNED ON THE *ROCKY* SERIES ENDURING AS LONG AS IT HAS.

Through the years, Stallone has made some definitive declarations about the *Rocky* series. Speaking with movie critic Roger Ebert in 1979, shortly before the release of *Rocky II*, Stallone indicated that *Rocky III* would conclude the series. "There'll never be a *Rocky IV*," he said. "You gotta call it a halt."

In 1985, while filming *Rocky IV*, Stallone told *Interview* magazine that he was finished. "Oh, this is it for Rocky," he said. "Because I don't know where you go after you battle Russia." In 1990, following the release of *Rocky V*, Stallone declared that "There's no *Rocky VI*. He's done." Upon the release of *Rocky Balboa* in 2006, Stallone once more declared he was finished. "I couldn't top this," he told *People*. "I would have to wait another ten years to build up a head of steam, and by that point, come on." *Creed* was released nine years later.

WINNING
SPORTS
MOVIES

If Rocky Balboa taught moviegoers—and moviemakers—anything, it's that you don't necessarily have to win in order to claim a victory. Fellow filmmakers listened.

The Bad News Bears (1976)

Walter Matthau is at his grumpiest in this classic about washout Morris Buttermaker, who coaches a juvenile delinquent baseball team from a losing record to less of a losing record.

Bang the Drum Slowly (1973)

Robert De Niro stars in the baseball equivalent of *Brian's Song* as a major league player with a terminal illness who bonds with teammate Michael Moriarty (*Q: The Winged Serpent*, *The Stuff*).

Breaking Away (1979)

Dennis Christopher stars as Dave, an aspiring cyclist in Indiana who wavers between pursuing his ambitions and falling in with childhood friends (including Dennis Quaid) content with a career in stonecutting.

Bull Durham (1988)

Kevin Costner's other baseball classic (see below) may be full of heart, but it's *Bull Durham* that nails the game's hedonistic side. As "Crash" Davis, Costner tries to polish a rookie pitcher (Tim Robbins) while fielding Susan Sarandon.

Caddyshack (1980)

The power of *Saturday Night Live* to excavate comedic genius was evident from the start. Few films helped prove the point better than *Caddyshack*, which paired *SNL* alums Chevy Chase and Bill Murray as part of a cast of eccentrics who make life intolerable for the stuffy clientele at a country club. Long believed to be one of the funniest movies ever made, it's also easily the best to feature a gopher puppet jamming to Kenny Loggins.

Major League (1989)
Charlie Sheen and Wesley Snipes throw curveballs at the sports film in this baseball comedy about the Cleveland Indians falling under the thumb of a new owner who wants to relocate—and thinks that recruiting the game's worst players can achieve it.

The Natural (1984)
Robert Redford actually glows as Roy Hobbs, a baseball player who excels through trials and tribulations, ascending to a kind of baseball deity. It shouldn't work, but it does, mostly thanks to Redford's inescapable charisma. Bonus points for Wonderboy, Hobbs's bat—and the best inanimate co-star next to *Cast Away*'s Wilson.

Rudy (1993)
Sean Astin defined the underdog genre in this true story about Gabe "Rudy" Ruettiger, who overcomes a lack of physical size and a learning disability to realize his dream of playing football for the University of Notre Dame.

The Sandlot (1993)
If *Stand by Me* had baseball instead of a dead body, it would look like *The Sandlot*. The ever-quotable Disney film follows a group of kids in 1962 Los Angeles who chase fly balls and summer memories that will last a lifetime.

Slap Shot (1977)
Paul Newman leads a group of ragtag hockey players who turn to violent play in an effort to bolster attendance in a small New England factory town. Both Newman and the movie confront sports movie clichés by skating right past them, with Newman calling *Slap Shot*'s Reg Dunlop one of his favorite roles.

Eight Men Out (1988)
The true story of the 1919 Chicago White Sox, who threw the World Series to appease bettors, is a solemn look at how America's pastime lost America's trust.

Field of Dreams (1989)
This sentimental favorite from writer-director Phil Alden Robinson contains the catchphrase that everyone knows: "If you build it, he will come." "It" is a baseball field; "he" is for the viewer to discover as Kevin Costner brings tears to your eyes with a story of fathers, sons, and the all-American sport of baseball.

Hoop Dreams (1994)
Lost in the shuffle of the NBA's star players are the thousands of aspiring athletes who struggle to make it to the court. This documentary does an exceptional job of spotlighting two: William Gates and Arthur Agee, who see the game as a way out of poverty.

Hoosiers (1986)
Gene Hackman stars as a basketball coach in small-town 1950s Indiana looking to start over with a clean slate. His performance in the film manages to take the conventional trappings of the sports underdog genre and bring a multilayered portrait of a man plagued by a past who's getting one last chance to get it right.

A League of Their Own (1992)
There's no crying in baseball— just in the audience for this classic comedy about the All-American Girls Professional Baseball League, which took to the field while men players were absent during World War II.

The Longest Yard (1974)
Burt Reynolds stars in the best prison football film ever made. As a jock who lands in prison after a joyride, Reynolds recruits convicts in a game against the guards that's as much about their humanity as it is bragging rights.

THE ROCKY HORROR PICTURE SHOW (1975)

WRITTEN BY: Richard O'Brien and Jim Sharman

DIRECTED BY: Jim Sharman

OTHER MOVIES DIRECTED BY JIM SHARMAN:
The Night, the Prowler (1978);
Shock Treatment (1981)

Many movies can claim the title "cult classic," but few have ever embodied that term quite like *The Rocky Horror Picture Show*. When sweet young lovebirds Brad (Barry Bostwick) and Janet (Susan Sarandon) find themselves with a flat tire in the midst of a terrible storm, they seek help at the nearest home they can find, which just happens to be the residence of mad scientist named Dr. Frank-N-Furter (Tim Curry). As the night progresses, songs are sung, dances are danced, and Brad and Janet lose some of their innocence as they mingle with a colorful cast of partygoers.

The movie was first written as a small stage production by an out-of-work actor who wanted to pay homage to the B movies he loved. The film version flopped at the box office when it premiered in 1975. Then, as midnight showings continued, its following grew, and grew, and grew. Today, nearly fifty years later, its fan base continues to grow. People don't just watch *The Rocky Horror Picture Show*, they live it— complete with costumes, props, and very vulgar audience participation.

DR. FRANK-N-FURTER ORIGINALLY HAD A GERMAN ACCENT.

Taking a cue from the character's name, Tim Curry began the stage production of *The Rocky Horror Show* by playing Frank-N-Furter as German. Then, one day, he heard a woman on a bus speaking with a particularly posh accent and decided, "Yes, he should sound like the Queen."

JIM SHARMAN AGREED TO A SMALLER BUDGET IN ORDER TO KEEP THE ORIGINAL STAGE CAST.

According to Sharman, 20th Century Fox offered him a decent budget if he would cast "currently fashionable rock stars" in the lead roles for *The Rocky Horror Picture Show*. Sharman lobbied instead to keep the original stage cast (with some exceptions, like the addition of Barry Bostwick and Susan Sarandon as Brad and Janet), and instead got a "modest budget" and a very tight shooting schedule. Sharman now calls the decision "crucial" to the film's cult success.

THE MOVIE'S LOOK WAS INSPIRED BY AN ACTUAL ROTTING MANSION.

While preparing to shoot the film, set designer Brian Thomson kept hearing about "the old house" near Bray Studios outside of London. When he finally got to see the house, a nineteenth-century mansion called Oakley Court, he realized it was exactly what they needed for the film, in part because its owners had essentially left it to rot (they wanted to demolish it, but it was designated a historic site). "The minute we saw it, we realized that this gave us the basis for the whole look of the movie," Thomson said. (Today, that rotting mansion is a posh hotel.)

THE REVEAL OF EDDIE'S BODY GENUINELY SHOCKED THE CAST.

For the iconic dinner party scene, in which Furter reveals that his guests have been dining on Eddie, Sharman elected to tell only Curry— who had to pull away the tablecloth to reveal Eddie's corpse—what the surprise of the scene was. He wanted the rest of the cast to be genuinely shocked.

The Rocky Horror Picture Show has had many famous fans, including the late Diana, Princess of Wales. Once, while doing a theater performance in Austria, Curry was informed that the princess wanted to meet him. When they met, she told him that the film "quite completed my education," apparently flashing a "wicked smile" as she did so.

TIM CURRY WAS ONCE KICKED OUT OF A SCREENING FOR BEING AN "IMPOSTOR."

As the film's cult following grew, Curry was living in New York, just down the street from the Waverly Theater, so he often witnessed fans going to midnight showings in costume. Intrigued, he called the theater, told them who he was, and asked if he could attend. The theater initially didn't believe him, until he actually showed up one night. While fans were delighted by Curry's presence, the theater staff still wasn't convinced, and an usher grabbed him, called him an "impostor," and threw him out.

5 ESSENTIAL MIDNIGHT MOVIES

In the early 1970s, a new kind of moviegoing experience began to evolve in American repertory theaters: the midnight movie. Yes, people were watching movies at midnight well before then, but this wasn't just about the time of night. It was about the experience of seeing a movie like *The Rocky Horror Picture Show*—something you wouldn't normally find during a prime theatrical matinee or evening slot. This was a place for movies that fell between the cracks, because they were too strange or too campy or too experimental. So they were sent out into the night, and there they found their audiences—with some careful curating by Ben Barenholtz, owner of New York City's legendary Elgin Theater.

1 The Adventures of Priscilla, Queen of the Desert (1994)

The story of two drag queens (Hugo Weaving and Guy Pearce) and one trans woman (Terence Stamp) who head out across Australia on a battered tour bus to perform a drag show at a casino, *The Adventures of Priscilla, Queen of the Desert* is both an intimate portrayal of LGBTQ characters and a glitzy celebration of Australia, with a killer soundtrack headlined by ABBA and Gloria Gaynor to make everything extra entertaining. The film was a surprise worldwide hit, spawned a stage musical, and remains one of the most important landmarks in both LGBTQ and Australian cinema.

2 El Topo (1970)

Alejandro Jodorowsky's bizarre "acid Western" is generally accepted to be the first "midnight movie." It got this reputation not out of some weird copyright loophole or from being hidden away for decades, but from one theater owner's fascination with it. Following a special screening of the film, Ben Barenholtz asked if he could begin running *El Topo* at the Elgin Theater. Barenholtz showed the film at midnight on weekdays and at 1:00 a.m. on weekends, and people (including John Lennon, who was a fan) started showing up in droves to see what all the fuss was about.

3 Eraserhead (1977)

David Lynch's imaginative, disturbing, and intensely compelling feature film debut is one of the most fully realized arrivals of a filmmaking voice you're ever likely to see. And while it probably never would have caught on with a mainstream audience, the midnight movie circuit made it a fast cult classic. Stanley Kubrick considered it one of his favorite films; George Lucas loved it so much that he asked Lynch to make the film that would become *Return of the Jedi*; and Mel Brooks admired the movie—and Lynch—so much that he hired Lynch to direct his 1980 production of *The Elephant Man*.

4 Pink Flamingos (1972)

John Waters's self-proclaimed "exercise in poor taste," which centers on a competition to determine the filthiest person in America, wasn't just made to shock you. It was made to threaten, to dare, and to challenge, and it did so in what remains an almost impossibly fascinating way. The Elgin's Ben Barenholtz thought so, too. After the success of his midnight showings of *El Topo*, he chose *Pink Flamingos* to be its successor.

5 The Harder They Come (1972)

The Harder They Come was the first major Jamaican feature film, and it was such an instant hit in its home country that its star could barely make their way to the theater where it premiered because of the crowds. In America, though, it took longer to catch on. The crime drama about a young songwriter (Jimmy Cliff) trying to find work was picked up for U.S. distribution by Roger Corman's New World Pictures, and while it was not an instant box office success, it began to gain traction on the repertory circuit. It became one of the films that followed *El Topo* in the Elgin Theater's midnight slot, and it enjoyed similarly successful midnight runs around the country in the years that followed.

WRITTEN BY: Craig Pearce and Baz Luhrmann (based on the play by William Shakespeare)

DIRECTED BY: Baz Luhrmann

OTHER MOVIES DIRECTED BY BAZ LUHRMANN:
Strictly Ballroom (1992); *Moulin Rouge!* (2001); *Australia* (2008); *The Great Gatsby* (2013)

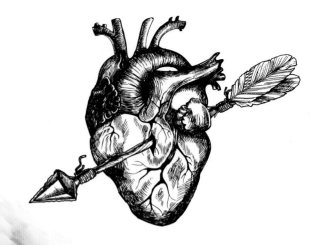

ROMEO + JULIET (1996)

When adapting William Shakespeare, most movie directors spend a lot of time fussing over Elizabethan gowns and crumbling castles. Baz Luhrmann was more concerned with guns, slang, and ecstasy trips. For his 1996 take on *Romeo and Juliet*, the Australian director dropped those famously star-crossed lovers into a contemporary city with contemporary problems. The resulting *Romeo + Juliet* was a bombastic update that struck a chord with teens, who turned it into a major hit.

BAZ LUHRMANN WANTED TO PROVE THAT SHAKESPEARE WASN'T FOR SNOBS.

In retelling *Romeo and Juliet* as a modern story, Luhrmann hoped to shake up Shakespeare's accessibility. "The thing I really set out to do was to smash what I call 'club Shakespeare,'" Luhrmann told ScreenSlam. "[The idea that] you have to be a member of the club to understand it." Luhrmann was especially committed to this goal because he was intimidated by Shakespeare as a school kid. It took a psychedelic performance of *Twelfth Night* to bring him over to the Bard's side, and he hoped to do the same for moviegoers with his equally brazen vision.

LEONARDO DICAPRIO FLEW TO AUSTRALIA ON HIS OWN DIME TO GET THE MOVIE MADE.

Romeo + Juliet came out a year before *Titanic*, before "Leo Mania" had struck. Without that star power behind him, DiCaprio had to fight hard to get the movie made. Luhrmann told SFGATE that when 20th Century Fox was still on the fence, DiCaprio flew down to Australia to help Luhrmann convince the studio of the project's viability. "He did a video workshop, so we could persuade the studio to do it," Luhrmann explained. "He was extremely passionate about it."

THE MOVIE'S HAIRSTYLIST WAS KIDNAPPED DURING PRODUCTION.

At one point, *Romeo + Juliet*'s key hairstylist, Aldo Signoretti, was kidnapped and held for ransom. "The bandidos rang up and said, 'For $300 you can have him back,'" Luhrmann told Cinema Papers. Maurizio Silvi, the key makeup artist, left the hotel to make the exchange: He threw the kidnappers a bag of money and they threw Aldo out of a car door, breaking his leg in the process.

DICAPRIO WAS IMPRESSED BY CLAIRE DANES.

Luhrmann was dazzled by Danes's maturity, but there was another quality that helped her land the job: DiCaprio said she was the only actress who looked him in the eye during auditions. "Claire just came in and was just so in the moment, and so there, and so not trying to do like this little angelic flower [version of] Juliet," DiCaprio told ScreenSlam.

FREEZE-FRAME

Almost every billboard, sign, and scrap of paper seen on-screen contains a Shakespeare reference. Just look at the opening gas station fight alone: You'll immediately see signs for Montague Construction and Phoenix Gas. The motto for Montague Construction is "retail'd to prosperity," which is a reference to *Richard III*. Meanwhile the slogan for Phoenix Gas is "add more fuel to your fire," a fragment from *Henry VI, Part 3*, which also has a Phoenix reference.

MARLON BRANDO WAS INTERESTED IN THE MOVIE, BUT CONCERNED ABOUT WORKING WITH DICAPRIO.

Pete Postlethwaite ended up playing Father Laurence, the priest who marries Romeo and Juliet. But Marlon Brando was initially interested in the role. Luhrmann said that Brando sent him letters about the part, but eventually took himself out of the running due to "personal family problems" surrounding his son, Christian. Even before Brando officially withdrew his interest, though, he had some reservations—mainly over DiCaprio, who had been far too convincing in a previous role. "He said he saw Leonardo in [*What's Eating*] *Gilbert Grape*," Luhrmann recalled. "[He asked,] 'Why is it you are going to cast a young man who's not entirely in control of his mental faculties?'"

THE FINAL SCENE REFERENCES ANOTHER PAIR OF STAR-CROSSED LOVERS.

For the famous double-suicide finale, Luhrmann chose a classical composition. It's called "Liebestod" (or "love death") and it comes from the Richard Wagner opera *Tristan und Isolde*. That medieval story also concerns a doomed couple who die in the final act—but with more love potions and maritime mishaps.

WRITTEN BY: Kevin Williamson

DIRECTED BY: Wes Craven

OTHER MOVIES DIRECTED BY WES CRAVEN:
The Last House on the Left (1972); *The Hills Have Eyes* (1977); *A Nightmare on Elm Street* (1984); *The Serpent and the Rainbow* (1988); *Red Eye* (2005); *My Soul to Take* (2010)

SCREAM (1996)

Where John Carpenter's *Halloween* (1978) invented the slasher genre, *Scream* reinvented it for a new generation, combining horror with meta comedy that skewers years of slasher movie tropes. *Scream* also revitalized the career of Wes Craven, a founding father of horror who had made a name for himself with films like *The Last House on the Left*, *The Hills Have Eyes*, and *A Nightmare on Elm Street*. Still, in the mid-nineties Craven was trying to move away from the dark, violent cinema he was associated with in an effort to avoid being pigeonholed. As such, he initially turned *Scream* down.

"The turning point was when a kid came up to me at a film conference or a panel I was on," Craven later recalled. "The kid said, 'You know, you should really do a movie like *The Last House on the Left* again. You really kicked ass back then, and you haven't done it since.'" Worried that he might be "getting soft" with his filmmaking choices, Craven thought it over, realized that the tone of *Scream* was a perfect fit for his voice, and finally said yes.

THE SCRIPT WAS PARTIALLY INSPIRED BY A REAL-LIFE STORY.

In addition to being inspired by John Carpenter's *Halloween*—screenwriter Kevin Williamson's favorite movie—*Scream* was partially inspired by a real-life series of student murders in Gainesville, Florida, in 1990. The killings were perpetrated by Danny Harold Rolling, who was later dubbed "The Gainesville Ripper."

IT COULD HAVE BEEN DIRECTED BY GEORGE ROMERO OR SAM RAIMI.

Both George A. Romero and Sam Raimi were originally approached about directing *Scream*, but both turned the project down.

DREW BARRYMORE WAS SET TO STAR, BUT CHANGED HER MIND.

Barrymore changed her mind about playing the lead five weeks before production was set to begin. Barrymore instead suggested she play Casey Becker, the teen terrorized by the killer in the opening scene, to cleverly subvert audience expectations that a star of her stature would survive the movie. Casting directors approached Alicia Witt, Brittany Murphy, and Reese Witherspoon to take over the Sidney Prescott role before eventually casting Neve Campbell.

THE FILM'S ICONIC MASK WAS FOUND DURING A LOCATION SCOUT.

The killer's now-iconic mask was a simple off-the-shelf Halloween mask. Craven and a producer found it at a house they were location scouting. Studio head Bob Weinstein didn't think the mask was scary enough and actually considered replacing Craven with another director. But Craven and editor Patrick Lussier created a work print out of dailies of the opening scene that quickly convinced Weinstein to change his mind.

LINDA BLAIR HAD A CAMEO.

The Exorcist star Linda Blair made a cameo as one of the news reporters outside of the school. She's the one with the bright orange blouse. Later on, she's the reporter who confronts Sidney in Dewey's police car. (Craven had previously directed Blair in the 1978 TV movie *Stranger in Our House*.)

THE FINAL SCENE TOOK TWENTY-ONE NIGHTS TO SHOOT.

The forty-two-minute final act, which takes place entirely during a party at Matthew Lillard's character Stu's house, took twenty-one successive nights to shoot. The cast and crew jokingly called it "the longest night in horror history."

IT WAS INITIALLY SLAPPED WITH AN NC-17 RATING.

The MPAA thought the film was too gruesome. Despite the fact that Craven initially refused to cut anything, the movie was edited and resubmitted by the studio nine times before it was given an R rating.

FREEZE-FRAME

Wes Craven makes a cameo as a janitor. He's wearing Freddy Krueger's hat and sweater.

6 KILLER FINAL GIRLS

SPOILERS!

The "final girl"—a term coined by Carol J. Clover in her 1992 book *Men, Women, and Chain Saws: Gender in the Modern Horror Film*—is a slasher-movie trope wherein one woman (usually a teen) is the sole survivor of a brutal massacre. She either narrowly escapes by being rescued by someone else or bravely faces off against her attacker(s) and kills them herself. Here are six of the most significant final girls in horror history.

1. Laurie Strode

// Halloween

Jamie Lee Curtis made her big-screen debut as Laurie Strode—the sweet-natured babysitter who became the archetype by which all subsequent final girls would be judged—in 1978's Halloween. In the nearly forty-five years since the original, Curtis has returned to square off against Michael Myers several more times. Yet she actually wasn't John Carpenter's first choice for the role; it reportedly wasn't until co-writer and producer Debra Hill learned that Curtis's mother was Janet Leigh, star of Alfred Hitchcock's Psycho (1960), that the director was persuaded to cast the then-unknown actress in the role.

PLAYED BY: Jamie Lee Curtis; Scout Taylor-Compton

KNOWN LOCATIONS: Various homes, including the Myers house, and Haddonfield Memorial Hospital in Haddonfield, Illinois; Hillcrest Academy in Summer Glen, California; Grace Andersen Sanitarium

OCCUPATION: High School Student, Babysitter, Headmistress

SQUARES OFF AGAINST: Michael Myers/The Shape (Nick Castle; Dick Warlock; Chris Durand; Brad Loree; Tyler Mane; James Jude Courtney)

WORST MOMENT: Discovers the bodies of friends Annie Brackett (Nancy Kyes), Lynda Van der Klok (P. J. Soles), and Bob Simms (John Michael Graham) across the street from the Doyle house, where she's babysitting for the night

SECRET TALENT: Grade-A pumpkin carver

GREATEST WEAKNESS: Her untreated trauma, which leads her to self-isolate; fake her own death and go into hiding; assume a new identity; self-medicate with alcohol; and get into too many spats with her kids, of which she has three across the series: Jamie Lloyd (Danielle Harris; J. C. Brandy); John Tate (Josh Hartnett); and Karen Nelson (Judy Greer)—although only one is ever acknowledged per continuity

THE MISTAKE THAT DOES GET HER KILLED: After accidentally killing an innocent man she believes to be Michael Myers, she's committed to a sanitarium. When Michael attacks her there, she quickly gains the upper hand, but hesitates—fearing another mistake—which gives him just enough time to fatally wound her with a knife, then toss her off a rooftop (an act that was retroactively, and purposely, forgotten for the sake of David Gordon Green's most recent trilogy of sequels).

BEST FLEX: Lures Michael into her "safe room" with the help of her daughter Karen and granddaughter Allyson (Andi Matichak), only to reveal it was a bait-and-switch the whole time. Once he's trapped, she proceeds to set the whole house ablaze.

BEST QUOTE: "Was that the boogeyman?"

ODDS OF SURVIVAL: 65 percent

2. Ginny Field

// Friday the 13th

There's no single enduring final girl of the *Friday the 13th* franchise (1980–present), but would-be child psychologist Ginny Field from *Part 2* offers a strong case. Ron Kurtz, who took over script duties from *Friday the 13th* (1980) writer Victor Miller, wanted to create a "smart" final girl—one who would use her wits to subdue Jason Voorhees, not just another machete. Plans for a follow-up sequel focusing on Ginny's trauma after the events at Crystal Lake were in the works, but ultimately never made it past the slush pile.

PLAYED BY: Amy Steel

KNOWN LOCATION: Packanack Lodge at Crystal Lake

OCCUPATION: College Student; Counselor Training Center Assistant

SQUARES OFF AGAINST: "Baghead" Jason Voorhees (Steve Daskewisz)

WORST MOMENT: Returns to Packanack Lodge after a night on the town, only to discover the sliced-and-diced remains of all the former camp counselors in training who stayed behind

SECRET TALENT: Studies child psychology and knows how to put it to use

GREATEST WEAKNESS: Her car

THE MISTAKE THAT NEARLY GETS HER KILLED: Crawls under a bed to hide from Jason, but gets so scared while he's in the room that she accidentally pees her pants

BEST FLEX: Discovers Jason's shack in the woods, then puts on the blue sweater worn by Pamela Voorhees (Jason's mom) in *Friday the 13th* (1980) and impersonates her, tricking him into believing she's his mother—for a few minutes, anyway

BEST QUOTE: "Come to Mama."

ODDS OF SURVIVAL: 70 percent

3. Nancy Thompson

// A Nightmare on Elm Street

Wes Craven originally envisioned Nancy Thompson, the resourceful final girl of the *Nightmare on Elm Street* franchise (1984–present), as the wholesome all-American type. In some ways, this was a big departure for the horror legend, who cut his teeth as a director in the porn industry and later gained mainstream attention with exploitation schlockfests like *The Last House on the Left* (1972) and *The Hills Have Eyes* (1977). Instead, it's Nancy's persona as a sleep-deprived warrior, unafraid to duke it out with Freddy Krueger whether in or out of dreamland, that gives the character such an unforgettable edge.

PLAYED BY: Heather Langenkamp; Rooney Mara

KNOWN LOCATIONS: 1428 Elm Street and Westin Hills Psychiatric Hospital in Springwood, Ohio; The Beautiful Dream

OCCUPATION: High School Student; Grad School Intern; OG Dream Warrior

SQUARES OFF AGAINST: Freddy Krueger (Robert Englund; Jackie Earle Haley); her parents, Marge (Ronee Blakley) and Lt. Don Thompson (John Saxon); Dr. Elizabeth Simms (Priscilla Pointer); the town's toxic culture of silence surrounding a known child murderer

WORST MOMENT: Discovers she's been locked in her house at the same moment as her boyfriend (Johnny Depp) is being eaten by a bed across the street

SECRET TALENT: Can consume ungodly amounts of coffee

GREATEST WEAKNESS: Still has to fall asleep eventually

THE MISTAKE THAT DOES GET HER KILLED: Gets pulled into Kristen's (Patricia Arquette) nightmare and helps her and the other Dream Warriors in their battle against Freddy. Believing he's been defeated, she lets her guard down and hugs her father, who has suddenly appeared in spirit form. In fact, it's Freddy in disguise. He fatally wounds her—but not before she manages to stab him in the gut with his own glove.

BEST FLEX: Tricks her house out with booby traps, then falls asleep, finds Freddy and yanks him out of her nightmare, and proceeds to kick the ever-living hell out of him before setting him on fire—again

BEST QUOTE: "All of you have this inner strength—some special power that you've had in your most wonderful dreams. Together, we can learn to use that power if we try."

ODDS OF SURVIVAL: 60 percent

4. Kirsty Cotton
// Hellraiser

As the final girl who knows how to drive a hard bargain, Kirsty first appears in Clive Barker's 1986 novella The Hellbound Heart, but her role is slightly different— she's not the daughter of Larry Cotton (known in the novella as Rory), but rather just a concerned friend. The decision to make her his daughter for the 1987 adaptation Hellraiser works to the film's advantage, heightening the fairy-tale horror vibes and upping the ante on the ick factor immensely, especially once Frank Cotton—her uncle—tries to put the moves on her.

PLAYED BY: Ashley Laurence

KNOWN LOCATIONS: England; Channard Institute Psychiatric Hospital; Hell

OCCUPATION: Puzzle Solver

SQUARES OFF AGAINST: Frank Cotton (Sean Chapman); Julia Cotton (Clare Higgins); Pinhead (Doug Bradley) and the rest of the Cenobites; Dr. Channard (Kenneth Cranham); Trevor Gooden (Dean Winters)

WORST MOMENT: Discovers the flayed remains of her father and realizes Uncle Frank and Julia are to blame

SECRET TALENT: Knows how to cut a deal with the bad guys

GREATEST WEAKNESS: Cuts too many deals with the bad guys

THE MISTAKE THAT NEARLY GETS HER KILLED: Knowingly descends into hell because she believes her father needs her help. In fact, it's just her uncle Frank, pulling another fast one.

BEST FLEX: Puts on Julia's skin in order to distract the newly Cenobited form of Dr. Channard, giving Tiffany (Imogen Boorman) just enough time to solve the Lament Configuration and close the portal to hell—until the sequel

BEST QUOTE: "Go to hell!"

ODDS OF SURVIVAL: 90 percent

5. Jeryline //
Tales from the Crypt

Inspired by the HBO horror-anthology series Tales from the Crypt (1989– 1996) and the 1950s comic book series of the same name, 1995's Demon Knight was one of three planned theatrical spin-offs. After a far campier follow-up, Tales from the Crypt: Bordello of Blood (1996), was panned by critics and bombed at the box office, plans for a third film were scrapped. But it's this flick—and specifically, Jada Pinkett-Smith's (then credited as Jada Pinkett) memorable turn as final girl Jeryline— that stands the test of time.

PLAYED BY: Jada Pinkett-Smith (credited as Jada Pinkett)

KNOWN LOCATION: New Mexico

OCCUPATION: Former Thief; Maid; Guardian of the Key

SQUARES OFF AGAINST: The Collector (Billy Zane); a legion of gnarly demons

WORST MOMENT: Discovers that demons are real and only an ancient relic known as the Key—which is filled with the blood of Jesus Christ and all the former Guardians of the Key— can save the world

SECRET TALENT: Sheer willpower, which prompts her to reject the Collector's overtures, even as almost everyone around her falls prey to similar temptations (and then become possessed as demons)

GREATEST WEAKNESS: Her cat

THE MISTAKE THAT NEARLY GETS HER KILLED: Doesn't kill the possessed form of Uncle Willy (Dick Miller) when she has the chance, nearly getting Brayker (William Sadler) killed, too. She repeats it again with Danny (Ryan O'Donohue), only this time Brayker isn't so lucky.

BEST FLEX: Covers herself in blood from the Key so the Collector can't touch her, then holds the last of it in her mouth and spits it in his face, ensuring his demise and humankind's survival (for now).

BEST QUOTE: "It's not my blood."

ODDS OF SURVIVAL: 85 percent

6. Sidney Prescott // *Scream*

Drew Barrymore was originally cast in the role of Sidney Prescott, the no-nonsense final girl of the Scream franchise (1996–present), but ended up dropping down to a more limited—but still iconic—role in the film's opening scene. Neve Campbell, who had gained fame on Fox's *Party of Five* (1994–2000) and had previously starred in *The Craft* (1996), was hesitant about taking on another horror film, but ultimately did because she "adored" the character.

PLAYED BY: Neve Campbell

KNOWN LOCATIONS: Woodsboro, California; Windsor College, Ohio; Hollywood, California

OCCUPATION: High School Student; College Student; Crisis Counselor; Author

SQUARES OFF AGAINST: Cotton Weary (Liev Schreiber); Gale Weathers (Courteney Cox); Ghostface, aka Billy Loomis (Skeet Ulrich); aka Stu Macher (Matthew Lillard); aka Mickey Altieri (Timothy Olyphant); aka Mrs. Loomis (Laurie Metcalf); aka Roman Bridger (Scott Foley); aka Jill Roberts (Emma Roberts); aka Charlie Walker (Rory Culkin); aka Amber Freeman (Mikey Madison); aka Sam Carpenter (Melissa Barrera)

WORST MOMENT: Discovering her mother's dead body, then finding out a year later that her boyfriend is one of the serial killers who slaughtered her, along with most of their friends. (Honorable mention: Discovering that Tori Spelling does, in fact, star as her in the Stab movies.)

SECRET TALENT: Doesn't actually like horror movies, which means she doesn't follow their rules

GREATEST WEAKNESS: Her taste in men

THE MISTAKE THAT NEARLY GETS HER KILLED: Has sex with Billy before she learns he's one of the killers, thereby breaking the "rule" that all final girls have to be virgins in order to survive.

BEST FLEX: Puts on the Ghostface costume and calls Billy and Stu, taunting them in the same way they terrorized their victims, before finally hitting Billy with an umbrella and dropping a TV set on Stu's head.

BEST QUOTE: "What's the point? They're all the same. Some stupid killer stalking some big-breasted girl who can't act, who is always running up the stairs when she should be running out the front door. It's insulting."

ODDS OF SURVIVAL: 99.9 percent

HONORABLE MENTIONS:

Lisa Fortier (Pam Grier) // *Scream Blacula Scream* (1973)

Sally Hardesty (Marilyn Burns; Olwen Fouéré) // *The Texas Chain Saw Massacre* (1974); *Texas Chainsaw Massacre: The Next Generation* (1995); *Texas Chainsaw Massacre* (2022)

Jess Bradford (Olivia Hussey) // *Black Christmas* (1974)

Sue Snell (Amy Irving; Gabriella Wilde) // *Carrie* (1976); *The Rage: Carrie 2* (1999); *Carrie* (2013)

Alice Hardy (Adrienne King) // *Friday the 13th* (1980); *Friday the 13th Part II* (1981)

Liz Blake (Nancy Allen) // *Dressed to Kill* (1980)

Courtney Bates (Jennifer Meyers; Crystal Bernard) // *The Slumber Party Massacre* (1982); *Slumber Party Massacre II* (1987)

Alice Johnson (Lisa Wilcox) // *A Nightmare on Elm Street 4: The Dream Master* (1988); *A Nightmare on Elm Street 5: The Dream Child* (1989)

Jamie Lloyd (Danielle Harris; J. C. Brandy) // *Halloween 4: The Return of Michael Myers* (1988); *Halloween 5: The Revenge of Michael Myers* (1989); *Halloween: The Curse of Michael Myers* (1995)

Rita Veder (Angela Bassett) // *Vampire in Brooklyn* (1995)

Julie James (Jennifer Love Hewitt) // *I Know What You Did Last Summer* (1997); *I Still Know What You Did Last Summer* (1998)

Brigitte Fitzgerald (Emily Perkins) // *Ginger Snaps* (2000); *Ginger Snaps: Unleashed* (2004); *Ginger Snaps Back: The Beginning* (2004)

Sarah Carter (Shauna Macdonald) // *The Descent* (2005); *The Descent Part 2* (2009)

Dana Polk (Kristen Connolly) // *The Cabin in the Woods* (2011)

Erin Harson (Sharni Vinson) // *You're Next* (2011)

Jay Height (Maika Monroe) // *It Follows* (2014)

Estrella (Paola Lara) // *Tigers Are Not Afraid* (2017)

Deena Johnson (Kiana Madeira) // *The Fear Street Trilogy* (2021)

SHAFT

(1971)

WRITTEN BY: Ernest Tidyman and John D. F. Black
(Based on the book by Ernest Tidyman)

DIRECTED BY: Gordon Parks

OTHER MOVIES DIRECTED BY GORDON PARKS:
The Learning Tree (1969); *Shaft's Big Score!* (1972);
Leadbelly (1976); *Moments Without Proper Names* (1987)

In 1971, moviegoers caught their first glimpse of John Shaft (Richard Roundtree), the "Black private dick that's a sex machine to all the chicks." Today, *Shaft* is considered one of the grandfathers of the blaxploitation genre—and it's got one of the most recognizable soundtracks of all time. While Samuel L. Jackson has taken on the role for a new generation in two separate films—one in 2000, the other in 2019—it's still impossible to compete with the original.

SHAFT WAS CREATED BY A WHITE NEWSPAPER REPORTER.

John Shaft made his debut in *Shaft*, a novel by Ernest Tidyman. Tidyman was a reporter for the *Cleveland News,* the *New York Post,* and the *New York Times* before he began writing the *Shaft* series, which included seven detective stories. Along with John D. F. Black, he adapted his first *Shaft* book into the screenplay for the first film. He would go on to write the screenplays for *The French Connection* (1971) and *High Plains Drifter* (1973) as well as *Shaft's Big Score!* (1972) and the *Shaft* TV series (1973–1974). His work earned him an NAACP Image Award.

THE STUDIO WANTED TO SHOOT SHAFT IN LOS ANGELES.

Shaft was filmed entirely in New York City, but it nearly wasn't. In his autobiography, *Voices in the Mirror,* Gordon Parks recalled how he received word from MGM mere hours before he was set to commence filming that he needed to return to Los Angeles and shoot the movie there. Apparently it was a budgetary issue, but Parks wasn't having it. He flew back to the West Coast and essentially told the studio heads he would quit if he couldn't shoot in Manhattan. "It has to have the smell of New York," Parks insisted.

SHAFT'S MUSTACHE WAS NON-NEGOTIABLE.

The Los Angeles fiasco was behind him, but Parks immediately faced another scare when he spied his star, Richard Roundtree, heading to the bathroom with a towel and razor. Producer Joel Freeman had asked him to get rid of his soon-to-be legendary mustache. Parks told Roundtree emphatically, "Shave it off and you're out of a job." And with that, the 'stache stayed in the picture.

PARKS MADE A CAMEO.

Parks appears briefly in the montage of Shaft searching for Ben Buford. He's the landlord with the pipe, who complains that he's also looking for Buford, who owes him six months of rent.

"SKLOOT INSURANCE" WAS A NOD TO A CREW MEMBER.

Shaft's office is sandwiched in between Acme Imports Exports Inc. and Skloot Insurance. The latter is a reference to Steven P. Skloot, the movie's unit production manager.

PARKS HAD TO EXPLAIN WHAT "SHAFT" AND "MOTHER" MEANT TO A REPORTER.

When Parks flew to London to do publicity for the film, he ended up giving an impromptu vocabulary lesson. At a press screening, a confused British reporter asked the director what "shaft" really meant. Parks replied by smiling and sticking his middle finger up in the air, explaining that was "the most honest answer" he could give. But the reporter was persistent and followed up by asking why the characters called each other "mother." Parks really didn't know how to answer that one, but luckily, a woman in the audience swooped in. "You've heard of Smucker's jam, young man," she said. "Just snip out the first two letters and add an 'f' and you'll get the message."

ISAAC HAYES WAS THE FIRST BLACK COMPOSER TO WIN AN OSCAR.

In 1972, Isaac Hayes's ubiquitous "Theme from Shaft" earned him an Oscar for Best Original Song. This win was historic for many reasons: For one, Hayes was the first Black composer to win an Oscar—but he was also only the third Black artist to win an Oscar, period. Prior to 1973, the only other Black Academy Award winners were Hattie McDaniel (Best Supporting Actress for *Gone with the Wind* in 1940) and Sidney Poitier (Best Actor for *Lilies of the Field* in 1964).

WRITTEN BY: Simon Pegg and Edgar Wright

DIRECTED BY: Edgar Wright

OTHER MOVIES DIRECTED BY EDGAR WRIGHT:
Hot Fuzz (2007); *Scott Pilgrim vs. the World* (2010);
Baby Driver (2017); *Last Night in Soho* (2021)

SHAUN OF THE DEAD
(2004)

Few comedies made in the past twenty years have inspired a devoted following quite like *Shaun of the Dead*. The film, about the beginning of a zombie apocalypse in London and the layabouts who are forced to reckon with it, made stars of director Edgar Wright, co-writer–star Nick Frost, and co-star Simon Pegg.

The film also launched what has come to be known as the "Three Flavours Cornetto Trilogy," which concluded with *Hot Fuzz* (2007) and *The World's End* (2013). *Shaun of the Dead* is one of those films that can make fellow fans into fast friends, and it's now considered one of the best zombie movies ever made.

SHAUN OF THE DEAD BEGAN WITH A SINGLE EPISODE OF *SPACED*.

According to Edgar Wright, the idea that would grow into *Shaun of the Dead* came from a single episode of *Spaced*, the comedy series he and Pegg co-created with Jessica Stevenson. In the first season episode "Art," Pegg's character Tim takes a dose of bad speed and stays up all night playing *Resident Evil 2*, which causes him to hallucinate that he's actually fighting zombies. After the episode was filmed, Wright pitched the idea of a feature-length zombie comedy.

THE ZOMBIE EXTRAS ARE MOSTLY MAJOR *SPACED* FANS.

To find extras willing to be made up as zombies, the filmmakers put out the call to *Spaced* fans. About two hundred extras were eventually recruited.

SHAUN'S NICKNAME HAS A VERY SWEET ORIGIN.

In the film, Shaun's mother Barbara (*Downton Abbey*'s Penelope Wilton) calls him "pickle," and apparently that's not just something the filmmakers made up. Wright's own mother called him that as a boy—and apparently while she taught some of his classes at school, much to his embarrassment.

ONE CHARACTER'S DEATH CAUSED ACTUAL TEARS ON THE SET.

Shaun of the Dead is full of comedy-laden deaths, but one particular character's demise caused real grief: the death of Shaun's mother. According to Wright and Pegg, this was incredibly emotional for everyone, and after her death scene was filmed, Pegg cried real tears.

GEORGE A. ROMERO WAS A FAN OF THE MOVIE.

Knowing that they were borrowing heavily from his zombie filmmaking style and that they'd taken their title from *Dawn of the Dead* (1978), Wright and Pegg reached out to zombie legend George A. Romero to ask if he'd see the film and give it his blessing.

According to Wright, Romero watched the movie in a theater in Florida by himself (except for a lone security guard) and quite enjoyed it. "We got a call from him later that night," Wright said. "He couldn't have been sweeter about it."

WRIGHT AND PEGG WERE IMMORTALIZED AS ZOMBIES AFTER THE MOVIE.

After they won over Romero with *Shaun of the Dead*, Pegg and Wright were both invited to cameo as zombies in Romero's fourth *Dead* film, 2005's *Land of the Dead*. They are both credited as "Photo Booth Zombie," and can be glimpsed during a scene in which rich humans get their photos taken next to chained-up zombies.

10

28 Days Later **(2002)**
Danny Boyle's apocalyptic thriller is best known for introducing fast-moving zombies, but it deserves endless credit for the creativity and logistical maneuvering required to pull off its depiction of an eerily deserted London. The crew sometimes had only an hour or two to shoot key scenes in early-morning hours, using up to eight small digital cameras simultaneously so filming could be completed as quickly as possible while police used rolling roadblocks to keep traffic at bay. To lend added realism, Boyle and cinematographer Anthony Dod Mantle often modeled their shots after iconic news footage from real-life crises, including images from Bosnia, Rwanda, and Northern Ireland.

BRAINY ZOMBIE FLICKS

It's been nearly a century since zombies first shambled onto the big screen, and our fascination with them is still going strong. They've changed dramatically since Bela Lugosi zombified his victims in 1932's *White Zombie*, which was in large part inspired by a 1929 book about Haitian folklore. But maybe their mutability is the secret of their appeal.

Thanks to constant reinvention, zombies have given form to our fears of other cultures, loss of agency, communism, atomic warfare, race relations and the civil rights movement, capitalism, mass contagions, the space race, and, most importantly, our bone-deep fear of one another.

2 Braindead (1992)

Before Peter Jackson scored an Oscar nomination for *Heavenly Creatures* (1994) and became the king of big-budget epic fantasy, he made a trio of hard-R exploitation films in his native New Zealand. One of those is *Braindead* (released in North America as *Dead Alive*), a ridiculously gory and strangely good-humored zombie movie that finds its hero wrestling an undead baby, dispatching a horde of flesh-eaters with a lawn mower, and returning to the womb of his zombified mother.

3 Dawn of the Dead (1978)

Night of the Living Dead was released a month before the MPAA's rating system went into effect, so there was nothing to stop theaters from selling tickets to kids—which they happily did, to the horror of film critic Roger Ebert, who saw the movie at a "kiddie matinee" full of unaccompanied children. When the ratings board previewed *Dawn of the Dead* a decade later, they had a powerful tool at their disposal: the dreaded "X" rating, which was such a deterrent that Romero declined the rating—which technically meant it was an X, but without the stigma. The *Dallas Times Herald* called it "the most horrific, brutal, nightmarish descent into Hell ever put on the screen," and the *New York Times* film critic Janet Maslin famously walked out after fifteen minutes. *Dawn of the Dead* still packs a punch today, though the gore is tempered by Romero's sly humor and the fact that almost everyone involved seems to be having the time of their life.

4 Day of the Dead (1985)

George Romero wanted the third entry in his *Dead* series to be, in his words, "the *Gone with the Wind* of zombie films." His producers offered him a $7 million budget, with the caveat that he'd have to deliver an R-rated movie so that the film's backers could recoup their investment. Romero refused, opting to pare back his vision rather than water it down to accommodate the MPAA's subjective restrictions. His original script was an adventure story that explored the wider ramifications of the zombie outbreak, but the version that made it to the screen confines most of the action to a Florida military bunker. It's a bleak, intensely nihilistic movie that has nevertheless found a devoted and ever-growing fan base in the decades since its release. Romero has singled it out as his favorite installment in the *Dead* series.

5 Night of the Comet (1984)

Writer-director Thom Eberhardt has maintained that *Night of the Comet* isn't a zombie movie, but it's hard to take him at his word when stars Catherine Mary Stewart and Kelli Maroney and production designer John Muto have all insisted that an early version of the script was titled *Teenage Comet Zombies* (a phrase that's also spoken in the movie). According to Stewart, Eberhardt and the film's producers had two very different ideas of what the movie should be. "The producers wanted a zombie horror movie with a couple of cute young female victims," Stewart said. "Thom . . . had a whole different concept. There were scenes that we shot two different ways to accommodate the two visions. Fortunately, Thom's concept won out."

6 Night of the Creeps (1986)

If you're a horror fan of a certain age, there's a good chance that your first brush with *Night of the Creeps* was the iconic image that was plastered all over video store walls in the eighties, depicting a zombified frat dude in a bloody tux and the memorable tagline "The good news is your date is here. The bad news is . . . he's dead." It's an attention-grabbing visual, but it doesn't convey the heady mix of throwback science fiction, grisly practical FX, and frat-house humor that make up Fred Dekker's directorial feature debut. *Night of the Creeps* bombed at the box office before slowly amassing a cult following on home video.

7 Pontypool (2008)

Director Bruce McDonald has insisted that *Pontypool*'s aggressors aren't zombies at all, referring to them as *conversationalists* instead. The virus in the film is spread through certain words, which drive the infected to commit gruesome acts of violence, mostly out of frustration with their inability to communicate. (Note that the word *typo* is embedded in the title.) Screenwriter Tony Burgess adapted the script from his 1995 novel *Pontypool Changes Everything*, reportedly drawing inspiration from Orson Welles's infamous 1938 radio broadcast of *War of the Worlds*. Set in a radio station as a possible apocalypse unfolds outside, *Pontypool* is a cerebral, inventive take on the subgenre.

8 [Rec] (2007)

Besides being one of the scariest zombie movies in recent memory, this Spanish shocker is one of the keystones of the modern found-footage cycle. Writer-directors Paco Plaza and Jaume Balagueró were both working for Spanish production company Filmax when they began talking about what new elements they could bring to the horror genre. Soon after, the pair had secured funding from their employer and began shooting *[Rec]*, a single-camera, one-location movie staged as a real-time television news report. Though it takes a few cues from *The Blair Witch Project*, *[Rec]* is very much a product of the gothic-tinged Spanish horror boom of the early 2000s. It's also one of the few movies to put an unnerving religious spin on the zombie-outbreak trope.

9 Train to Busan (2016)

Train to Busan was a massive hit in its native South Korea, grossing more than $80 million in its domestic theatrical run. It's the first live-action feature directed by Yeon Sang-ho, who was highly regarded for a pair of adult-oriented animated films before he set out to make South Korea's first feature-length, live-action zombie movie. He came up with the idea for *Train to Busan* while he was working on an animated feature called *Seoul Station*, a zombie apocalypse story inspired by the plight of people experiencing homelessness and living in one of Seoul's largest train terminals. According to an interview with the newspaper *Korea JoongAng Daily*, Yeon was more heavily influenced by close-quarter, single-location thrillers such as *United 93* and *Captain Phillips* than other zombie films.

10 Zombi 2 (1979)

When *Dawn of the Dead* was released in Italy, it was re-edited by Dario Argento, re-scored by Italian prog rockers Goblin, and titled simply *Zombi*. Because of a quirk in Italian copyright law that allows for unauthorized sequels, enterprising Italian producers quickly set out to capitalize on *Zombi*'s success with an unofficial sequel helmed by Lucio Fulci. *Zombi 2* features some infamous gore gags and gnarly, worm-eaten zombies, and it's notable for reintroducing the element of black magic that had fallen out of favor in post–*Night of the Living Dead* zombie cinema. But its most memorable scene is a weird underwater showstopper that pits a zombie against a live shark.

WRITTEN BY: **Frank Darabont**
(based on the novella by Stephen King)

DIRECTED BY: **Frank Darabont**

OTHER MOVIES DIRECTED BY FRANK DARABONT:
The Green Mile (1999); *The Majestic* (2001);
The Mist (2007)

THE SHAWSHANK REDEMPTION (1994)

Beloved as it may be now, *The Shawshank Redemption* was an abject box-office bomb when it was first released in 1994. Overshadowed by the likes of *Forrest Gump*, it took years—and numerous cable airings—for the movie to find its audience. Once it did, viewers became attached to the story of Andy Dufresne (Tim Robbins), who tries to find both metaphorical and literal escape from the confines of a life sentence at Maine's Shawshank State Penitentiary with the help of fellow inmate "Red" (Morgan Freeman).

FREEZE-FRAME

Shooting Tim Robbins in the rain was no easy task. Every take of the film's signature shot of Andy raising his arms outstretched in the rain after breaking out of prison was out of focus except the one in the film. It was the final take.

IT'S BASED ON A STEPHEN KING NOVELLA.

The film is based on Stephen King's novella *Rita Hayworth and the Shawshank Redemption*, which was published in his 1982 collection *Different Seasons*. Two other novellas in the collection were made into films: 1986's *Stand by Me* (based on "The Body") and 1998's *Apt Pupil*.

IT SHARES A THEME WITH TOLSTOY.

King's novella shares several plot points with a nine-page short story written by Leo Tolstoy called "God Sees the Truth, but Waits." Both are about men sent to prison for murders they didn't commit.

DARABONT GOT A GOOD DEAL ON THE RIGHTS TO KING'S STORY.

Prior to *Shawshank*, Darabont adapted King's "The Woman in the Room," the rights to which he bought for $1. (The bestselling author has long made a policy of granting the rights to his short stories to promising up-and-coming filmmakers for just a dollar.) But for *Shawshank*, King wanted more—something like $5,000. Darabont sent a check, which King didn't cash. After the film was made, King sent the check back along with a note saying, "In case you ever need bail money."

THE PRODUCTION COMPANY THAT MADE THE FILM HAS A NOD TO KING IN ITS NAME.

Castle Rock Entertainment, the production company that made *The Shawshank Redemption*, was co-founded by *Stand by Me* director Rob Reiner and is named after the mythical Maine town that provides the setting for many of King's books. After director Darabont pitched *The Shawshank Redemption* to Castle Rock, Reiner offered a rumored $3 million so he could direct the film, for which he planned to cast Tom Cruise as Andy and Harrison Ford as Red. Darabont said no.

DARABONT WROTE THE SCRIPT IN EIGHT WEEKS.

He decided to drop the "Rita Hayworth" part of the novella because actresses sent their résumés in for consideration thinking it was a Rita Hayworth biopic. During the casting process, Darabont even received a call from an agent who represented a supermodel; he swore the script was the best she had ever read and that she'd be perfect for the (nonexistent) part of Hayworth.

GOODFELLAS INSPIRED THE FILM'S STYLE.

Darabont says his main source of inspiration was Martin Scorsese's *Goodfellas*, because of its use of voice-over narration and editing techniques.

FREEMAN RECORDED HIS VOICE-OVER BEFORE ANY FILM WAS SHOT.

Originally, all of Freeman's voice-over was recorded before any of the film was shot. The fact that much of it syncs up to the on-screen action (see the scene on the roof where the inmates drink beer) isn't simple editing; Darabont would play back the recorded voice-over on set during each take for the actors to specifically play off the audio. But the audio quality of his voice-over was too poor to include in the movie, so Freeman had to re-record the entire voice-over in postproduction.

The scene where Andy first approaches Red about getting him a rock hammer as Red plays catch in the main yard took nine hours to shoot. Freeman continued to play catch for the whole nine hours without complaining and showed up the next day with his arm in a sling.

FLOP FLIP: 5 BELOVED MOVIES THAT FLOPPED AT THE BOX OFFICE

It's hard to believe that some beloved films didn't find immediate success when they were released, but sometimes movies are just ahead of their time.

1 The Big Lebowski (1998)

The Dude abides, but moviegoers didn't when this black comedy from Joel and Ethan Coen first arrived in theaters back in 1998. It opened in the U.S. to tepid reviews (the *Guardian* called it a "loose, meandering outline" of a film) and earned a disappointing $5.5 million during its first weekend against a $15 million budget, but it found new life thanks to home video. In the years since, it has come to be regarded as that rarest of gems: a cult flick that's as weird as they come, but also a masterstroke from its creators. That rug really tied the room together, and when it comes to the Coen brothers' filmography, *The Big Lebowski* does, too.

2 Brazil (1985)

Terry Gilliam earned plenty of good faith from general audiences and movie studios, thanks to his work with Monty Python. However, after he finished *Brazil* in 1985, Universal Pictures refused to release the film because of its anti-corporate undertones and strange narrative. Terry Gilliam screened *Brazil* privately without Universal's approval and took out a full-page ad in *Variety* to address studio boss Sid Sheinberg that simply read, "When are you going to release my film, *BRAZIL?*" An edited-down version was ultimately released, but it didn't get much traction in the United States, where it only grossed around $10 million.

3 Children of Men (2006)

Seven years before Alfonso Cuarón dazzled audiences with *Gravity* in 2013, his dystopian science fiction film *Children of Men*—which imagines a world in which rampant infertility is pushing humankind to the brink of extinction—hit theaters. Although it received positive reviews and three Academy Award nominations, including one for Best Adapted Screenplay, it didn't make much of an impact on moviegoers: It took in just $35.5 million during its domestic release.

4 Dazed and Confused (1993)

While Richard Linklater's sophomore film featured loads of current-day stars such as Ben Affleck, Milla Jovovich, and Matthew McConaughey, the young cast weren't household names at the time. Gramercy Pictures and Universal Pictures didn't know how to market a stoner coming-of-age movie without raunchy sex scenes or gross-out humor to a general audience. While the movie was virtually forgotten in 1993, it survived and managed to eventually find a massive following among cinephiles.

5 Willy Wonka & the Chocolate Factory (1971)

While *Willy Wonka & the Chocolate Factory* is considered a family classic today, audiences didn't enthusiastically respond to it when it first arrived in theaters. As the film wasn't profitable, Paramount Pictures decided not to renew its seven-year copyright, and Warner Bros. bought the rights for $500,000 in 1977. Under new ownership, Warner Bros. licensed *Willy Wonka & the Chocolate Factory* for TV broadcast, where it found a widespread audience after repeated airings and further home video sales.

(2010)

THE SOCIAL NETWORK

The *Social Network*—a movie released when Facebook was less than seven years old and the social media era was relatively new—seemed destined to age poorly. But this exhilarating account of how a college student started the behemoth social media site is even more alarming given what we've learned about Mark Zuckerberg and the company since then.

Jesse Eisenberg's crisp lead performance, Aaron Sorkin's verbose dialogue, and David Fincher's energetic direction combine to make this a cautionary tale of Shakespearean proportions. It might be the best document of how the internet and social media have fundamentally changed us.

FREEZE-FRAME

Fincher has been known to regularly leave Easter eggs in his movies. Sharp-eyed viewers may have noticed the *Fight Club* Easter egg that Fincher snuck into the scene where Zuckerberg is checking someone's Facebook to cheat on a test. The name Tyler Durden (aka Brad Pitt's character) can be seen in the top-left corner of the profile.

AARON SORKIN STARTED WRITING THE SCRIPT BEFORE THE BOOK IT'S BASED ON WAS PUBLISHED.

The Social Network is officially an adaptation of *The Accidental Billionaires*, Ben Mezrich's 2009 book detailing the founding of Facebook. But according to screenwriter Aaron Sorkin, he had already completed 80 percent of the script by the time he read the book (though they had compared notes). The project came to him in the form of a fourteen-page book proposal the publisher was shopping around to filmmakers ahead of the title's release. "I said yes on page three," Sorkin told Deadline in 2011. "That's the fastest I've ever said yes to anything."

THE SOCIAL NETWORK WASN'T FILMED AT HARVARD.

Harvard University is integral to the legend of Facebook, and setting the first half of *The Social Network* there was non-negotiable. Filmmakers ran into trouble, however, when attempting to get the school's blessing. The 1970 adaptation of *Love Story* had been shot there, but various productions had damaged the campus; the school has reportedly banned all commercial filming on the premises since then. To get around this, *The Social Network* crew shot the Harvard scenes at Johns Hopkins University in Maryland and two Massachusetts prep schools, Phillips Academy Andover and Milton Academy.

FINCHER DID SNEAK ONE SHOT OF HARVARD INTO THE MOVIE.

To convince the audience that they were indeed seeing Harvard, Fincher couldn't resist sneaking in a shot of the campus's iconic architecture. When Eisenberg runs across Harvard Square (which is not on Harvard property) in the beginning of the film, some nearby arches (which *are* on Harvard property) appear in the background. Fincher got the lighting he needed for this scene by hiring a street mime to roll a cart with lights on it onto the campus. "If security were to stop him, the mime wouldn't talk," cinematographer Jeff Cronenweth told *Variety*. "By the time they got him out of there, we would have accomplished our shot."

NATALIE PORTMAN GAVE SORKIN THE INSIDE SCOOP ON HARVARD.

Portman attended Harvard from 1999 to 2003, briefly overlapping with Zuckerberg's time there. While enrolled, she dated a member of one of the university's elite final clubs, which are an important part of the movie's plot. When she learned that Sorkin was writing the screenplay for the movie, she invited the writer over to hear her insider knowledge. Sorkin gave the actress a shout-out in the final script.

MARK ZUCKERBERG WASN'T A FAN OF THE MOVIE.

The Social Network doesn't paint Zuckerberg in the most flattering light, and unsurprisingly, the real-life Facebook founder wasn't happy about it. Following the movie's release, he called out its "hurtful" inaccuracies, specifically citing the fictional Mara Rooney character that's used as his motivation for founding the website. But even he admits that some details were spot-on. "Like every single fleece and shirt I had in that movie is actually a shirt or fleece that I own," Zuckerberg said at a Stanford event.

STAR WARS:
THE ORIGINAL TRILOGY
(1977–1983)

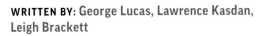

WRITTEN BY: George Lucas, Lawrence Kasdan, Leigh Brackett

DIRECTED BY: George Lucas, Irvin Kershner, and Richard Marquand

OTHER MOVIES DIRECTED BY GEORGE LUCAS: *THX 1138* (1971); *American Graffiti* (1973); *Star Wars: The Phantom Menace* (1999); *Star Wars: Attack of the Clones* (2002); *Star Wars: Revenge of the Sith* (2005)

For some, it's the most concentrated expression of mythological storytelling ever put on film. For others, it's a story about a space farm boy who runs into a galactic drifter and his talking-carpet sidekick. However you interpret *Star Wars*, there's no denying it has grown into something far beyond a series of films and into something approaching a pop culture religion. But still, what films they are. As ambitious but naïve Luke Skywalker, Mark Hamill falls under the tutelage of wizened Obi-Wan Kenobi (Alec Guinness, lending gravitas to the fantasy trappings). Alongside Harrison Ford's Han Solo, who verbalizes the audience's skepticism of the all-encompassing Force, and Carrie Fisher's capable Princess Leia, young Luke evolves into a stoic Jedi Knight capable of confronting Darth Vader.

Conceived by George Lucas but burnished to a sheen by the talents of his effects artists and John Williams's rousing score, the original trilogy bridged the gap between the nihilism of seventies cinema and the neon optimism of the eighties. Ewoks aside, it's the series virtually every major Hollywood franchise aspires to be—movie magic as mysterious and hard to capture as the Force itself.

THE FIRST DRAFT OF *A NEW HOPE* WAS REPORTEDLY TWO HUNDRED PAGES LONG.

In 1974, 20th Century Fox head Alan Ladd Jr. gave Lucas a preliminary deal to eventually make the movie. But the "final" screenplay Lucas turned in was more than two hundred pages long, so Lucas excised the final two acts and presented the first act of the screenplay as the finished story. The script would be reworked into *Star Wars* (before it was known as *A New Hope*) and he placed the other two acts on the shelf, hoping to come back to them later.

HARRISON FORD'S CASTING WAS SORT OF ACCIDENTAL.

Lucas spent seven months holding casting sessions for *Star Wars* with his friend Brian De Palma, who was casting for *Carrie* at the same time. Lucas was looking for unknown faces whom he had never worked with before, and initially brought in Harrison Ford—whom he had worked with on *American Graffiti*—to feed lines to the auditioning actors. Lucas saw dozens of actors, including a young Kurt Russell, for the part of Han, but liked Ford's delivery as he fed lines to the other actors so much that he caved and cast him in the part.

George Lucas originally wanted Orson Welles as the voice of Darth Vader, but dropped the idea when he thought Welles's famous baritone would be too recognizable.

THEATERS BALKED AT SHOWING *STAR WARS*.

Fewer than forty theaters agreed to book showings of *Star Wars* after its release date was moved up to before Memorial Day (the studio thought it would bomb in a crowded summer movie slate). Around the same time, 20th Century Fox was going to release a highly anticipated adaptation of a bestselling book called *The Other Side of Midnight*, which theaters were eager to show. Fox then stipulated that any theater showing *The Other Side of Midnight* must also show *Star Wars*, which inflated the number of screens for the movie.

Needless to say, *Star Wars* eventually became the highest-grossing movie ever made up to that time, while *The Other Side of Midnight* didn't even break the $25 million mark. And as requiring movie theaters to show one movie in exchange for another movie was actually illegal, 20th Century Fox ended up being fined $25,000 by the Department of Justice.

THAT ICONIC OPENING CRAWL WAS CREATED WITH PRACTICAL EFFECTS.

The opening crawl for the original movie (which was cribbed from the *Flash Gordon* serials that also inspired the film) was done using practical effects (or special effects that are created live on the set using tangible objects versus digitally after the fact). It was created by carefully placing two-foot-wide die-cut yellow letters over a six-foot-long black paper background with a camera making a slow pass over them to mimic the crawl. In total, it took three hours to shoot.

GEORGE LUCAS WANTED JIM HENSON AS YODA.

In an interview with Leonard Maltin, Lucas admitted that he wanted Muppets maestro Jim Henson to play the role of Yoda. "I went to Jim [Henson] and said, 'Do you want to do this?' And he said, 'Well, I'm busy, I'm doing this, and doing that, I'm making a movie and all that—I really can't, but . . . how about Frank [Oz]? You know, Frank's the other half of me.' And I said, 'Well, that'd be fantastic.'"

THE EMPEROR USED TO BE A CHIMP.

In the original version of *The Empire Strikes Back*, the scene in which Darth Vader converses with the Emperor looked a lot different. Though many viewers automatically associate the character with actor Ian McDiarmid, the original Emperor was an old woman with chimpanzee eyes and the voice of distinguished voice actor and Royal Shakespeare Company alum Clive Revill.

ALEC GUINNESS WAS PAID A LOT FOR VERY LITTLE WORK.

Sir Alec had a testy history with his legacy when it came to *Star Wars*. He described the first film as "fairy-tale rubbish" before he even started filming, and although he had come around on that film, he wanted nothing to do with *The Empire Strikes Back*. Lucas and the filmmakers eventually persuaded the actor to appear as the ghostly version of Obi-Wan with Yoda on Dagobah, but Guinness would only do it under very strict conditions: He would work only one day but would start at 8:30 a.m. and be done by 1:00 p.m., and would have to be paid one-fourth of a percent of the movie's total gross. That four and a half hours' worth of work netted Guinness millions of dollars.

DARTH VADER COULD HAVE BEEN CHEWBACCA.

David Prowse, who ended up portraying the in-costume version of Darth Vader, originally turned down the role of Chewbacca. When given the choice between portraying the two characters, Prowse said, "I turned down the role of Chewbacca at once. I know that people remember villains longer than heroes. At the time I didn't know I'd be wearing a mask, and throughout production I thought Vader's voice would be mine."

DUTCH AND GERMAN SPEAKERS MAY HAVE HAD A CLUE ABOUT LUKE'S PARENTAGE.

Dutch and German speakers should have known Darth Vader was Luke's father from the get-go, as the Dutch and German words for father are *vader* and *Vater*, respectively (though it remains unknown whether this was intentional).

SOME BIG NAMES WERE ON THE SHORTLIST TO DIRECT *RETURN OF THE JEDI*.

Steven Spielberg was reportedly Lucas's first choice to direct the third installment of the series, but Spielberg was forced to bow out due to Lucas's unceremonious exit from the Directors Guild of America, of which Spielberg was a prominent member. (Lucas opted to leave the DGA following *The Empire Strikes Back* over the organization's rules about title credits, so he could not hire a DGA member to work on the film.) Relative newcomers David Lynch and David Cronenberg were also tapped to potentially direct. Lynch was coming off the commercial success of his movie *The Elephant Man* (1980), but turned Lucas down to direct the big-screen adaptation of *Dune* instead. Cronenberg was also coming off a hit—the horror classic *Scanners* (1981)—but he hesitated, due to generally not directing other people's material, and said he was immediately hung up on.

Lucas eventually settled on Welsh director Richard Marquand because he liked his previous movie, the 1981 World War II spy thriller *Eye of the Needle*, and because he wasn't a DGA union member.

IT TOOK UP TO SEVEN DIFFERENT PUPPETEERS TO BE JABBA THE HUTT.

The Jabba puppet was partly inspired by stout British actor Sydney Greenstreet, who had appeared in such movies as *The Maltese Falcon* (1941) and *Casablanca* (1942). Created by Yoda designer Stuart Freeborn, the massive puppet was controlled by a handful of puppeteers: Inside, one controlled the right arm and jaw, while another handled the left hand and jaw, tongue, and head movements; both of them moved the body, and a third person was in the tail. Outside, there were one or two people on radio controllers for the eyes, someone under the stage to blow cigar smoke up a tube, and another working bellows for the lungs.

AN EWOK GOT HIS BIG BREAK BECAUSE OF FOOD POISONING.

Then-eleven-year-old Warwick Davis was initially cast as an Ewok extra after his grandmother heard about an open casting call on the radio in England. When Kenny Baker, who played R2-D2 and was also originally cast as the main Ewok named Wicket, fell ill with food poisoning on the day he was supposed to begin shooting his Ewok scenes, the filmmakers had Davis play Wicket instead. Davis allegedly based his performance of the inquisitive little critter on his dog.

THE FILMMAKERS WANTED A MOVIE STAR TO BE THE UNMASKED VADER.

The one moment at the end of *Return of the Jedi* that fans had been waiting years for was seeing Darth Vader's actual face. When the time came, audiences finally got that moment, and the face they saw was . . . Sebastian Shaw's.

Shaw, who was primarily known as a British stage actor before making his *Jedi* cameo, wasn't the first person the filmmakers had in mind. They initially wanted to make it a momentous occasion by casting a well-known movie star like Laurence Olivier or John Gielgud to be behind the mask, but later changed their minds. Instead of a recognizable star, they thought it would be better if Vader turned out to be a nondescript person who still had to be a veteran actor to handle the emotions, and Shaw fit the role.

CLOSE-UP

In early drafts of the screenplay, Yoda was actually named "Buffy," which was completely changed in subsequent drafts to the full name "Minch Yoda," and then shortened to just Yoda.

"No, I am your father."

STAR WARS'S MOST MEMORABLE LINE IS ALSO ITS MOST MISQUOTED.

When Darth Vader drops the paternal bomb on Luke, he does so by stating, "No, I am your father." The line is one of the most often misquoted in cinema history, and usually repeated as "Luke, I am your father." (Even Chris Farley got it wrong in *Tommy Boy*.)

SOME OF THE ASTEROIDS YOU SEE ARE SPRAY-PAINTED POTATOES.

When the filmmakers needed asteroids in the background during the *Millennium Falcon*'s escape through an asteroid belt in *The Empire Strikes Back*, they simply spray-painted potatoes and filmed them in front of a blue screen to composite later.

THE SAGA COULD HAVE ENDED VERY DIFFERENTLY.

During an early story meeting, Lucas pitched an idea for the end of *Return of the Jedi* that would have irrevocably changed the entire *Star Wars* saga as we know it.

His idea started out very much like the end of *Jedi* now: Luke and Vader engage in a lightsaber battle with Vader ultimately sacrificing himself to save Luke by killing the Emperor, then Luke watches his father die after taking his mask off. But then, in the proposed ending, Lucas suggested, "Luke takes his mask off. The mask is the very last thing—and then Luke puts it on and says, 'Now I am Vader.'" The idea was scrapped because Lucas didn't want the story to go that dark and wanted a happy ending after all.

THE STING

(1973)

Four years after partnering up for *Butch Cassidy and the Sundance Kid*, the dynamic duo of Paul Newman and Robert Redford—two of the biggest movie stars of the day—collaborated once again on *The Sting*. While their partnership as Butch and Sundance might be the better remembered one, partly because Redford really latched onto that whole "Sundance" thing, *The Sting* was actually the bigger hit. In it, Redford and Newman play wannabe con artist Johnny Hooker and veteran flimflammer Henry Gondorff, respectively, who are both out for revenge. Fortunately, they're after the same man: merciless crime boss Doyle Lonnegan (Robert Shaw), who is responsible for the murder of their mutual friend.

While they attempt to plan the perfect con, Hooker and Gondorff learn that even the best-laid plans don't always work out. Fortunately, they're crafty enough to improvise. And it's that feeling of never knowing what will happen next that makes the film, which won the Oscar for Best Picture, a timeless gem.

WRITTEN BY: David S. Ward

DIRECTED BY: George Roy Hill

OTHER MOVIES DIRECTED BY GEORGE ROY HILL:
Butch Cassidy and the Sundance Kid (1969);
Slap Shot (1977); *A Little Romance* (1979);
The World According to Garp (1982);
Funny Farm (1988)

PAUL NEWMAN'S ROLE WAS WRITTEN FOR AN OVERWEIGHT, OVER-THE-HILL SLOB, AND WAS A MINOR CHARACTER.

Henry Gondorff was only in about half of David S. Ward's original screenplay and was intended to be an older, paunchier fellow—a sort of gruff mentor to Johnny Hooker (who was written as a nineteen-year-old). The producers were thinking of someone like Peter Boyle to play the role, but Newman loved the screenplay and wanted to play Gondorff no matter what. So Ward slimmed down the character and beefed up the role.

REUNITING BUTCH AND SUNDANCE WASN'T THE NO-BRAINER YOU'D EXPECT.

Separately, Redford and Newman were two of the biggest movie stars in the world in the early 1970s. As a duo, they were perhaps even more popular, with mega-hit *Butch Cassidy and the Sundance Kid* (1969) fresh in people's memories. When the director of that film, George Roy Hill, signed on for *The Sting*, Redford soon followed. Then came Newman, as described above. But while a Butch and Sundance reunion sounded tempting (and lucrative), the studio had a concern: In the movie, the two con men's partnership hinges on the possibility that one (or both) will try to double-cross the other. With Redford and Newman so famously chummy,

Robert Redford and Paul Newman were each paid $500,000 for *The Sting*. That was the top rate for an actor in those days. That's about $3.1 million in 2022 dollars, which is well below the $10 to $20 million big stars get paid nowadays.

Universal was concerned that audiences wouldn't believe such a betrayal was possible, and the film would thus lose some of its suspense. Hill assuaged their fears.

THE SCREENWRITER WANTED TO DIRECT THE MOVIE HIMSELF.

When the producers first optioned Ward's screenplay—before it was finished, based only on his telling them the story—the deal had been for him to direct it, too. That was nixed when Redford, sniffing around the project, said he wouldn't do such a complicated movie with a first-timer at the helm. Once Ward saw the caliber of talent his screenplay was attracting, he came to agree with the producers that it deserved a more experienced director. Ward did eventually direct a few of his own screenplays, including *Major League* (1989), *King Ralph* (1991), and *The Program* (1993).

ROBERT SHAW'S LIMP WAS REAL.

Per producer Julia Phillips's memoir, *You'll Never Eat Lunch in This Town Again*, Shaw, who played crime boss Doyle Lonnegan in the film, tore the ligaments in his knee on a handball court just days before shooting began and had to keep his leg in a brace. Director Hill decided to work with it and had Shaw turn his injury into a character trait.

THE DIRECTOR RESHOT THE FIRST WEEK'S WORTH OF FOOTAGE.

Production got off to a rather rocky start. Screenwriter Ward told the *Sydney Morning Herald* that "George [Roy Hill] reshot his first week. He didn't like what he did the first week of shooting, and thought it could be better, so he reshot it." (It was the first sequence in the movie, the one where Hooker and Luther Coleman fleece a mobster in the alley.) Things went smoothly after that, and people praised Hill for running an efficient, happy, and well-organized set.

WRITTEN BY: Mario Puzo,
David Newman, Leslie Newman,
and Robert Benton

DIRECTED BY: Richard Donner

**OTHER MOVIES DIRECTED BY
RICHARD DONNER:**
The Omen (1976); *The Goonies*
(1985); *Lethal Weapon* (1987);
Scrooged (1988); *16 Blocks* (2006)

SUPERMAN: THE MOVIE (1978)

Today, comic book movies are ubiquitous—a fact that's largely due to the success of Richard Donner's *Superman*. In the 1970s, superhero movies were an untested gamble. To make *Superman*, a trio of ambitious producers teamed up with a talented director, a great cast, and an unprecedented special effects team to create something unlike anything anyone had ever seen on the big screen before. The result was a storied, often tense, filmmaking experience that, even in the age of the Marvel Cinematic Universe, remains one of the greatest superhero movies ever made.

RICHARD DONNER ACCEPTED THE *SUPERMAN* DIRECTING JOB WHILE ON THE TOILET.

According to Donner, who was riding high after the success of 1976's *The Omen*, he was actually sitting on the toilet when he got the call from producer Alexander Salkind offering him the chance to shoot *Superman* and *Superman II* back-to-back.

THE ORIGINAL SCRIPT WAS FIVE HUNDRED PAGES LONG . . . AND DONNER HATED IT.

When producers Ilya and Alexander Salkind began the project, they wanted a high-profile writer to boost the film's profile, and decided on *The Godfather* author Mario Puzo. After spending some time with editors and DC Comics to familiarize himself with Superman lore, Puzo got to work and produced a massive script spanning two films and five hundred pages. The script was later rewritten by David and Leslie Newman and Robert Benton. When Donner joined the film, he demanded additional rewrites.

MARLON BRANDO WANTED TO PLAY JOR-EL "LIKE A BAGEL."

To further boost the film's profile, the Salkinds went after major stars for key supporting roles, and pursued Marlon Brando for the role of Superman's father, Jor-El. Before he met the actor, Donner asked famed Hollywood agent Jay Kanter for any negotiating hints, at which point he learned that Brando was going to attempt to do as little work as possible. "He said, 'He's going to want to play it like a green suitcase,'" Donner recalled. "I said, 'What does that mean?' 'It means he hates to work and he loves money, so if he can talk you into the fact that the people on Krypton look like green suitcases and you only photograph green suitcases, he'll get paid just to do the voice-over. That's the way his mind works.'"

When the director actually met with Brando, the actor proposed that he play Jor-El not as a green suitcase, but as a "bagel." He also pitched the idea that maybe Kryptonians don't even talk. They simply make electronic sounds that are translated through subtitles.

MARGOT KIDDER'S CLUMSINESS WON HER THE ROLE OF LOIS LANE.

For the role of Lois Lane, several actresses—including Lesley Ann Warren and Anne Archer—were considered, but Kidder ultimately won the role by simply being herself. "When I met her in the casting office, she tripped coming in and I just fell in love with her," Donner said. "It was perfect, this clumsy [behavior]. She was one of the few [actresses] we flew to London to test with Chris [Reeve]."

THE MOVIE'S KRYPTONIAN COSTUMES COULDN'T BE TOUCHED BY BARE HANDS.

For the scenes on Krypton, costume designer Yvonne Blake wanted costumes that reflected some kind of "energy," and ultimately decided to craft the suits from material traditionally used for movie screens "made out of minuscule balls of glass." The glowing effect the material produced was fantastic, but because of its delicate nature, the crew could only touch it while wearing cotton gloves.

THE MOVIE'S CREW CRIED WHEN SUPERMAN FLEW FOR THE FIRST TIME.

Perhaps the biggest challenge in making *Superman* was creating a convincing special effect that would allow Superman to fly. Donner was adamant that it had to feel authentic, and that meant the special effects team had to essentially invent new methods of on-screen flight. Finally, optics expert Zoran Perisic designed a system that used two zoom lenses interacting with each other to create a flight effect.

"Christopher Reeve would be basically in one place, on a pole arm . . . that you don't see, and all he does is sort of make the moves, and it's the camera and the projector that make him look like he comes straight up," Perisic said. According to Donner, crew members actually cried the first time they saw Reeve take flight.

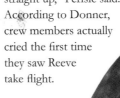

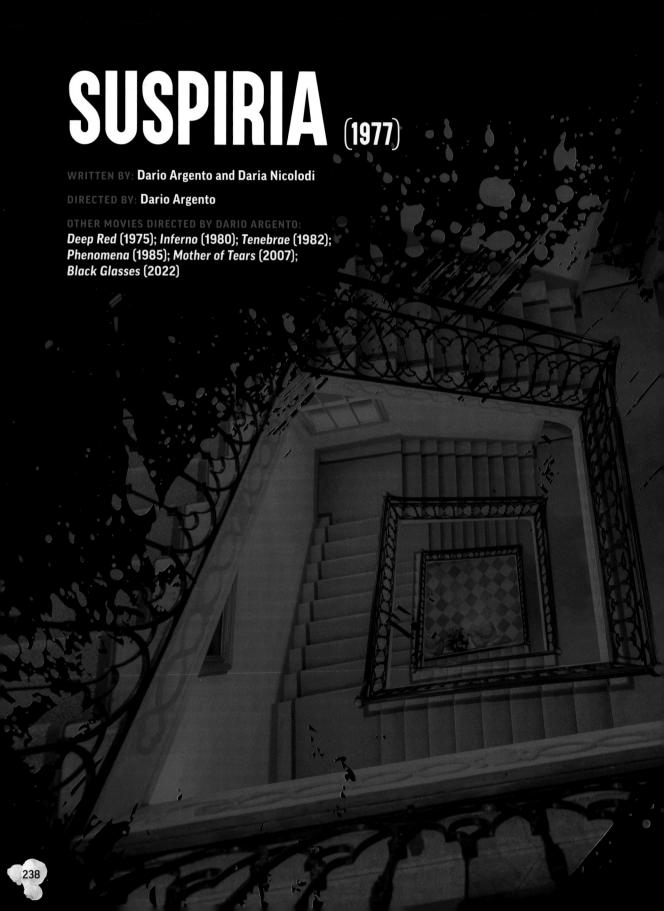

SUSPIRIA (1977)

WRITTEN BY: **Dario Argento and Daria Nicolodi**

DIRECTED BY: **Dario Argento**

OTHER MOVIES DIRECTED BY DARIO ARGENTO:
Deep Red (1975); *Inferno* (1980); *Tenebrae* (1982);
Phenomena (1985); *Mother of Tears* (2007);
Black Glasses (2022)

By 1977, Dario Argento was already on his way to becoming a cinema legend. He'd proved himself a master of the Italian *giallo* genre with thrillers like *The Bird with the Crystal Plumage* (1970) and *Deep Red* (1975), but for his sixth directorial effort he had something else in mind. A story about witches lurking in a boarding school from his co-writer and partner Daria Nicolodi became the seed of a landmark film, and Argento turned from violent thrillers to dreamlike supernatural terror.

With its vivid color palette, nightmarish story, and evocative score, *Suspiria* became an instant horror classic, elevating Argento and Nicolodi to icon status and cementing the director's reputation. More than forty-five years later, Argento's fairy tale–inspired, ultraviolent masterpiece is still terrifying new audiences.

IT IS PARTIALLY INSPIRED BY A TRUE STORY.

Though *Suspiria*'s unique Technicolor horrors are often described as a "fairy tale," the original seed of the story apparently emerged from something quite real. According to co-writer Daria Nicolodi, her grandmother was once sent away to a prestigious boarding school, only to find that black magic was actually being practiced there. When Nicolodi heard the story, she filed it away in her head and it became the inspiration for *Suspiria*.

THE CHARACTERS WERE ORIGINALLY MUCH YOUNGER.

Because the film was so heavily influenced by fairy tales, the original screenplay called for the students at the dance school to be very young girls, aged eight to ten. This made producers nervous, not just because of the idea of brutally murdering little girls on-screen—which Argento thought could only improve the horror—but because Argento's tendency toward perfectionism was not a good fit for child actors.

Eventually, Argento agreed to recast the students as teenagers. However, he and Nicolodi did not update the script to reflect this, hence the often unnerving childlike dialogue between the girls. Also, the doorknobs in the film are deliberately placed high up to make the actors appear more childlike.

THE SCORE WAS INNOVATIVE.

To craft the music for *Suspiria*, Argento turned to the Italian band Goblin, whom he'd previously worked with on *Deep Red*. Argento wanted the score to sound otherworldly, so the band developed innovative sounds using a variety of methods. In addition to their standard instruments, Goblin brought in African drums and a Greek stringed instrument called a bouzouki (recommended by Argento). Then the band got even more inventive, squeezing plastic cups against the microphones to create echoing sounds, hitting metal buckets full of water with hammers, incorporating disembodied voices, and more.

ONE DEATH SCENE REALLY WAS PAINFUL.

Suspiria delivered an unforgettable death scene when Sara (Stefania Casini) dives into a room full of razor wire and becomes trapped. While Casini knew that she was filming a death scene, she was unaware of how her character would be killed. When she saw the wire, Argento told her to simply dive in and struggle to reach the window on the other side of the room; Casini eagerly obliged. While the barbs were, of course, removed from the wire, it was still real wire. As she struggled, the wire kept tangling and wrapping itself around Casini's limbs, pinching her flesh. Luckily, it was shot in one take.

IT WAS A CRITICAL FLOP.

Today, *Suspiria* is an essential genre film and regarded as Argento's masterpiece, but not everyone thought so in 1977, when it was often critically savaged. "It is a horror movie that is a horror of a movie, where no one or nothing makes sense: not one plot element, psychological reaction, minor character, piece of dialogue, or ambience," John Simon wrote for *New York* magazine.

ARGENTO WASN'T THRILLED ABOUT THE REMAKE.

When asked about Luca Guadagnino's *Suspiria* remake in 2016, Argento argued against the film being made at all. "The film has a specific mood," Argento told IndieWire. "Either you do it exactly the same way—in which case, it's not a remake, it's a copy, which is pointless—or you change things and make another movie. In that case, why call it *Suspiria*?"

THE TERMINATOR

(1984)

WRITTEN BY: James Cameron, Gale Anne Hurd, and William Wisher

DIRECTED BY: James Cameron

OTHER MOVIES DIRECTED BY JAMES CAMERON:
Aliens (1986); *The Abyss* (1989); *Titanic* (1997); *Avatar* (2009); *Avatar 2* (2022)

Arnold Schwarzenegger told you he'd be back: The Austrian American action star has reprised his role as the Terminator in four movie sequels plus a theme park attraction. But the original *Terminator*, which was director James Cameron's breakout movie (unless you count *Piranha II: The Spawning*), wasn't intended to be part of a franchise. It's a tight, lean thriller about a cyborg (Schwarzenegger) traveling through time to kill the mother of the man who will lead the resistance against the machines. It was only after the success of the original film that it morphed into an ever-growing franchise.

THE TERMINATOR CAME FROM A NIGHTMARE.

Cameron first thought of the idea for *The Terminator* while stressed out and fever-stricken in Rome during production on his low-budget horror movie, *Piranha II: The Spawning*. Though Cameron had been hired in a different role, he was recruited to move into the director's chair when the original director left. Weeks later, Cameron was also fired. Through a complex sequence of events he found himself in Italy trying to get his own cut of the film made when he fell ill. Cameron dreamed of a chrome skeleton crawling out of a fire and dragging itself across the floor. The director quickly cooked up the story of a robot assassin sent back in time to kill the woman whose son will become the savior of humankind, and *The Terminator* was born.

THE MOVIE HAD A UNIQUE PITCH MEETING.

The script found its way to the desk of John Daly, the head of low-budget movie studio Hemdale Pictures, who called Cameron in for a pitch meeting to get financing after Orion Pictures had already agreed to distribute the film nationwide. To woo the studio, Cameron had actor Lance Henriksen (whom he had worked with on *Piranha II*) show up to the meeting decked out in costume as the title cyborg. Henriksen broke down the studio's office door while wearing a ripped shirt, leather jacket, combat boots, and gold foil from a cigarette pack folded around his teeth. The gimmick clearly worked.

THE STUDIO WANTED O. J. SIMPSON TO PLAY THE TERMINATOR.

When *The Terminator* came around, Schwarzenegger's only legitimate acting experience had been in 1982's *Conan the Barbarian*. A studio executive wanted Schwarzenegger to play Kyle Reese, the human fighter sent back in time, and wanted former NFL star O. J. Simpson to play the Terminator. Cameron didn't like either choice, but took a meeting with Schwarzenegger with the intention of picking a fight with him, then going back to the studio and demanding a new actor. Instead, the two clicked over Schwarzenegger's vision for the killer cyborg, which led Cameron to suggest that Schwarzenegger play the title role instead; the actor was signed the next day.

CREATING THE TERMINATOR SKELETON WAS NO EASY TASK.

Seven artists worked around the clock for six months to create Cameron's vision of the Terminator skeleton puppet. It was made using clay, plaster, and urethane moldings, which was then cast in a mixture of epoxy and fiberglass with reinforced steel throughout the rig. The whole skeleton was chrome-plated and distressed to look more realistic, and the final skeleton weighed more than a hundred pounds.

AUTHOR HARLAN ELLISON ACCUSED JAMES CAMERON OF STEALING HIS IDEAS.

After the movie was released, writer Harlan Ellison sued the makers of *The Terminator* for allegedly stealing the idea for the movie from an episode of the 1960s sci-fi anthology series *The Outer Limits* that he had written. Ellison alleged that Cameron took the idea of two future warriors battling in the past from an episode entitled "Soldier" (it's long been claimed that elements were also taken from the episode "Demon with a Glass Hand," but in 2001 Ellison said that was wrong and it was just "Soldier"). Rather than battling him in costly court proceedings, Orion Pictures simply settled out of court and agreed to add an "acknowledgment to the works of" credit in subsequent prints of the movie. Cameron wasn't too happy about Orion capitulating to Ellison, mostly because he felt he came up with an original idea and any resemblance to Ellison's work was because they both dealt with similar genre tropes. Cameron would later go on to call Ellison a "parasite who can kiss my ass."

ACTORS WHO ALMOST TURNED DOWN VERY FAMOUS ROLES

Can you imagine *The Terminator* without Arnold Schwarzenegger? Think about how different film history would've been—let alone California. It's true: The Terminator-turned-Governator almost skipped out on the part, and Universal Studios amusement parks everywhere would have forever felt a little bit emptier without us knowing entirely why. So would the movies.

The same could be said for a handful of other actors who almost turned down some of their most famous parts, and, in some cases, the roles that made them superstars in the first place.

1 Leonardo DiCaprio // *Titanic* (1997)

Does anyone even *want* to imagine *Titanic* without Leonardo DiCaprio? According to *People*, DiCaprio wasn't interested in playing a romantic leading man. "It became my job to convince him that it was a challenge to do what Gregory Peck and Jimmy Stewart did in previous generations, to stand there and be strong and hold the audience's eye without seeming to do very much," James Cameron said. "[It was] only when I convinced him that was actually the harder thing to do that he got excited."

2 Richard Dreyfuss // *Jaws* (1975)

According to an old BBC documentary on *Jaws*, Richard Dreyfuss wasn't interested in playing oceanographer Matt Hooper in what would become Hollywood's defining "blockbuster." However, after seeing—and hating—his performance in 1974's *The Apprenticeship of Duddy Kravitz*, Dreyfuss reportedly begged Spielberg for another shot.

3 Tom Hanks // *Big* (1988)

Tom Hanks came very close to not playing *Big*'s thirty-year-old man-child Josh Baskin at all. Hanks originally passed on the role due to scheduling conflicts, so the role went to Robert De Niro. However, a failed deal cleared the way for Hanks to shift things around and reconsider. "We had a thing with the negotiation . . . so it went the way it went," De Niro said. "So, it's fine."

4 Richard Harris // *Harry Potter and the Sorcerer's Stone* (2001)

Richard Harris turned down a place in the Harry Potter universe not once, not twice, but three times. "Anyone involved has to agree to be in the sequels . . . and that's not how I wanted to spend the last years of my life," Harris told the *Guardian* in 2001. It was Harris's granddaughter who eventually changed his mind when she told him: "If you don't play Dumbledore, then I will never speak to you again." Harris played Dumbledore in the first two movies; following his death in 2002, Michael Gambon assumed the role.

5 Bill Murray // *Lost in Translation* (2003)

Lost in Translation isn't necessarily Bill Murray's most famous role, but it's the movie that gained him a bit of recognition for his capabilities as a dramatic actor—and earned him his first Oscar nomination. Sofia Coppola wrote the role of fading star Bob Harris specifically for Murray, but for months he ignored Coppola's phone calls, emails, and requests for contact. Eventually, producer Mitch Glazer connected the two—still, it wasn't a done deal. "We went to Japan without knowing if Bill was going to show up—he wouldn't even tell us what flight he was on because he's so elusive—so it was nerve-racking," Coppola said. "But he showed up right before we started shooting."

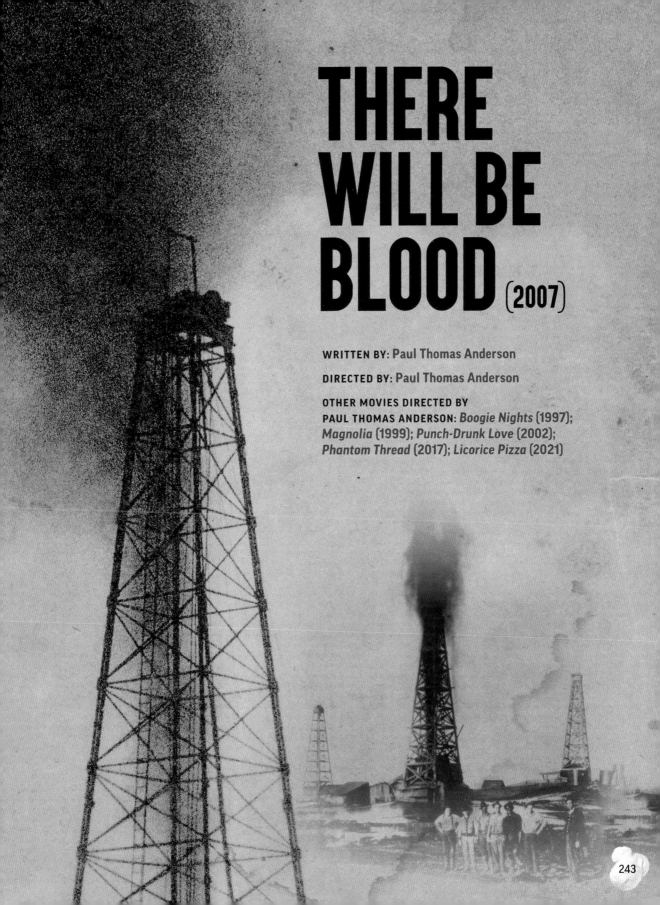

THERE WILL BE BLOOD (2007)

WRITTEN BY: Paul Thomas Anderson

DIRECTED BY: Paul Thomas Anderson

OTHER MOVIES DIRECTED BY
PAUL THOMAS ANDERSON: *Boogie Nights* (1997);
Magnolia (1999); *Punch-Drunk Love* (2002);
Phantom Thread (2017); *Licorice Pizza* (2021)

Family, greed, religion, madness, and milkshakes came together in unexpected and jarring ways in *There Will Be Blood*, Paul Thomas Anderson's sprawling tale of a wealthy oilman named Daniel Plainview (Daniel Day-Lewis) who uses his cunning and charm to convince a small California town to let him drill their land for oil in the early 1900s. His manipulation tactics work on all but one member of the community: Eli Sunday (Paul Dano), a young preacher who proves to be a surprisingly deft opponent for Plainview.

CLOSE-UP

When Daniel Day-Lewis won a Best Actor Oscar for his work in *There Will Be Blood* in 2008, he thanked Dillon Freasier, the then-twelve-year-old who played his son. But Freasier missed it; he was already asleep.

DANIEL DAY-LEWIS PUT A LOT OF THOUGHT INTO WHAT HIS CHARACTER'S HAT SHOULD LOOK LIKE.

In an interview with the *Washington Post*, costume designer Mark Bridges explained that hats were extremely important to both the character of Daniel Plainview and Daniel Day-Lewis for finding the character. "There were three [hat] choices that were all good, and he took them and lived with them for days," Bridges said. "[He] just took them for a spin, so to speak, and settled on that one as what he felt most comfortable with and most represented in his mind the character he was creating."

PAUL DANO DIDN'T KNOW WHAT TO EXPECT FROM DAY-LEWIS.

When asked about what it was like to work opposite Day-Lewis in such an intense, antagonistic way, Dano told Collider that there were "definitely some moments where, you know, I was going, 'Holy shit.' . . . Because we didn't really rehearse and so sometimes, I didn't know how big something that was gonna come out of him was gonna be, because he's so powerful."

DILLON FREASIER, WHO PLAYED HW, HAD NEVER ACTED BEFORE.

Anderson and his team had trouble casting the role of HW, Plainfield's son. They looked at a number of professional actors, but Anderson realized they "needed a boy from Texas who knew how to shoot shotguns and live in that world." So casting director Cassandra Kulukundis contacted a number of schools around Marfa, Texas, where they were shooting, and asked for help, which is how they were introduced to Dillon Freasier.

FREASIER'S MOM WAS NERVOUS ABOUT HER SON WORKING WITH DAY-LEWIS.

Freasier's mom wasn't overly familiar with Day-Lewis's work, so before allowing her son to spend so much time with him, she decided to watch one of his films. Unfortunately, she chose *Gangs of New York* "and was absolutely appalled," Day-Lewis is quoted as saying. "She thought she was releasing her dear child into the hands of this monster. So there was a flurry of phone calls and someone sent her *The Age of Innocence* and apparently that did the trick."

THE OIL WAS MADE FROM THE SAME LIQUID MCDONALD'S USES IN ITS MILKSHAKES.

When discussing the production design with *Entertainment Weekly*, Anderson explained how they built an eighty-foot oil derrick and filled it with fake oil. The recipe for that oil, according to Anderson, included "the stuff they put in chocolate milkshakes at McDonald's."

NO, DAY-LEWIS DID NOT BUILD AN OIL RIG IN HIS BACKYARD.

Many outlets reported that Day-Lewis built his very own oil rig in preparation for his role. "I must say when I read that I thought: 'That's not a bad idea, I might try that!'" Day-Lewis told IndieLondon. He also claimed that his dedication to the Method acting process has "been soundly misrepresented so many times that there's almost no point in even talking about it."

IT'S ANDERSON'S MOST PROFITABLE MOVIE.

There Will Be Blood remains Anderson's most profitable movie, with an estimated $77 million worldwide gross.

THIS IS SPINAL TAP (1984)

WRITTEN BY: Christopher Guest, Michael McKean, Harry Shearer, and Rob Reiner

DIRECTED BY: Rob Reiner

OTHER MOVIES DIRECTED BY ROB REINER:
Stand by Me (1986); *The Princess Bride* (1987); *When Harry Met Sally . . .* (1989); *Misery* (1990); *The American President* (1995); *The Bucket List* (2007)

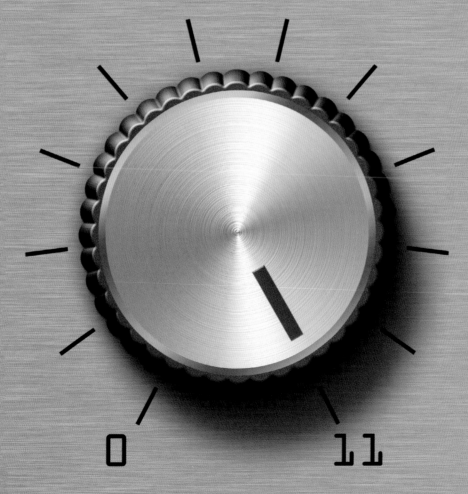

0   11

VOLUME

This Is Spinal Tap may not have invented the mockumentary genre, but it certainly popularized it. Rob Reiner's cult classic comedy—which starred Michael McKean, Christopher Guest, and Harry Shearer—turned the fictional heavy metal band of its title into bona fide musical superstars. It also called into question what the exact dimensions of an on-stage Stonehenge should be, and paved the way for Guest to bring movies like *Waiting for Guffman*, *Best in Show*, and *A Mighty Wind* to the comedy forefront.

MANY PEOPLE BELIEVED IT WAS AN ACTUAL DOCUMENTARY.

Like *Smell the Glove*, the new album that the band is promoting in the film, *This Is Spinal Tap* didn't immediately find its audience. Reiner thinks he knows the reason why. "When *Spinal Tap* initially came out, everybody thought it was a real band," Reiner told *Newsweek* in 2010. "Everyone said, 'Why would you make a movie about a band that no one has heard of?' The reason it did go over everybody's head was it was very close to the bone." This despite the fact that the credits state the band is fictional, "and there's no Easter Bunny, either!"

ANY SIMILARITIES TO BLACK SABBATH ARE PURELY COINCIDENTAL.

In one of the film's most iconic moments, a miscommunication in measurements causes what is supposed to be a life-size version of Stonehenge to end up being very, very tiny. A similar incident occurred on Black Sabbath's "Born Again" tour in 1983, except their monument was too big to fit on the stage. Given that *This Is Spinal Tap* was released a year later, that Black Sabbath would have influenced the film seems logical. But the scene in question was actually filmed in 1982, as part of a twenty-minute short the production team used to get a green light.

THE FILM HIT TOO CLOSE TO HOME FOR MANY MUSICIANS.

"We do love that, the musicians who have said, 'Man, I can't watch *Spinal Tap*, it's too much like my life,'" Shearer said in John Kenneth Muir's book *Best in Show: The Films of Christopher Guest and Company*. "That's the highest compliment of all. It beats all the Oscar nominations we never got." Robert Plant, Jimmy Page, Eddie Van Halen, Eddie Vedder, and Dee Snider are just a few of the musicians who have referenced similarities between their own lives and the movie's plot.

MOST OF THE DIALOGUE WAS AD-LIBBED.

Because the vast majority of the film was improvised, all four of the film's main stars—Reiner, McKean, Guest, and Shearer—received equal billing in the script. But because all of the actors contributed to the script, the foursome lobbied the Writers Guild of America to give every member of the cast a writing credit. The request was promptly denied.

ALL THAT IMPROVISATION RESULTED IN MORE THAN A HUNDRED HOURS OF FOOTAGE.

Reiner managed to edit the film's original theatrical release down to eighty-two minutes, but fans of the film have very actively sought out the unedited footage. In 1998, the Criterion Collection released its only single-layer, double-sided disc that included more than an hour of additional footage (it's now out of print, but can be found used on Amazon for about $200). MGM's DVD features an additional seventy minutes of footage. But the holy grail of alternate versions is a four-and-a-half-hour bootleg edition.

A HERPES-RELATED SUBPLOT WAS REMOVED.

The film's original script included a subplot that explained why the band members are often seen with cold sores on their lips: All three of them had slept with the lead singer of their opening act, and she gave them all herpes.

NORWEGIANS KNOW THE FILM AS *HELP! WE ARE IN THE POP BUSINESS!*

When *This Is Spinal Tap* was released on video in Norway in 1984, its title was translated as *Hjelp vi er i popbransjen*, or *Help! We Are in the Pop Business!* This caused some Norwegian filmgoers to believe it was related to *Airplane!*, as that had been released as *Hjelp, vi flyr!*, or *Help! We Are Flying!* a few years earlier.

FUNNY BUSINESS: ESSENTIAL COMEDIES

Comedy generates an immediate, undeniable audience response. If audiences are smiling and laughing, then there's a good chance you made an effective funny movie. Thousands of comedies fall under the "effective funny movie" umbrella, of course, but what about the movies that exist beyond that, in another sphere? What about the films that are both hilarious and emotional, hilarious and innovative, and hilarious and profound in a way that keeps us thinking about them years and even decades later? Here are fifteen films that do just that.

9 to 5 (1980)

There's something about seeing Jane Fonda, Lily Tomlin, and Dolly Parton on-screen together that basically insists you love the movie, as it's impossible to not be charmed by the sheer star power. Look past the glare of their collective glow, though, and you've still got an all-time great film that mixes elements of Golden Age screwball comedies with a very modern look at bureaucracy, office politics, unvarnished sexism, and the strength of found sisterhood.

Airplane! (1980)

Airplane! isn't the first film to play the "pick a genre and just do a straightforward spoof" card successfully, but it remains the standard against which all other films that apply its brand of rapid-fire, throw-spaghetti-at-the-wall humor are measured—and with good reason. There's a timeless purity to the zaniness of it, the sense that anything can and might happen for the sake of a joke—with Leslie Nielsen, who was primarily known as a dramatic actor before this, leading the charge. *Airplane!* exists in its own hilarious little world, and it's one that new viewers can still be welcomed into.

Anchorman: The Legend of Ron Burgundy (2004)

The team of writer-star Will Ferrell and writer-director Adam McKay has made several films in the "lovable manchild makes good" genre, but—with all due respect to other triumphs like *Step Brothers*—*Anchorman* is the one that's held up the best. The story of an egotistical, clueless, unrepentantly sexist news anchor from the seventies resisting a world rapidly changing around him manages to be a showcase of both Ferrell's boundless comedic energy and of the commitment and laugh-generating power of fellow all-stars like Christina Applegate, Paul Rudd, and of course Steve Carell, who won the movie's most-quoted moment simply by saying he loves a lamp.

Animal House (1978)

More than forty years after its original release, *National Lampoon's Animal House* remains one of the most influential comedies of all time. It laid the framework for the many fraternity comedies that would follow, from *Revenge of the Nerds* to *Old School*, and turned its director (John Landis) and writer (Harold Ramis) into household names. It also elevated John Belushi's status from *SNL* star to comedy icon and is regularly cited as the original "gross-out" comedy.

Best in Show (2000)

After Rob Reiner proved it would work in *This Is Spinal Tap*, writer-director-actor Christopher Guest decided to make much of the rest of his career about the joys of improvisational mockumentary-making. The result is a handful of unforgettably funny movies, with *Best in Show* rising above the rest to become arguably the best mockumentary ever made. The cast is packed with comedic superstars, the format allows for endless playful forays into absurdity, and it all builds to a genuinely emotionally satisfying conclusion. Plus, it might be the only film that's ever wrung laughs out of simply listing different varieties of nuts.

Blazing Saddles (1974)

Whenever *Blazing Saddles* comes up in conversation, someone always manages to remark that "you could never make that movie today," and that observation remains an extreme oversimplification of Mel Brooks's achievement with his classic western satire. Yes, the jokes are dirty, transgressive, and in some cases haven't aged well, but "you couldn't make it today" ignores the larger point: You don't need to make it today. *Blazing Saddles* is still as blisteringly funny and relevant as it was when it was released, and that go-for-broke ending remains one of the gutsiest comedy moves of all time.

Bridesmaids (2011)

In the 2000s, raunchy hard-R buddy comedies had a wave of massive box office success, so on some level the cynical view is that a movie like *Bridesmaids* was inevitable just from a business standpoint. That said, it certainly wasn't inevitable that the film would be this good. Writers

Kristen Wiig and Annie Mumolo went far beyond making a "female *Hangover*" or some other commodification of a comedy moment when they wrote the story of a directionless baker (Wiig) whose lifelong best friend (Maya Rudolph) is about to get married, which sends Wiig's character on a downward spiral. They teamed with director Paul Feig and an all-star cast to eventually produce a film of tremendous heart and insight into both the black humor of human despair and the silly joy of having nowhere to go but up.

Friday (1995)

Friday began as the fulfillment of Ice Cube and DJ Pooh's desire to craft a story that showed that the kinds of neighborhoods depicted in movies like *Boyz n the Hood* were also places of great joy and peace, and the result is a film with an absolutely undeniable sense of comedic personality. It remains one of the ultimate "guys hanging out all day" comfort comedies because it's wall-to-wall funny, but it also feels honest in a way that other stoner comedies just aren't. Craig and Smokey's day is full of funny mishaps, but there's also a real emotional payoff there, and *Friday* never lets you forget those two things go hand in hand.

Ghostbusters (1984)

Ghostbusters has famously been called a film about "nothing" because of the perceived way in which its characters don't really grow or change. However, the fact that we're still talking about the meaning behind a movie in which guys in jumpsuits shoot sci-fi guns at a giant marshmallow monster is proof of its greatness.

Groundhog Day (1993)

It's not often you come across a film that takes the name of a well-known holiday and literally redefines it, which tells you something about the power of Harold Ramis's legendary time-loop comedy. Yes, watching Bill Murray suffer for an hour and a half is great fun, but *Groundhog Day* is after something bigger than a memorable premise. It turned out, jokes and all, to be one of the great life-affirming American movies—a film about smiling through the pain and finding meaning when the world around you feels endless.

The Jerk (1979)

Some roles are so universal you can imagine a number of actors playing and nailing them. Others are so specific, so informed by a particular comedic sensibility, that they can only come through one performer. No one but Steve Martin could have made Navin Johnson the character he is. No one but Martin could have made an extended sequence of violence as funny by simply yelling, "He hates these cans!" And, of course, no one but comedy legend Carl Reiner could have turned the story of a wide-eyed innocent attempting to make his way in the city—and finding that his sweet-but-simple nature is both a blessing and a curse—into the comic heart-warmer that is *The Jerk*.

Lost in America (1985)

Albert Brooks's comedies are very hyper-focused films that say a lot about the time in which they were made while also remaining almost paradoxically timeless. They're all great, but *Lost in America* stands as perhaps Brooks's greatest statement on the kind of comedy that interests

him. The story of a couple who set out to find themselves, only to discover that they're not really interested in growth, is one that won't leave your brain for weeks after you've seen it. And though it was aimed at Reagan's America when it was made, it still has a point to make about the capitalist traps set for us even now.

Monty Python and the Holy Grail (1975)

There was no guarantee that the absurdist humor of Monty Python would translate from small screen to big. But with *Monty Python and the Holy Grail*, the legendary comedy troupe proved that they could arguably make their brand of comedy work even better with a longer story in which to plan numerous running gags, side quests, and wacky characters. Plus, nearly fifty years after its release, *Holy Grail*—a comedic retelling of the legend of King Arthur, but framed with a murder investigation—remains one of the most quotable movies of all time.

Planes, Trains and Automobiles (1987)

Though John Hughes is best known for his teen comedies like *Sixteen Candles* and *The Breakfast Club*, his greatest success may be this Thanksgiving road movie starring two of the best comedic actors of all time. Steve Martin and John Candy's incredible chemistry is on display as they navigate mishap after mishap in Hughes's slapstick but heartfelt comedy.

Tootsie (1982)

So many things about *Tootsie* could have gone so wrong. The film could have been wildly, tonally mismatched, too subtle (or not subtle enough), or just plain offensive. Instead, this funny story about an egotistical actor literally and metaphorically getting in touch with his feminine side just works. In director Sydney Pollack's hands, though, the film managed to poke fun at everything from oblivious sexism and gender roles to the strange egos of actors and writers.

Wayne's World (1992)

A lot of films have come out of the sketch mines at *SNL* over the years, but many of them fail to outlast the premise that worked for four minutes on late-night television. *Wayne's World* is the rare example of that effort going as well as it possibly can. The plot is pretty minimal: A Hollywood producer (Rob Lowe) wants to bring Wayne (Mike Myers) and Garth's (Dana Carvey) public access TV show to a national audience, but also wants to reinvent what they created in the first place, and steal Wayne's girlfriend (Tia Carrere) at the same time. There's a sense in this film that Myers, Carvey, and director Penelope Spheeris were willing to try just about anything to make the jokes land, and their success rate is uncommonly high. A clear grasp of character, a great supporting cast, and a simple warmth that persists through the whole film do the rest.

TITANIC

(1997)

WRITTEN BY: James Cameron

DIRECTED BY: James Cameron

OTHER MOVIES DIRECTED BY JAMES CAMERON:
The Terminator (1984); *Aliens* (1986); *True Lies* (1994); *Avatar* (2009); *Avatar 2* (2022)

Titanic is one of those rare movies that wasn't just a hit—it was a phenomenon. James Cameron's action-packed historical romance follows the budding relationship between an upper-class young woman named Rose (Kate Winslet) and a penniless artist named Jack (Leonardo DiCaprio), whose doomed love intensifies while the doomed ship they're traveling on advances closer and closer to the iceberg we all know is coming.

Though the movie, which quickly became the highest-grossing film of all time, had its fair share of detractors at the time of its release, pendulums have now swung the other way: It's not the top earner anymore (Cameron's own *Avatar*, among other films, eventually surpassed it), and people seem okay with openly admitting it's a sweeping, rousing, entertaining epic that achieved the rare combination of incredible financial success and artistic merit (regardless of how much room there was on that floating door frame).

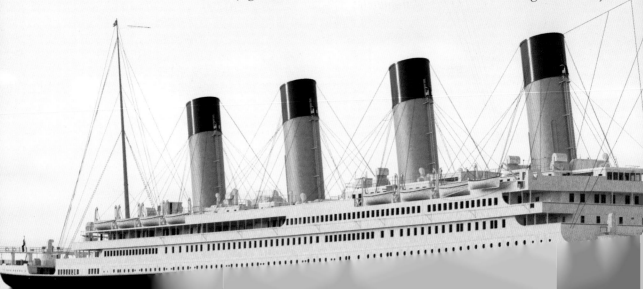

TITANIC'S MOST ICONIC LINE WASN'T IN THE SCRIPT.

When DiCaprio first got up on the end of the ship, there wasn't a line there. Trying to get some level of cinematic epicness, Cameron yelled at DiCaprio to say "I'm the King of the World." According to Cameron, DiCaprio was originally hesitant, but Cameron told him it was probably stupid enough that it wouldn't wind up in the film. Though the line would go on to be parodied countless times—including at the Oscars—it landed at no. 100 on the American Film Institute's list of the greatest movie quotes.

A NAKED DRAWING OF WINSLET SOLD FOR THOUSANDS.

In 2011, a company called Premiere Props auctioned off one of the movie's most evocative pieces of memorabilia: one of the drawings Jack made of Rose, who is wearing nothing but the Heart of the Ocean necklace. Although the identity of the buyer was unknown, the final price was reportedly $17,000. The drawing was done by Cameron, not DiCaprio.

NEIL DEGRASSE TYSON MADE AN IMPORTANT CHANGE TO THE MOVIE.

The noted astrophysicist didn't see *Titanic* until years after it was released, but he took issue with the scene where Rose is lying on the piece of driftwood and looking up at the sky. He sent James Cameron "quite a snarky email" (Cameron's words) explaining that the star field Rose saw in the movie isn't the one she would have seen in real life at that place and time. Cameron—ever the perfectionist—reshot the scene for the 3D edition of the movie.

AN ALTERNATE ENDING WAS FILMED.

In the scene, Bill Paxton's character finally does get to hold the Heart of the Ocean necklace in his hand, and Gloria Stuart, playing a much older version of Winslet's Rose, gives him a speech about making every day count.

Because it remained in cinemas for so long, *Titanic* was released on VHS while it was still playing in theaters. Its popularity was so massive, with people lining up for repeat viewings, that some theaters reportedly had to get new film reels to replace the ones they'd worn out.

NO, JACK DIDN'T HAVE TO DIE.

One question that has plagued Cameron since the movie's release, mostly because so many fans and even scientists have taken issue with it, is: Did Jack *really* have to die? The short answer is: no. In an episode of *MythBusters* that examined whether both Jack and Rose could have stayed on the wooden door (though some would argue it's a door frame) without it sinking, they determined it would have been possible—but only if they had secured Rose's life jacket to the underside of the door for added buoyancy. Cameron himself came on the show to defend his decision and admit that the movie's dramatic ending depended on Jack dying. "If [he] lives, the movie makes a tenth as much," Cameron quipped.

In 2017, twenty years after the movie's release, Cameron was still being grilled about it in an interview with *Vanity Fair*. Though he repeated that the decision to kill Jack was "an artistic choice," as the movie "is about death and separation," he still defended the means, saying he tested the floating board prop itself to gauge its buoyancy. "So whether it was that, or whether a smoke stack fell on him, he was going down," Cameron said. "It's called art, things happen for artistic reasons, not for physics reasons."

TRAINSPOTTING

(1996)

WRITTEN BY: John Hodge
(based on the book by Irvine Welsh)

DIRECTED BY: Danny Boyle

OTHER MOVIES DIRECTED BY DANNY BOYLE:
Shallow Grave (1994); *28 Days Later . . .* (2002);
Slumdog Millionaire (2008); *Steve Jobs* (2015);
Yesterday (2019)

FREEZE-FRAME

The infamous "worst toilet in Scotland" scene is a horror to behold, but it was much less disturbing on set. To create the ghastly bathroom stall, Boyle's props team simply smeared the toilet with copious amounts of chocolate mousse. This trick apparently stayed with him; Boyle used the same stuff (mixed with crunchy peanut butter) for a similar scene in *Slumdog Millionaire* (2008).

In 1996, a young Scottish actor named Ewan McGregor careened onto the movie screen, daring viewers to "Choose life. Choose a job. Choose a career. Choose a family. Choose a fucking big television." This was just the beginning of McGregor's star-making turn in *Trainspotting*, a darkly comic yet harrowing tale of five friends—most with heroin addictions—trying to make their way in the world, and occasionally attempting to abstain from drug use.

In addition to being McGregor's breakout role, the pulse-pounding movie announced Danny Boyle as a fiercely innovative director to be reckoned with—and grossed audiences out with the "worst toilet in Scotland."

EWAN MCGREGOR LOST TWENTY-SIX POUNDS FOR THE PART.

In order to look the part of a heroin addict, McGregor lost twenty-six pounds, and his diet was surprisingly simple. "I grilled everything, and stopped drinking beer," he told *Neon* magazine. "I drank wine and lots of gin instead. The weight just falls off."

JONNY LEE MILLER HAS A REAL-LIFE JAMES BOND CONNECTION.

Jonny Lee Miller's character, Sick Boy, is a major 007 fan. Appropriately, the actor himself has family ties to the franchise. Miller's grandfather was Bernard Lee, the original M.

MCGREGOR DID A LOT OF RESEARCH FOR THE ROLE.

To prepare for the movie, McGregor read several books on crack and heroin addiction and spoke with members of the Calton Athletic Recovery Group (who served as consultants for the movie). Along with some of his co-stars, he even attended "cookery" classes hosted by the Calton crew, who used glucose powder in place of the real thing. But McGregor almost took his research to extremes. As he noted in *Neon*, "I thought about actually taking heroin—and the more research I did, the less I wanted to do it. I've had to die on-screen before, and I don't know what that's like either. I'm not a Method actor at all, so to take heroin for the part would just be an excuse to take heroin, really. So I didn't."

A PROSTHETIC ARM WAS USED FOR CLOSE-UPS OF MCGREGOR SHOOTING UP.

That wasn't McGregor's arm in the many close-ups of Renton shooting up. The props team took a mold of the actor's arm instead and created a prosthetic with a plastic pipeline of fake blood, so it would bleed upon injection.

RENTON AND DIANE'S SEX SCENE WAS EDITED FOR AMERICAN AUDIENCES.

When *Trainspotting* made its way overseas, it apparently lost a few frames from the sex scene between Renton and Diane. McGregor trashed the decision in an interview with the *Los Angeles Times*. "The American censors cut a few seconds from the movie, from a scene between me and Kelly [Macdonald]. It was a sex scene, which her character was obviously enjoying. They obviously didn't like the idea of a young girl having enjoyable sex, whereas the shooting up and violence was acceptable to them."

BOB DOLE CONDEMNED THE MOVIE.

Trainspotting was a huge critical and commercial success—but then–presidential candidate Bob Dole wasn't a fan. While speaking to a school in L.A., he blasted both *Trainspotting* and *Pulp Fiction* for promoting "the romance of heroin," which is something *Trainspotting* does not do. Dole's press secretary later clarified that he had not actually seen either movie, but based his comments on reviews he had read.

"Choose your future. Choose life."

WAITING FOR GUFFMAN (1996)

WRITTEN BY: Christopher Guest and Eugene Levy

DIRECTED BY: Christopher Guest

OTHER MOVIES DIRECTED BY CHRISTOPHER GUEST:
Best in Show (2000); *A Mighty Wind* (2003);
For Your Consideration (2006); *Mascots* (2016)

Though it didn't make much of a dent in the box office when it hit theaters nearly thirty years ago, Christopher Guest's mockumentary *Waiting for Guffman* has become a cult hit in the years since. This movie follows a group of small-town residents-turned-amateur-actors from Blaine, Missouri, and their eccentric director, Corky St. Clair, as they put on a production called *Red, White and Blaine* in honor of the sesquicentennial (that's a 150th anniversary) of the town's founding by Blaine Fabin. When they get word that New York film critic Mort Guffman is coming to their performance, they begin to dream about taking their show out of Blaine's high school gym and onto the Broadway stage—until fate intervenes.

THE MOVIE WAS INSPIRED BY A JUNIOR HIGH PRODUCTION OF *ANNIE, GET YOUR GUN*.

Christopher Guest told Deborah Theaker, who plays *Guffman*'s Gwen Fabin-Blunt, that he was watching one of his kids perform in *Annie, Get Your Gun* when inspiration struck. "There were all these little kids with handlebar moustaches, and he thought it was just hilarious and sweet at the same time," Theaker said in *Best in Show: The Films of Christopher Guest and Company*.

"I was just drawn to the idea of how earnest everyone was, how devoted they were to do the best performance they could, albeit at the level that they were working at," Guest said.

THERE WASN'T AN OFFICIAL SCRIPT.

Guest's mockumentaries famously have no scripts. Instead, they're mostly improvised by the actors based on outlines written by Guest and his collaborators—a tradition that began with *Waiting for Guffman*.

SOME ELEMENTS OF THE FILM DID NEED TO BE SCRIPTED AND REHEARSED.

Namely, the songs and dialogue of *Red, White and Blaine*, the play at the center of the film. Guest turned to his *This Is Spinal Tap* (1984) collaborators to help him with the music: He and Harry Shearer co-wrote "Stool Boom" and "Nothing Ever Happens on Mars," while Guest and Michael McKean co-wrote "Covered Wagons, Open Toed Shoes" and "Penny for Your Thoughts."

The dialogue in *Red, White and Blaine* is the only dialogue in all of *Waiting for Guffman* that isn't improvised; Guest said that "writing the book for [*Red, White and Blaine*] was one of the most fun parts."

THE CAST SPENT FOUR DAYS REHEARSING THE PLAY'S CHOREOGRAPHY.

While the song-and-dance numbers featured in *Red, White and Blaine* required some rehearsal, Guest decided to cap it at four days, which he said was "just the right amount, because when we eventually did the show, it was at the level it should have been: Under-rehearsed, and if you watch closely, there are many things being screwed up."

THE CAST WATCHED DAILIES TOGETHER AT THEIR HOTEL.

The cast stayed in a hotel in Austin and, as Catherine O'Hara said in 2010, "Every night was movie night . . . when Chris invited us to watch dailies. You want to go to dailies on a Chris Guest movie, because we shoot 80 hours of improvisation . . . and then he cuts it down to 86 minutes, so if you don't go to dailies, you miss 90 percent of the movie."

GUEST HAD TO WHITTLE FIFTY-EIGHT HOURS OF FOOTAGE DOWN TO NINETY MINUTES.

That meant that entire characters and musical numbers had to be cut. Frances Fisher, who played Johnny Savage's mother, appeared in the movie's trailer but didn't make it into the movie. *Red, White and Blaine* itself ran forty minutes long, so the numbers "Nothing Ever Happens in Blaine" (which came before "Nothing Ever Happens on Mars") and "This Bulging River" were cut for time, and a dance sequence and solo were trimmed from "Penny for Your Thoughts."

GUEST EDITED HIS CHARACTER OUT OF THE MOVIE ENTIRELY.

Editing the movie took eighteen months, and Levy recalled that at one point, Guest had cut Corky out completely. "In the initial edit, when you cut this thing for the first time, you had literally cut yourself out of the movie," Levy told Guest in the movie's DVD commentary. "I looked at the first cut, there was no Corky in the movie . . . You thought your little runs were a little too insane and maybe not grounded, and everybody said 'Let's put them all back in, how about that.'"

FREEZE-FRAME

Look closely and you'll catch a glimpse of *Better Call Saul*'s Bob Odenkirk. He's in the hallway during the audition scenes dressed as a vampire. Odenkirk had been cast as the town minister, but the part was cut when he had a scheduling conflict.

WHIPLASH (2014)

WRITTEN BY: Damien Chazelle

DIRECTED BY: Damien Chazelle

OTHER MOVIES BY DAMIEN CHAZELLE:
La La Land (2016); *First Man* (2018); *Babylon* (2022)

The most thrilling movie of 2014 doesn't feature shoot-outs or car chases (though one particularly nail-biting scene does take place behind the wheel). *Whiplash* follows an ambitious jazz drummer named Andrew Neiman (Miles Teller). When Andrew joins his school's studio band, the band's leader, Terence Fletcher (J. K. Simmons), pushes him to his mental and physical limits.

The concept sounds like fodder for an inspirational story about a young musician and his mentor, but writer-director Damien Chazelle's brutal feature borders on horror. The movie owes many of its thrills to Simmons, who gives a career-defining (and Oscar-winning) performance as every music student's worst nightmare. Viewers will never be able to hear the phrase "not quite my tempo" without flinching again.

DAMIEN CHAZELLE BASED *WHIPLASH* ON HIS OWN SCHOOL EXPERIENCE.

When writing and directing *Whiplash*, Chazelle drew inspiration from his days in a high school jazz band. Like Teller's character, Chazelle was obsessed with playing the drums. He also had a teacher who served as the model for Simmons's bandleader, though the real person wasn't quite as ruthless as the character that ended up in the film.

IT STARTED AS A SHORT FILM (KIND OF).

Whiplash took an unconventional path from concept to feature film. After writing the first draft of the script in 2012, Chazelle struggled to find a production company to produce it. He decided to prove the story would work on-screen by turning one of the movie's explosive rehearsal scenes into a fifteen-minute short. Jason Reitman, the Oscar-nominated director of *Juno* (2007) and *Up in the Air* (2009), suggested that Chazelle talk to J. K. Simmons about the role of the teacher. Simmons said yes with the hope that if and when it was turned into a feature, he would get the chance to explore the character further.

That short premiered at the Sundance Film Festival in 2013 and attracted the funding necessary to make a full-length movie. The rehearsal scene shot for the feature is nearly identical to the short film: Both star Simmons as the overly demanding instructor, but the role of Andrew was played by actor Johnny Simmons (no relation to J. K.).

MILES TELLER REALLY DOES PLAY THE DRUMS.

In addition to selling the emotional stakes of the story, Teller needed to make his character believable as a drummer. Fortunately, he had been playing the instrument for over a decade when he signed on for the role. When you see Andrew at a drum set, it really is Teller playing. The actor's biggest challenge on the musical side of the performance was teaching himself to play in the style of a jazz drummer rather than a rock musician.

J. K. SIMMONS CRACKED HIS RIBS SHOOTING ONE SCENE.

Just like a more traditional thriller, filming *Whiplash* required some stunt work. Teller accidentally cracked two of Simmons's ribs when he had to tackle him to the ground for a scene. That wasn't the only case of the two actors getting physical: During the infamous "not my tempo" sequence, some of the slaps Simmons deals to Teller are real.

THE MOVIE WAS SHOT IN JUST NINETEEN DAYS.

Most movies take at least a couple of months to shoot, but *Whiplash* was filmed at a breakneck pace. Principal photography wrapped in just nineteen days, thanks to Chazelle's meticulous planning and the eighteen-hour workdays put in by the cast and crew. The movie's speedy schedule stood in stark contrast to one of its biggest competitors that awards season: Richard Linklater's *Boyhood*, another Oscar contender for Best Picture in 2015, took twelve years to shoot. But a quick turnaround doesn't necessarily hurt quality, at least in the eyes of the Academy's voters. The work Simmons did in just a couple of weeks beat out Ethan Hawke's multigenerational performance in the Best Supporting Actor category.

THE BAND CONSISTED OF REAL MUSICIANS.

Teller wasn't the only performer in the cast with real-life music experience. Chazelle cast actual jazz musicians as his bandmates to add to the realism of the rehearsal and performance scenes.

"Not quite my tempo."

41 MUST-SEE MOVIES OF THE 2010S

The 1910s were a critical decade in film history, as California became a moviemaking center and many studios that are still around today were founded. Filmmakers marked the centennial by finding new ways to amuse, shock, and thrill us (and bore us, but those movies aren't on this list).

Anna Karenina (2012)

Much of director Joe Wright's reimagining of Leo Tolstoy's classic nineteenth-century Russian tragedy takes place on an opulent-yet-crumbling theater set designed by Sarah Greenwood, who earned an Oscar nomination for her work (along with set decorator Katie Spencer). With Keira Knightley as the adulterous Anna, Aaron Taylor-Johnson as her lover Count Vronsky, and a sweeping score by Dario Marianelli—not to mention Oscar-winning costume designs by Jacqueline Durran—the result is nothing short of operatic.

Arrival (2016)

This is optimistic, life-affirming science fiction of the highest order, using an alien first-contact scenario to tell a wholly engrossing story in which humankind's worst tendencies—selfishness, suspicion, aggression—threaten to overtake our best ones. Directed by Denis Villeneuve and starring Amy Adams, it's a steadily paced drama of discovery that makes us feel more hopeful about humanity.

Beasts of No Nation (2015)

Idris Elba astounds in this harrowing tale of child soldiers kidnapped and exploited by an African paramilitary group. Poignant and unflinching, the story will squeeze your heart until it bursts.

Beginners (2010)

Beginners, which is told in flashback, follows the evolution of the relationship between Oliver (Ewan McGregor) and his now-deceased father Hal (Christopher Plummer), who spent his last five years living as an out gay man for the first time—a joyful metamorphosis that helps Oliver navigate his own hopeful journey of self-discovery. The film, which earned Plummer an Oscar for Best Supporting Actor, is based on writer-director Mike Mills's real-life experience with his father.

Bone Tomahawk (2015)

Tombstone meets the horror genre when a local sheriff (Kurt Russell) leads a posse into uncharted territory in this tense thriller, which marked the directorial debut of S. Craig Zahler. After several townsfolk begin going missing, it's up to the sheriff to rescue them from a band of savage cannibals. The third act is a cover-your-eyes endurance test.

Boyhood (2014)

Boyhood works as a kind of time travel movie, as director Richard Linklater spent twelve years filming the adolescence of a Texan (Ellar Coltrane) from age six to eighteen. This lengthy production process made it possible for Coltrane to portray the character at various stages, from coming to grips with his parents' divorce as a young child to his going to college. In lesser hands, it would be a gimmick. For Linklater, it's a chance to meditate on encroaching independence.

Dunkirk (2017)

Christopher Nolan first considered basing a film on World War II's Battle of Dunkirk after a choppy, somewhat harrowing yacht ride to Dunkirk in the early 1990s. "It actually felt at times life-threatening," Nolan said. When he returned to the idea roughly two decades later, he thought about doing the entire movie without a script, establishing character and story through action alone. Nolan's wife and collaborator Emma Thomas talked him out of it, but the end result—which follows the battle through the eyes of several fictional players from the air, ground, and sea—is still light on dialogue. As Nolan told *Entertainment Weekly*, it's a "survival story," rather than a "war story." All of it is urged on by Hans Zimmer's tick-tock musical score.

Enemy (2013)

Jake Gyllenhaal has an uneasy feeling that his exact double— a man who looks like him but is living a very different life—is intruding on his own world. The Gyllenhaal collision is the foundation for this psychological thriller from director Denis Villeneuve, who offers no pat answers but an effective undercurrent of dread.

The Fighter (2010)

Mark Wahlberg and director David O. Russell strip away the conventions of standard boxing movies and deliver a potent blend of pugilism and family drama. As real-life fighter Mickey Ward, Wahlberg tries to juggle his ring aspirations with the emotional challenges presented by his drug-addled half brother Dicky (Christian Bale).

Green Room (2015)

Here's a film that starts with an uncomfortable arrangement (a young punk band has booked a gig for a den of Nazi skinheads) and descends from there into expertly crafted, cold-sweat terror. Though it's primarily a siege scenario, with the band locking themselves in their dressing room after witnessing a skinhead-on-skinhead murder, the story goes in more directions (figuratively and geographically) than you'd expect. Writer-director Jeremy Saulnier never lets it get stagnant. He barely lets you catch your breath.

Hell or High Water (2016)

David Mackenzie's *Hell or High Water* follows two brothers (Chris Pine and Ben Foster) who take to bank robberies in an effort to save their family ranch from foreclosure; Jeff Bridges is the drawling, laconic lawman on their tail.

The Imitation Game (2014)

Benedict Cumberbatch earned his first Oscar nomination for his depiction of genius Alan Turing, who led the team of mathematicians who cracked the Enigma code during World War II. But the film delves into the personal: When it's discovered that Turing is gay, he's turned from a hero into a criminal.

Inside Llewyn Davis (2013)

Like many of Joel and Ethan Coen's films, this one—about a struggling folk singer in 1961 determining once and for all whether he's cut out for this—has a dark whimsy to it, peculiar and funny but run through with deep melancholy. Oscar Isaac's heartfelt turn in the lead role is one of the best the Coens have ever directed, and memorable performances by Adam Driver, Carey Mulligan, and John Goodman help it along.

The Irishman (2019)

The culmination of themes that Martin Scorsese has addressed throughout his incredible five-decade (and counting) career, this gangster story stars Robert De Niro as a man reflecting, at the end of his life, on the multitude of regrets he refuses to acknowledge, the apologies he should have offered, and the loneliness that has always plagued him. It's sad, thrilling, funny, and introspective, with outstanding performances by De Niro and Joe Pesci (though the digital de-aging of their characters drew of lot of chatter, not all of it positive).

It Follows (2014)

The premise of this horror movie couldn't be simpler: What if you were followed by a supernatural entity that never relents, no matter how far you run? The film delivers on this idea with plenty of heart-hammering moments—from slow-burn frights to one of the best jump scares the genre has produced. Preceding other creepy classics of the 2010s like *The Witch* (2015), *Get Out* (2017), and *Hereditary* (2018), *It Follows* marked an early entry in the run of elevated horror that defined the decade.

Jackass 3D (2010)

If you think *Jackass 3D* is yet another movie where a group of guys hang around and attempt to pull off a series of increasingly dangerous and painful stunts when they're not attempting to viciously prank each other, well, okay, you'd be right. But seeing it all play out in glorious 3D is truly one of the best uses of the three-dimensional format.

The King's Speech (2010)

From laughingstock to maestro of one of Great Britain's finest public addresses, *The King's Speech* tells the true story of King George VI's triumph over stuttering. The film took home Oscars for Best Picture, Best Director (Tom Hooper), Best Actor (Colin Firth), and Best Original Screenplay (David Seidler).

Lady Bird (2017)

Christine MacPherson (Saoirse Ronan)—who insists you call her "Lady Bird"—is simultaneously sure-footed and self-conscious, often frustrated, and always passionate. Her experiences navigating romance, cool kids, mother-daughter disputes, and everything else feel universal. But the film also functions as a time capsule for anyone who attended a Sacramento Catholic high school in the early 2000s, as writer-director Greta Gerwig did. She gave her young actors homework to help them better grasp their characters, including Joan Didion books and John Hughes movies for Ronan; Stephen Sondheim musicals for Lucas Hedges; and Howard Zinn's *A People's History of the United States* for Timothée Chalamet.

The Lobster (2015)

Colin Farrell stars in a black comedy that feels reminiscent of screenwriter Charlie Kaufman's work: A slump-shouldered loner (Farrell) has just forty-five days to find a life partner before he's turned into an animal. Can he make it work with Rachel Weisz, or is he doomed to a life on all fours (well, tens)? By turns absurd and provocative, *The Lobster* isn't a conventional date movie, but it might have more to say about relationships than a pile of Nicholas Sparks paperbacks.

Locke (2013)

The camera rarely wavers from Tom Hardy in this existential thriller, which takes place entirely in Hardy's vehicle. A construction foreman trying to make sure an important job is executed well, Hardy's Ivan Locke grapples with some surprising news from a mistress and the demands of his family. It's a one-act, one-man play, with Hardy making the repeated act of conversing on his cell phone as tense and compelling as if he were driving with a bomb in the trunk. (Oscar-winner Olivia Colman, *Fleabag*'s "Hot Priest" Andrew Scott, *Spider-Man*'s Tom Holland, and Ruth Wilson are the people whose voices we hear on the other end of the line.)

Magic Mike (2012)

Anyone who has pressed Play on *Magic Mike* hoping for a two-hour, high-octane striptease from Channing Tatum, Matt Bomer, and other Hollywood hunks might be disappointed to find that the film contains quite a bit of character development and plot, too. That's not to say it's anything less than wildly entertaining—even more so when you know that the actors had just as much fun leaning into their roles as they seem to on-screen. Matthew McConaughey wasn't initially given a dance sequence in the script, but pushed for one himself. He even helped create his own moves, one of which is named the "Lick It and Slick It."

The Master (2012)

Paul Thomas Anderson delivered an absorbing tale of a World War II veteran (Joaquin Phoenix) who falls under the spell of a charismatic philosopher (Philip Seymour Hoffman) whose teachings soon become the focus of a cult movement. Both Phoenix and Hoffman were nominated for Academy Awards.

Moonlight (2016)

Barry Jenkins's quiet, poignant Best Picture winner is about identity, race, sexuality, poverty, and masculinity (among other things)—several movies' worth of themes, all considered in a single, deeply felt drama of elegant, heartbreaking simplicity. The main character is played at different ages by Alex Hibbert, Ashton Sanders, and Trevante Rhodes, each giving a delicate performance that seems to borrow from and influence the other two.

Once upon a Time . . . in Hollywood (2019)

Quentin Tarantino's ninth film isn't driven by plot mechanics, but character. Fading '60s TV star Rick Dalton (Leonardo DiCaprio) wants to prove himself; Cliff Booth (Brad Pitt), Rick's Zen master stunt double, just wants to hang out with his dog. How Charles Manson upends both plans is best left to the movie, which practically drips with Tarantino's affection for a bygone L.A.

Pariah (2011)

By the very title, you know that the protagonist of Dee Rees's (*Mudbound*) skillfully told portrait focuses on an outsider. Alike (Adepero Oduye) is a teenage girl struggling with her lesbian desires and the expectations and conflict in her family, yet she is no standard coming-of-age heroine. Oduye is so self-possessed in her portrayal, it's impossible to look away.

Phantom Thread (2017)

In Paul Thomas Anderson's stylish 1950s period drama, the life of a fastidious, fussy couture dressmaker (Daniel Day-Lewis) is thrown into disarray when his wily new muse (Vicky Krieps) fails to follow the script. True to his Method roots, Day-Lewis learned to sew and took an active role in making costume decisions. He also named his own character: Reynolds Woodcock.

The Place Beyond the Pines (2012)

The legacies of fathers are visited upon their sons in this crime drama starring Ryan Gosling and Bradley Cooper as men on opposite sides of the law. Gosling turns to robbery; Cooper is a cop in pursuit. Their paths intersect and resonate in ways neither they—nor the viewer—could ever anticipate.

Roma (2018)

Alfonso Cuarón's semi-autobiographical story of growing up in a middle-class Mexico City home in the early 1970s is a tribute to the women who shaped him, told through the eyes of a live-in housekeeper and nanny who comes from a much poorer stratum of society. Impeccably, affectionately crafted, the film breaks down the language and class barriers that divide us to deliver an emotionally powerful story.

Room (2015)

A woman (Brie Larson) is held captive by a deeply disturbed man for seven years. During that time, her son (Jacob Tremblay) has never experienced the outside world. That kind of setup is usually reserved for thrillers, but *Room* is not as interested in Larson's potential escape as much as it is in her courage giving her son sanctuary in an unsafe space. Larson won an Academy Award for the role.

Scott Pilgrim vs. the World (2010)

A rare adaptation for writer-director Edgar Wright brings Bryan Lee O'Malley's popular graphic novel series to life. Michael Cera is perfectly cast in the title role as an awkward young man who is determined to win the heart of the woman he loves (Mary Elizabeth Winstead) by literally winning video game style battles against her "Seven Evil Exes." Wright throws every trick in his book at the screen, and the result is a film you can watch again and again.

The Shape of Water (2017)

In this imaginative Best Picture Oscar winner from Guillermo del Toro, a woman who can't speak (Sally Hawkins) falls in love with a humanoid amphibian (Doug Jones) imprisoned in the government lab where she works as a cleaner. Set in 1960s Maryland amid the Cold War, this *Creature from the Black Lagoon*–inspired story is equal parts romance, fantasy, and spy thriller.

Snowpiercer (2013)

Parasite's Bong Joon Ho wrote and directed this adaptation of the *Le Transperceneige* graphic novel series, which portrays a dystopian future in which a train carrying cars separated by social class circles the globe. Soon, the have-nots (led by Chris Evans) decide to defy authority and get answers from those in charge.

Take Shelter (2011)

Two-time Oscar nominee Michael Shannon is one of the finest actors working today, and few directors allow him to show off his rare mix of intensity and humor as Jeff Nichols. In *Take Shelter*, he plays Curtis, a devoted husband and father

who begins having intense nightmares and visions of an apocalyptic storm. Curtis becomes obsessed with building a shelter for his family, despite being unsure whether what he's experiencing is precognition or a break with reality.

Toy Story 3 (2010)

We see action movies all the time whose flesh-and-blood characters never convince us they're in any real danger, and existential dramas where we just wish people would shut up about their problems. Yet here we are wide-eyed with giddy tension over the fate of some toys—and not even actual toys, but computer-animated toys! This was the apex of Pixar's creative abilities, brilliantly funny and sophisticated yet accessible to five-year-olds.

The Tree of Life (2011)

Terrence Malick's rumination on the purpose of life, the meaning of suffering, and the nature of God is as poetic and philosophical as you'd expect a movie about those subjects to be, yet it's as down-to-earth and unpretentious as possible. Malick uses the gentle rhythms of poetry and the majestic images of the natural world to put us in a meditative state. It's a movie that wants us to ponder the big questions.

Uncut Gems (2019)

Adam Sandler takes a dramatic turn as Howard Ratner, a jeweler who can't control his betting urges, in this anxiety-inducing crime-drama directed by Benny and Josh Safdie. When he gets hold of an expensive ring from NBA star Kevin Garnett, he takes a gamble with his life. *Uncut Gems* is an effectively grubby movie that will have you sweating the results of Ratner's wagers right along with him.

Under the Skin (2014)

This uniquely surreal and understated film by Jonathan Glazer was based on a novel, but Glazer revised it into something you can scarcely imagine existing in book form at all. Scarlett Johansson plays a nameless extraterrestrial roaming the streets of Scotland, looking for humans to feed on before starting to develop empathy. Unnerving and unforgettable, the film is frequently mesmerizing, using sound, music, and silence to great effect.

We Need to Talk About Kevin (2011)

Lynne Ramsay's *We Need to Talk About Kevin* (2011) isn't technically a horror film, but it may feel that way to new parents. Eva (Tilda Swinton) has a strained relationship with her son Kevin from the time he's born. His difficult behavior as a toddler becomes full-on sociopathy when he grows into a teenager (played by Ezra Miller). The question of how evil is made haunts the characters in the film, and it will haunt viewers long after the credits roll.

Winter's Bone (2010)

Jennifer Lawrence's breakthrough film is nothing flashy. As Ree Dolly, Lawrence is a teen in the Ozarks of Missouri charged with finding her missing father before her family loses their home. Her journey takes her through hostile territories and reveals truths that were best left uncovered.

The Witch (2015)

Delicately crafted with an eye toward historical accuracy, this existential horror film focuses on a New England farming family in the wilds of 1630 who believe a witch has cursed them. Anya Taylor-Joy's standout performance acts as a guide through the possessed-goat-filled insanity.

The Wolf of Wall Street (2013)

Based on a memoir by stockbroker-turned-felon Jordan Belfort (Leonardo DiCaprio), *The Wolf of Wall Street* follows Belfort's meteoric, drug-filed rise to the top. Belfort's misfortune became director Martin Scorsese's prize cash cow: it remains his highest-grossing film to date.

YOUNG FRANKENSTEIN (1974)

WRITTEN BY:
Gene Wilder and Mel Brooks

DIRECTED BY: Mel Brooks

OTHER MOVIES DIRECTED BY MEL BROOKS:
The Producers (1967); *Blazing Saddles* (1974); *History of the World: Part I* (1981); *Spaceballs* (1987); *Robin Hood: Men in Tights* (1993)

In 1974, Brooks had arguably the greatest year any comedy filmmaker has ever had. *Blazing Saddles* came out in February and became an instant classic, and then in December, Brooks released another all-time great laugh fest: The Universal Monsters send-up *Young Frankenstein*. Featuring Gene Wilder in full mad scientist mode, Madeline Kahn stealing every scene she's in, Marty Feldman delivering some of cinema's best one-liners, the greatest performance of "Puttin' on the Ritz" ever put to film, and so much more, *Young Frankenstein* is a brilliant, timeless film that showcased Brooks's skill as a visual artist almost as much as his skill as a humorist.

GENE WILDER WOULD ONLY AGREE TO STAR IN YOUNG FRANKENSTEIN IF MEL BROOKS DIDN'T APPEAR IN IT.

Like Alfred Hitchcock, Brooks usually gave himself a part in his own films. His characters regularly broke the fourth wall and "winked" at the audience, something Wilder felt would clash with *Young Frankenstein*'s tone. So, as a condition of his taking on the lead role, Wilder made Brooks agree to remain off camera.

ONE OF IGOR'S BEST MOMENTS INSPIRED A HIT AEROSMITH SONG.

"Walk this way!" Marty Feldman's Igor instructs his master, who proceeds to copy the hunchback's shuffling gait. Aerosmith frontman Steven Tyler found this line hilarious and repurposed it as the title of a track about high school lovers.

WILDER CONSTANTLY RUINED TAKES BY CRACKING UP.

According to Cloris Leachman, "[Wilder] killed every take [with his laughter] and nothing was done about it!" Shots would frequently have to be repeated as many as fifteen times before Wilder could finally summon a straight face.

HANS DELBRÜCK WAS A REAL PERSON.

As Wilder's Dr. Frederick Frankenstein readies his monster, he sends Igor to fetch a very special brain that rests in a jar labeled "Hans Delbrück: Scientist and Saint." The actual Delbrück (1848–1929) was an accomplished military historian whose son, Max, won a Nobel Prize for his work with viruses.

BROOKS WANTED TO CUT THE "PUTTIN' ON THE RITZ" NUMBER.

While making the movie, Brooks felt that having Dr. Frankenstein and his monster tap-dance to an old Irving Berlin song seemed "too crazy," so he was planning to cut Wilder and Boyle's "Puttin' on the Ritz" number. Upon hearing this, Wilder—who thought it was brilliant—snapped and came "close to rage and tears" before Brooks unexpectedly changed his tune. "I wanted to see how hard you'd fight for it," the director said. "If you gave up right away, I'd know it was wrong. But when you turned blue—I knew it must be right."

SEVERAL PROPS HAD PREVIOUSLY APPEARED IN JAMES WHALE'S FRANKENSTEIN.

Taking his feature-length tribute to the next level, Brooks included much of the faux lab equipment used in James Whale's iconic 1931 version of *Frankenstein*, in which Boris Karloff starred as Frankenstein's Monster.

GENE HACKMAN SPECIFICALLY ASKED WILDER FOR A PART IN YOUNG FRANKENSTEIN.

Hackman—who at the time had been thrice nominated for an Academy Award (and won one in 1972)—learned about *Young Frankenstein* through his frequent tennis partner Wilder and requested a role. Ultimately, Harold—the lonely blind character he briefly portrayed—sparked one of the most memorable sequences in comedic history.

A HUGE PERCENTAGE OF THE MOVIE HAD TO BE DELETED.

"For every joke that worked, there were three that fell flat," Brooks is quoted as saying. He whittled *Young Frankenstein* down to its current runtime after observing several mixed reactions from test audiences. This cut material included a clip in which Frederick's relatives listen to a recorded will left by his great-grandfather Beaufort von Frankenstein, whose message starts skipping and nonchalantly repeats the phrase "Up yours!"

ZODIAC
(2007)

WRITTEN BY: James Vanderbilt
(based on the book by
Robert Graysmith)

DIRECTED BY: David Fincher

**OTHER MOVIES DIRECTED BY
DAVID FINCHER:** *Se7en* (1995);
The Game (1997); *Fight Club*
(1999); *Gone Girl* (2014);
Mank (2020)

"**T**his is the Zodiac speaking . . .″

So began one of the first cryptic letters from one of history's most notorious murderers, whose identity remains unknown but whose story was brilliantly immortalized on-screen by David Fincher with *Zodiac*. This unsung masterpiece is about the infamous serial killer who terrorized the citizens of San Francisco in the 1960s, and who managed to evade police, all while sending taunting letters to the media to further promote his agenda. We're no closer to solving the mystery of the Zodiac's identity (there have been plenty of theories, but no actual evidence), but we can solve the mystery of how Fincher and his collaborators—including stars Jake Gyllenhaal, Mark Ruffalo, and Robert Downey Jr.—created one of the greatest procedural thrillers ever made.

IT WAS A FAX THAT GOT PRODUCTION STARTED.

According a making-of documentary, Robert Graysmith informed screenwriter James Vanderbilt and producer Bradley Fischer that he was personally taking pitches from a handful of filmmakers now that he owned the rights to his books again, but only via a fax number through a local Kinko's. The pair built their pitch—which Vanderbilt described as asking, "What if Garry Trudeau woke up one morning and tried to solve the Son of Sam?"—and eventually won the rights to make the film after they successfully sent the fax.

FINCHER HAD A PERSONAL CONNECTION TO THE ZODIAC STORY.

In addition to having an interest in the Zodiac killer's story from a filmmaking perspective, Fincher had a personal connection to the story, too. Though the director was born in Denver in 1962, his family relocated to California when he was two years old—just a few years before the Zodiac committed his first murder. So he grew up fearing the serial killer. "I grew up in Marin and now I know the geography of where the crimes took place, but when you're in grade school, children don't think about that," Fincher said in the film's production notes. "They think, 'He's going to show up at our school.'"

FINCHER, VANDERBILT, AND FISCHER CONDUCTED THEIR OWN INVESTIGATIONS.

Once Fincher was on board, he, Vanderbilt, and Fischer agreed to develop further drafts of the screenplay to emphasize fact over fiction. They spent months poring over police documents and interviewing witnesses, investigators, and the case's two surviving victims: Mike Mageau and Bryan Hartnell.

THE CAST LEARNED TO ENDURE FINCHER'S LEGENDARY MULTIPLE TAKES.

Fincher has an infamous habit of demanding many, many takes for particular scenes. His work on *Zodiac* was no different, which proved to be a challenge for the three main actors, all of whom were Fincher rookies.

"You get your chance to prove what you can do. You get a take, five takes, 10 takes. Some places, 90 takes," Gyllenhaal told the *New York Times*. "But there is a stopping point. There's a point at which you go, 'That's what we have to work with.' But we would reshoot things. So there came a point where I would say, 'Well, what do I do? Where's the risk?'"

THE MOVIE BROKE NEW GROUND IN DIGITAL MOVIEMAKING.

Zodiac was one of the first feature-length motion pictures to be primarily shot using a digital camera. Certain slow-motion scenes—including one during the Blue Rock Springs opening—were shot on film, but the rest was photographed using a Thomson Viper Filmstream camera, which Fincher had previously used for shooting commercials.

The decision wasn't meant to be some sort of revolutionary move to introduce what is now a nearly ubiquitous moviemaking method. Instead, Fincher simply hated how long it took to process daily film footage. "I liked the process of working digitally and I didn't like waiting until the next day to see what I had shot," Fincher explained.

Similarly, *Zodiac* was one of the first feature movies to be edited using the inexpensive consumer software program Final Cut Pro.

PERFECTLY EVER AFTER:
IMPECCABLE MOVIE ENDINGS

SPOILERS! We've all had the same feeling. You're watching a good movie, everything is moving forward exactly the way you feel it should, and then the ending comes and it just doesn't land. Plenty of great stories have been derailed by lackluster endings, or endings that simply chicken out on the bold promises the rest of the film made to its audience. These movies, thankfully, are not those stories.

Big Night (1996)

Baking a big tonal shift into the ending of your film is always a risk, but having one of the most endearing casts ever assembled certainly helps to pull it off. The final act of *Big Night* largely plays out as one big party put on to save a restaurant laced with some of the greatest food porn ever put on film. Then the ending comes, and the film deflates like a falling souffle, as our restaurateur heroes (Stanley Tucci and Tony Shalhoub) watch their dream fade.

Carrie (1976)

There's an element of impish glee running through Brian De Palma's *Carrie*, from the way the film showcases the often clueless arrogance of Carrie White's (Sissy Spacek) tormentors to the absolutely unhinged performance from Piper Laurie as Carrie's mother. In retrospect, it makes perfect sense that De Palma would want to pay off the devilish delight one last time with a jump scare that had popcorn sticking to movie-theater ceilings all over America.

Fargo (1996)

When it comes to *Fargo*, most people get the infamous woodchipper scene stuck in their heads right away. The more time you spend with this Coen brothers' classic, though, the more you come to appreciate the quiet moment that follows it: Marge Gunderson, back home with her husband, celebrating his art on a three-cent stamp and their impending baby. It's a reminder that, even in a world that seems determined to rip itself apart, you have to celebrate in your own quiet way whenever you can.

Invasion of the Body Snatchers (1978)

How do you top the climax of the 1956 *Invasion of the Body Snatchers*, which features Kevin McCarthy screaming, "You're next!" directly into the camera? If you're Philip Kaufman, you both pay homage to that ending in your new interpretation and you build up such a level of paranoia and dread that the audience clings to the one sane man in your narrative right up until the final, haunting shot. With that achieved, you ask Donald Sutherland to make one of the most horrifying faces in all of horror cinema, and unleash a primal scream that will have everyone squirming in their seats as the credits roll.

The Taking of Pelham One Two Three (1974)

For almost the entirety of *The Taking of Pelham One Two Three*, its main characters are static. The criminals are on the train, and the Transit Police lieutenant (Walter Matthau) trying to slow them down is behind a switchboard, begging for more time. When it all breaks down, it breaks down quickly and dramatically, which is why the film's ultimate ending is so sublime. After all that, the solution (or is it?) to the mystery comes down to a single, poorly timed sneeze.

Thelma & Louise (1991)

In the hands of the wrong storyteller, an ending like the one in *Thelma & Louise* would fall absolutely flat, be little more than a joke, or even transform into a misogynistic snipe at "dramatic" women. In the hands of Ridley Scott and his two shining stars, Geena Davis and Susan Sarandon, it becomes a primal shout in the face of an unfair world, a triumphant moment in which two women for whom the game has never been fair simply refuse to play anymore.

The Thing (1982)

John Carpenter's *The Thing* is perhaps best remembered among horror fans for its dazzling visual effects and, of course, the amazing blood test scene. But the sense of utter paranoia and tension running through those moments is present throughout the film, and it all builds to one of the greatest ambiguous endings in horror cinema: two men, alone in the frozen dark, each ready to be proven right and destroyed at the same time.

The Vanishing (1988)

The Vanishing is a film about obsessive search for truth, and the real brilliance of George Sluizer's filmmaking approach is in the way he makes us a part of that obsession rather than just observers of it. The audience gets to know more about the killer than the protagonist does, but we still never get the whole story. Sluizer pushes us, just as he pushes Rex (Gene Bervoets), to absolutely crave that last piece of the puzzle above all else. The horrifying payoff remains one of the most chilling conclusions ever put on film.

ACKNOWLEDGMENTS

You are holding *The Curious Movie Buff* in your hands right now because of the diligence, enthusiasm, and genuine love of cinema of many talented individuals. First, an enormous thank you to our agent, Dinah Dunn, and our designer, Carol Bobolts, from Indelible Editions, and to our publisher, Weldon Owen, Inc., especially Roger Shaw, Rachel Barry, and Karyn Gerhard.

Profound gratitude is also owed to editor-in-chief Erin McCarthy and the entire Mental Floss team—writers Michele Debczak, Ellen Gutoskey, and Jake Rossen; editors Kat Long, Shayna Murphy, Jason Serafino, and Kerry Wolfe; social media maestro Angela Trotti; and "V-boys" Jon Mayer and Justin Dodd—for their constant support, great ideas, and incredible contributions to this book. Very special thanks to the former Mental Floss staffers whose work appears in this book: Erika Berlin, Jason English, Hannah Keyser, and Andrew LaSane.

The Curious Movie Buff would not have been possible without the constant support of our Minute Media family, especially Matan Har, and everyone else who was so enthusiastic about this project.

Thanks to our amazing fact checker Austin Thompson, copyeditor Becky Maines, and proofreader Carrie Wicks.

Deepest thanks to the many amazing writers who contributed their work to this book: Tara Aquino (*Coming to America, Harold and Maude*); Scott Beggs (*Black Panther, The Cabin in the Woods, Call Me By Your Name, Casino Royale, Do The Right Thing, Get Out, The Godfather Part II, Grizzly Man, Mad Max: Fury Road*); Stacy Conradt (*Beauty and the Beast*); Meredith Danko (*Mulholland Drive*); Kate Erbland (*Pulp Fiction*); Todd Gilchrist (*The Godfather Part III*, Killer Gangster Films); Kristin Hunt (*The Muppet Movie, Princess Mononoke, Romeo + Juliet, Shaft, Trainspotting*); Sean Hutchinson (*Apocalypse Now, The Godfather, Halloween, Jaws, Jurassic Park, Raiders of the Lost Ark, Scream, The Shawshank Redemption, Star Wars*: The Original Trilogy, *The Terminator, Zodiac*); Matthew Jackson (*Batman, Clue, The French Connection, Hedwig and the Angry Inch, Iron Man, The Rocky Horror Picture Show, Shaun of the Dead, Superman: The Movie, Suspiria*, Thrilling Car Chases, Offbeat Romantic Comedies, Arresting Heist Movies, Explosive Action Movies, Essential Midnight Movies, Impeccable Movie Endings, Essential Comedies); Mark Mancini (*Young Frankenstein*); Rudie Obias (Movies That Were Supposed to Be Sequels to Other Movies, Horror Movies Inspired by Real-Life Events, Beloved Movies That Flopped at the Box Office); Rebecca Pahle (*Blade Runner, The Lord of the Rings* Trilogy, Obvious Movie Anachronisms, Casting Decisions That Infuriated Fans); Garin Pirnia (*Heat*); Kristy Puchko (*Clueless*); Mike Rampton (*Drive, Ex Machina, Parasite*, Why Is the World Obsessed with *Die Hard?*); Paul Schrodt (Essential LGBTQ Movies, Wild Movie Plot Twists); April Snellings (*Jennifer's Body*, Brainy Zombie Flicks); and Eric D. Snider (*All the President's Men, Chinatown, My Own Private Idaho, Pan's Labyrinth, The Sting*).

INDEX